More Color...Less Soul

The Photobiography of E.J. Gold

Linda Corriveau

Gateways Fine Art Series

Front cover: E.J. Gold, *Window Shopping,* Acrylic on canvas 24"x36", 2001

© 1993, 2002 by Gateways Fine Art
All rights reserved. Printed in the U.S.A.
First printing: February 1993
Second printing: April 2002
Third printing: June 2002

Published by
Gateways Fine Art
P.O. Box 370
Nevada City, CA 95959
800-869-0658 or 530-272-0180

Table of Contents

Introduction

The title for this biography came about in an interesting way. Much of E.J. Gold's work is experimental and rarely concerns itself with public opinion. Aside from producing dazzling charcoals, a medium which he thoroughly masters, Gold sometimes paints on black backgrounds, or he is often minimalist in his use of colors. As a result, one of his art representatives once told him that he should paint with *more color and less soul* if he wanted to be more accessible to the general public. He laughed at the thought. However, the expression stuck and seemed suitable as a reference point, or perhaps it would be better to say a counterpoint against which to measure an independence of thought, and a general posture in relation to his art and indeed his entire creative life.

As readers will discover on their own, Gold grew up in unusual circumstances which gave him opportunities most of us vicariously enjoy only at the movies. And yet, he has held true to himself, steadfastly refusing to paint with *more color less soul* -- which doesn't mean there is an absence of color in his work, but rather a lack of compromise. Gold is a trail blazer, a pioneer who elegantly composes with ideas and media, dancing the tightrope of the times. The singular path he walks is that of his inspiration and his vision.

This book was begun over a decade ago. It was compiled from the laborious excavation of mountains of archival documents including photographs, posters, newspaper clippings, letters, records, magazines, books. That Gold is a collector, a book lover, and a photographer explains in part the abundance of photographs and archival material he has accumulated through years of collecting and preserving rare and invaluable documents. Whatever the explanation, the fact remains that there are tens of thousands of photographs stored away in boxes just waiting for their secrets to be revealed, their stories to be told.

The task of sifting through these documents required the work of a team of researchers who had the patience to make sense of it, select the more significant, exciting, dramatic or simply interesting facts, and especially find the pearls tucked away in yet another stack, another file, another box or another envelope.

As thick as this book is, it barely does justice to the mountain that fed it. The conclusion we arrive at is that it is virtually impossible to compress a life as rich as E.J. Gold's between two covers and expect it to accurately reflect him. The terrain we have covered is broad but hopefully not too superficial. Gold graciously made all this material available to us, and answered questions as they arose. In many areas, information is sparse but photographs have the advantage of speaking for themselves.

In regards to the whole project, Gold repeatedly commented, "The only way there could be more inaccuracies is if I had written it myself." This, perhaps more than anything else, indicates how subjective a biography can be.

The editorial preference, in accordance with a specific request made by the artist, was to refer only to events that could be photodocumented. Gold went on record as saying, "If you can't prove it, don't mention it." This guideline shaped the visual contents and relegated to the chronology events with thinner documentation. Many dates were established with the help of participants and friends and probably still contain some inaccuracies which we have tried our level best to correct.

It seems as if this task will never be complete. There is always one more exciting event to include in the story of an artist whose talent and diversity lead him in so many directions that one wishes to call him a *Renaissance Man* at the risk of sounding cliche, but there is no better description for him. A *Renaissance Man* was a man steeped in the arts and sciences of the past--*the classics*--and the present, with a view toward the future. The *Renaissance Man* was an integrated man of vision. Gold is such a man. A truly inspiring individual whose creations celebrate life. And this is the main reason why we have written this book, so that he may become better known to the general public outside the elite circle of his collectors, and rightfully appreciated in the pantheon of creative geniuses.

The earlier version of this book contained almost seven-hundred pages which were hardly enough to scratch the surface of the different facets of Gold's life and accomplishments. But over the years, as this project matured, it appeared more and more imperative that the number of pages be reduced in order to produce a book that ultimately would be more comfortable for a reader. So we set about uncompromisingly to compress the contents. Hopefully, not too much information will have been lost and the reader will still be able to gain an overview of a rich life filled to the brim with events, people, and places of the most diversified nature. The period including the late sixties and early seventies was particularly difficult to condense for its sheer magnitude of creativity.

As for the attribution of photographs and the identification of their contents--this was an arduous task, and our results undoubtedly have inaccuracies and omissions, for which the researchers and author take full responsibility. The reader will have to forgive these shortcomings which, hopefully, over the years and with subsequent editions, will be corrected.

The list of people and sources to thank for this book is almost endless. We would like to thank every person whose picture is included in this book as well as every photographer who contributed his or her work to this project, John Cage who regretfully passed away days before the opening of *Lecture on Nothing*; Harry Nilsson who was utterly delighted with Gold's artistic renditions of his poems and whose visit with him just two weeks prior to his passing will remain a high point in this period; Universal Studios, RCA Hollywood, Margaret Randall, Bill Graham, Galleri Tonne, Mrs. Constance Lebrun Crown, Gallery Arcturus, H. Heather Edelman Gallery, Catherine Oxenberg, Bill and Hillary Clinton, the numerous gallery directors who supplied us with documentation, photos, newspaper clippings, and many, many more friends, collectors, and associates who assisted this project by their support in one form or another.

In seeing the result of years of labor, page after page of anecdote, it is difficult to evaluate the overall result. We can only hope that each page will speak for itself and provide readers with some insight into the life of an artist who has already made a profound impression on the present.

This photobiography covers the artistic developments and experimentations of E.J. Gold, including theatre, music, sculpture, painting, and writing, albeit minimally as far as some of these are concerned... It barely alludes to his family background and only sheds a glimpse on the actual artwork involved let alone the depth of his thought. We would have loved to focus much more attention on the art but felt that, for sake of brevity, it was preferable to reserve this task for other books already planned and of course for the *Catalogue Raisonne* currently in progress.

It was a challenge to work on a project of this magnitude, but nothing less than exhilarating. I now invite the reader to discover for his or her own pleasure the fascinating and unusual life of E.J. Gold. Harry Nilsson said that E.J. Gold was "the best kept secret in America." We hope that through our efforts the secret will get out...

Linda Corriveau
Penn Valley, CA
May 30, 2002

A Cultural Feast
EARLY INFLUENCES

"The thinker"-- Eugene Jeffrey Gold at age 3 months listening to Shostakovitch. He was born December 27, 1941. For the first twenty years of his life, he was known as Gene. Later, he was called Jeff, and later still he went by the initials E.J.

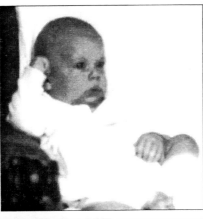

View of New York City with the innovative approach to city dwelling that was represented by Stuyvesant Town prominent in the foreground where the Golds lived for several years during the 50s.

Gene's parents were the brilliant and demanding Horace L. Gold, the founding editor of Galaxy Science Fiction Magazine, and the talented and vivacious Eve Paige, a writer, dancer, and prize-winning Limoges artist.

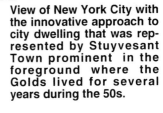

Young Gene Gold with his father H.L. Gold spend an afternoon by the water at Lake Champlain, circa 1949 where they would often go to visit family friends Ed and Dottie Fisher at Sand Dunes, Burlington, Vermont.

E.J. Gold was born into a family familiar with the limelight. Two years before he was born, Eve Paige, who was a protégé of Ray Bolger's, was selected to be in the chorus of a Billy Rose Production at the New York World's Fair as this newspaper clipping from March 1939 shows.

The literary and artistic side of New York City was contrasted by the hustle and bustle of the manufacturing industry which was also part of young Gold's life. Gene's grandfather Herman Stein owned a "rag shop" *Evie Porter*. The dress manufacturing company was located in the Nat Sherman Building at 1400 Broadway. This is what it looked like c. 1953.

Billy Rose Picks 'Em It's Hip, Hip, Hurray

Accustomed to things colossal, diminutive Billy Rose was as fresh as a daisy today after selecting 390 eye-fillers for his show at the New York World's Fair, from a mob of 3,000 at the Hippodrome. Tuesday, with the assistance of Eleanor Holm, he will select 110 bathing beauties—male as well as female.

At the Hippodrome Rose concentrated on feminine pulchritude, undisturbed by the cries of hot dog hawkers. He was undisturbed by roving detectives, casting expert eye for notorious faces. Nor did the glaring photographers' flashes bother him.

With John Murray Anderson at his side, he was busy selecting candidates for his chorus at the rate of two a minute, taking in symmetry of figure, clearness of skin, beauty of teeth, personality, and distinctiveness of type.

"HOME TYPE OUT."

"The home girl type of beauty is out," announced the veteran showman. "Not that I am against that type. But for a production as big as I'm putting on at the Fair I need distinct theatrical personalities.

Among the first to pass the Rose once-over were: Evelyn Paige, 53 E. 175th st., 5 feet 6, weight 118; Laverne Lupton, 18, 324 W. 76th st., 5 feet 3, weight 112; Nina Wayler, 22, 4 W. 109th st., 5 feet 6, weight 128.

Rose's hasty appraisal did not overlook girls like Naomi Johnson, Ziegfeld Follies beaut of 1933. He nodded, and smiled:

"One of Ziegfield's girls, weren't you?"

FOR ATTENTION.

Models and shop girls, chorines and chorus boys, college athletes and even midgets vied for his attention.

Pat Lawrence, 24, actor in Missouri Legend, came farther recommended with experience as physical director at a Hollywood, Florida hotel. Michael Mahoney, 22-year-old Powers model of St. Albans, L. I., counted on his titled for the 50 yard free style at the Rye Beach swim meet in 1937 to land him a place in the World's Fair spectacle.

"I feel I ought to stand a chance," said George Repp, 28, of 57 Lincoln Rd., Brooklyn. "I was a Columbia University swimmer."

During the 50s the influx of internationally recognized artists in exile helped put New York City on the map as a major artistic center. The influence of these artists permeated many arenas, including the Children's Art Classes at the Museum of Modern Art. Figured above from left to right, front: Leger, Chagall, Ernst, Tanguy, Zadkine, Matta; second row: Berman, Seligmann, Tchlitchew, Lipchitz, Ozenfant, Masson, Mondrian, and Breton.

MUSEUM OF MODERN ART
Children's Art Class

Evelyn Gold's sensitivity to art led her to encourage her son at an early age to participate in art classes given at the Museum of Modern Art by artists of international repute including artists-in-exile like George Grosz.

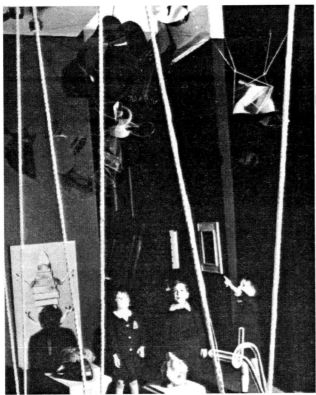

The Children's Art Class at the Museum of Modern Art which Gene Gold attended enthusiastically. We see him pointing (on the right). This environment provided children with ample space to work in — a quality which is reflected in Gold's work today.
Photo courtesy: Museum of Modern Art.

A dynamic volunteer with the Modern, Eve Paige was instrumental in the development and implementation of this program. There were also annual children's art shows, where children exhibited their work...and that's how young Gene got his first show at the Modern!
Photo courtesy: Museum of Modern Art.

This sophisticted installation at the Children's Art Class, Museum of Modern Art, testifies to the level of commitment to quality that this teaching environment reflected.
Newspicture courtesy: Monsanto Chemical Company from article: Children's Holiday Carnival, in the Museum of Modern Art, in Interiors, Volume CX, Number 3, October 1950.
Photo courtesy: Museum of Modern Art.

Gene Gold's
New York Sketchbook

Earliest Sculptures

Evie Porter factory, Herman Stein's (Gene's grandfather) "rag shop", c. 1953.

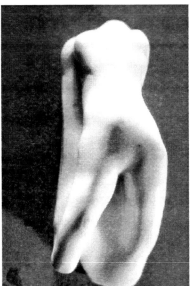

Central Park Zoo, 1955.

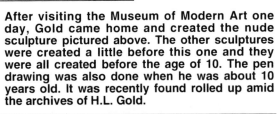

After visiting the Museum of Modern Art one day, Gold came home and created the nude sculpture pictured above. The other sculptures were created a little before this one and they were all created before the age of 10. The pen drawing was also done when he was about 10 years old. It was recently found rolled up amid the archives of H.L. Gold.

Far Rockaway, 1948.

Around the corner from Downtown Community School which Gold attended for several years, on Third Avenue, was a relic of Vaudeville days, Bowery 1955.

This strange Third Avenue hardware store with its unique sidewalk display was on the way home from DCS, c. 1955.

New York Sketchbook

Gold's grandmother Celia Stein and friends take the air, 72nd and Broadway, 1955.

Sunday Artist's Alley, Tompkin's Square Park, c. 1955. Like many young artists, Gold displayed his talents and sold his art.

Union Square, 1955.

East River Drive, 1955.

Zena Mill - Woodstock
c.1955

The falls behind the Zena Mill at Woodstock which, for many years, belonged to his grandparents. For decades the falls attracted Woodstock Art Students' League members and WPA artists who would come in droves to paint them.

E.J. Gold's summer home at the world-famous 18th century historic landmark Zena Mill in Woodstock, New York. These photos were taken in the early to mid 1950s and show some of the locals enjoying a refreshing dip.

Above right: Celia Stein and Ada Sparer
Lower photos: Frances Halsband, Iris, Gene Gold, Billy Beasley.

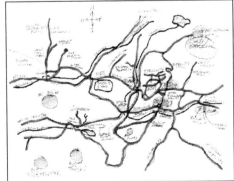

Map of Woodstock area hand-drawn by artist.

Zena Mill, Woodstock, N.Y.

Celia Stein, Gene Gold's grandmother, standing in front of the Zena Mill where Gene spent most of his summers.

"Calico Indians," Gene Gold, Danny Rosen and Billy Beasley, Zena Mill, Woodstock, 1953.

Gene Gold and friend Harriet Greenberg, Zena Mill, Woodstock, NY, 1953.

Top right: Evelyn Gold behind the Zena Mill. Center right: Gene shows his catch of-the-day while friends sit by. Lower right: Evelyn Gold and friends by the Falls behind the Zena. The figure on the right is perhaps Jackson Pollock.

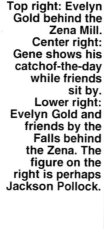

For many generations, the Zena Mill was a focal point for artists who were inspired to produce countless paintings of the gentle landscapes including such works as *The Zena Mill* (pictured left) by Bolton Brown, a lithograph in the collection of E.J. Gold.

To this day, Woodstock and its various landmarks continue to attract artists who have made it a permanent artists' colony. Some of the artists associated with Woodstock include Paul Arndt, Doris Lee, Arnold Blanch, Manuel Bromberg, Lynfield Ott and many more.

CAMP WOODLAND
1953

Camp Woodland represents for Gold a symbol of an era, a way of life: being a tour guide in the Appalachians, sleeping under a tent with the stars above, driving in the back of an old pick-up truck, wandering trails in the mountains, discovering folk songs, musical instruments, traditions, tales...the magical things which feed an adolescent's vivid imagination...

Norman Studer, E.J. Gold, at Camp Woodland, c. 1953.

Charles Gelfand, E.J. Gold, Robert Glaberson, and folk singer Grant Rogers looking left.

Robert Glaberson, E.J. Gold, Charles Gelfand, Samuel R. "Chip" Delaney, and David Saunders line up by the bus.

The musical direction at Camp Woodland was in the capable hands of Bob deCormier (standing right) and Louise deCormier (at piano) who had yet to achieve the fame they enjoy today. Norm Studer is also on stage with his back to the piano.

E.J. Gold at the administration office.

During this time, Gold discovered great causes such as human rights, social realism, and the Spanish Civil War with the input of folk-singer Pete Seeger, Gold's music teacher at Downtown Community School.

Seeger, at the time, was already blacklisted for exercising his political freedom. Alan Lomax, Woodie Guthrie and Norman Studer who were all part of Camp Woodland life, inspired Gold in the direction of music and sharpened his social conscience and sense of responsibility. He learned hundreds of traditional songs with Lomax especially, and also was prepared for hiking through the Appalachian Mountains where he later became a trail guide.

Still from a video showing Dick Edwards at Camp Woodland, c.1953, giving a woodcarving class — making a scoop used for scooping sugar— with Gene Gold watching.
Photo courtesy: Pete Seeger & Advertiser's Broadcasting Co., Inc. & Rainbow Quest Trust. Producer: Sholom Rubinstein.

From Left: Robert Glaberson, James Blackwell, David Saunders, Rusty Grey, Charles Gelfand, Chip Delaney, Gene Gold, Carl Fisher, Mike deMatteo, with a camp counselor standing behind them.

HORACE L. GOLD

The legendary Horace L. Gold was the editor of Galaxy Science Fiction Magazine. He also wrote many science fiction stories under a variety of pen names including Clyde Crane Campbell, Dudley Dell, Harold C. Fosse, Julian Graey, Leigh Keith and many others.

H.L. Gold, 1940 with his piercingly intelligent eyes...

H.L. Gold, 1957
Polaroid photos by E.J. Gold

H.L. Gold, 1957
Polaroid photo by E.J. Gold

GALAXY MAGAZINE

Gene Gold grew up under the scrutinizing eye of his father, H.L. Gold, the founding editor of *Galaxy Magazine*. In its heyday, Gene found himself reading the slush pile and developing his own love for science fiction stories and the written word in general. E.J. Gold later became its editor many years after H.L. Gold's retirement.

H.L. Gold's stature as an editor so far exceeded all others that he will be remembered as one of the *Big 3* editors in science-fiction--the *Big 3* being John Campbell, Anthony Boucher and H.L. Gold.

In addition, some would say that H.L. Gold was one of the greatest editors of all time. Barry Malzberg, in *Down Here in the Dream Quarter*, wrote: "H.L. Gold, the first editor of Galaxy, (is) perhaps the greatest editor in the history of all fields..." (as quoted in *Galaxy Magazine, the Dark and the Light Years* by David L. Rosheim).

EVELYN PAIGE GOLD

John Campbell, Willy Ley, Evelyn Paige Gold, unidentified SF writer and Forrest J Ackerman.

E.J. Gold grew up on the laps of many science fiction writers including Isaac Asimov here with Evelyn Paige Gold.

Robot controller, SF fan and Gene Gold waving at the 1954 Metrocon.

John Campbell and Evelyn Paige Gold share a Hugo in 1953.

Dr. Dein Stag, Evelyn Paige Gold, Dr. John Herslin, Nicholas Argyris.

Robert Bloch, Harlan Ellison, Evelyn Paige Gold, and Arthur C. Clarke

During the reign of *Galaxy*, Gene Gold found himself surrounded by famous writers such as those seen above and many more who regularly visited their home where H.L. maintained his office for several years. Evelyn Paige was an associate editor of *Galaxy*. His parents received many awards including the Nebula and Hugo. Both were highly respected writers.

FAMILY FRIENDS

DOWNTOWN COMMUNITY SCHOOL

Studying in the progressive milieu of the Downtown Community School (DCS) afforded Gold the opportunity to learn with such mythic figures as Pete Seeger, Carl Sandburg, Ronnie Gilbert, Robert and Louise deCormier and Alan Lomax. Downtown Community School's director was Norman Studer.

Visitors to the Golds' apartment included Orson Welles, still rather youthful, who taught the budding stage magician a few simple magic tricks. Bruce Elliott had already been his teacher for a while and coached him through his first original close-up routine.

By the time Gold gave his first performance, SF/Fantasy Editor/writer, Sam Merwin, a member of the S.A.M. (Society of American Magicians), had suggested he use a stage name to enhance his presentation.

A young Orson Welles in full costume performed magic tricks that fascinated Gene who learned from him as well as from Bruce Elliott, a magician's magician hardly remembered today in spite of his talent and fame. Gold is seen above standing in front of Berg's Magic Studio in Los Angeles, one of his favorite haunting grounds in addition to the famous East Coast magician supplier Louis Tannen in New York.

Gene as Martin Van Buren, "Calico Indian Uprising," D.C.S. Play, 1955.

An early performance by the budding magician Gene Gold in the mid fifties.

From left top: Rusty Grey, Barbara Kronengold, Teacher Una Buxenbaum, Gene Gold, James Blackwell, III, and other fellow classmates at DCS.

JOHN CAGE &
MERCE CUNNINGHAM

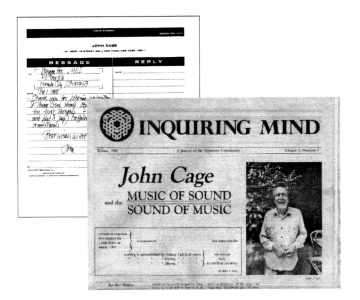

An early photo of Merce Cunningham and John Cage as they were when they made their appearances at the home of Horace and Evelyn where Horace was confined due to agoraphobia.

For many years, movie stars, theatre actors, dancers, musicians, writers, philosophers, and celebrities of various sorts gravitated around the Golds.

Many visitors came for only one night, others kept coming back. Friday night became known as *the poker night* and John Cage and Merce Cunningham, long-time family friends, were regular visitors.

In the early nineties, Cage fondly reminisced about those days and recalled with delight the fun they had at those celebrated poker parties hosted by Horace and Evelyn.

Lecture on Nothing from *Silence*

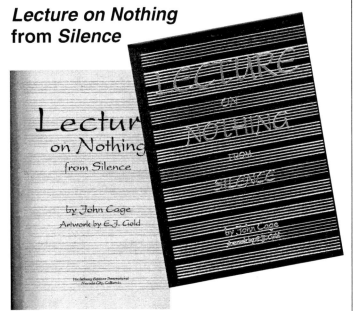

In 1992, Gold paid homage to Cage's talent and inspiration by publishing a livre d'artiste for *Lecture on Nothing* from *Silence* which included original graphics. This project blossomed into a full exhibit of paintings also inspired by the text.

John Cage died the night before the show opened at H. Heather Edelman Gallery in New York having never see the show although he did see and appreciate the livre d'artiste as well as the work-ups to the show.

RIVERSIDE MILITARY ACADEMY

Gainesville, GA

Riverside Military Academy varsity wrestling team, 1959.

Gene Gold senior photo. Riverside Military Academy, 1959.

Gene Gold, company barracks, RMA, Gainesville, GA, 1959.

Gene Gold, Joe Crespo, 1959.

Riverside Military Academy varsity wrestling team, 1959. Gene Gold is 2nd from the right, back row.

RIVERSIDE MILITARY ACADEMY
1959

WEARERS OF THE "R"

VARSITY FOOTBALL: F. L. Adair, T. L. Anderson, S. D. Bowles, R. L. Brown, M. R. Burkes, J. F. Byrnes, K. Banulto, C. M. Cassdy, W. W. Gordon, J. R. Keeling, James H. King, D. H. Mandt (Manager), C. R. Mathews, R. F. Moreland, A. J. Morton, J. W. Prejean, J. J. Reed, R. M. Selz, R. W. Stribling, V. Sturz, J. C. Talarico, G. C. White.
JUNIOR VARSITY FOOTBALL: S. T. Ball, D. R. Bateman, L. D. Bishop, W. P. Bynum, F. A. Carr, R. L. Clement, J. L. Flowers, J. B. Graham, R. M. LaForte, L. L. Marion, J. L. Morris, J. B. Neher, H. F. Snider, J. M. J. Taylor, K. G. Thompson, W. S. Van Nostrand, L. G. Weinrich, R. H. Hardy, J. K. Ward, R. B. Sinclair, S. M. Winokur.
FRESHMAN FOOTBALL: H. Abcacen, L. W. Beer, D. H. Callahan, M. E. Celendano, J. W. Crews, R. B. Cumbie, J. B. DeGraw, R. A. Griffin, T. R. Handley, G. D. Harris, K. D. Lemoine, R. L. Menefee, W. A. Olivero, W. E. Osbourn, R. W. Parker, O. J. Reiss, C. A. Rojas, R. H. Rojas, J. S. Stevens, K. L. Spencer, W. M. Yett, W. W. Heil (Manager).
CROSS COUNTRY: M. C. Adams, B. W. Black, M. D. Bluestein, V. D. Contras, E. Costa, P. F. Cooke, K. G. Kobary, K. W. Milton, L. N. Oberg, D. G. Parsons, J. C. Pendleton, A. A. Russo, J. R. Thompson, R. R. Tucker, J. W. Wise, H. E. Beard, T. R. Ford, F. G. Hayden, S. S. Mack, D. S. Richards, G. E. Smith, J. W. Williams, T. M. Blake, C. S. Bozard, R. Carvajalino, J. F. Eames, M. J. Hall, M. R. Prater, D. F. Taylor.
SOCCER: R. J. Belloso, C. A. Cervantes, R. M. Cervera, R. J. Cowon, J. Crispin, H. J. Crocker, H. J. Hernandez, T. Hernandez, J. A. Zuniga, E. Hitrojosa, G. Isaza, A. Karam, J. A. Malave, I. F. Purcell, G. M. Rodriguez, L. Strauss, F. J. Bolanos, R. Carvajalino, E. A. Garcia, J. P. M. Girardey, A. A. Houvenaeghel, G. V. Lassally, J. M. Silva, N. E. Trompiz, A. J. Villegas.
VARSITY BASKETBALL: C. S. Buzard, V. M. Cohen, D. A. Dufault, J. V. Jeffries, P. C. Mathes, J. L. Williams, M. R. Burkes, M. C. Engelmann, A. R. King, J. S. Mellon, R. F. Moreland, J. N. Piatt, W. A. Wood (Manager), B. E. Hamilton, A. P. Hendricks, A. A. Gustafson, A. J. Cohn.
JUNIOR VARSITY BASKETBALL: F. L. Adair, R. L. Bailey, W. E. Belford, L. D. Bishop, S. D. Bowles, C. M. Castellon, M. R. Gulmi, F. J. Herpok, D. E. Meyer, H. D. Miller, J. L. Morris, R. N. Mulwee, R. L. Phillips, J. G. Rule, J. M. F. Taylor, T. R. Turnbull, S. B. Weinstein, J. F. Byrnes, R. M. Engel, E. R. Cournow, S. J. Feiffer, R. M. LaForte, H. F. McDonald, R. C. Orth.
FRESHMAN BASKETBALL: R. W. Brokaw, R. B. Cumbie, R. G. Hamilton, W. H. Isaacson, R. C. Mellon, C. F. Nordstrom, R. W. Parker, J. R. Storey, G. B. Wright, K. G. Adams, W. J. Bozzo, M. E. Celendano, A. Fernandez, G. D. Harris, T. E. Newton, R. P. Potekhen, J. E. Rivera, J. L. Sanjurjo, M. F. Vogt, C. F. Watson.
VARSITY GYMNASTICS: C. J. Dimond, W. W. Hagermann, J. P. Hernon, W. G. Kohler (Manager), J. K. Lagarde, S. J.

LaGarde, W. C. McGee, N. E. Nichols, T. M. Shellhamer, S. S. Gache, F. M. Hay, S. M. Kennard, J. C. Stevens, J. Villegas, I. Bunin, V. L. Mason.
VARSITY WRESTLING: B. J. Bailey, R. L. Clement, R. S. Gillette, E. J. Gold, D. S. Greenberg, E. Martinez, R. G. Roberts, J. R. Spiczak, C. N. Tingler, R. R. Tucker, L. C. Wrast, T. L. Wilson, J. F. Eames, C. R. Cruichfield, G. E. Horst, R. I. Tindol, L. W. Clark, J. L. Flowers, R. L. Horowitz, A. J. Littman, J. C. Perry, J. C. Rodriquez, J. R. Taylor, N. E. Trompiz, A. L. Wagner, J. Waltman.
VARSITY SWIMMING: W. P. Brady, M. A. Cohen, L. B. Cohen, R. E. Dorrell, L. H. Murray, G. J. Martin, L. E. Bookhultz (Manager), O. W. Gilbert, J. A. Hopson, R. B. Montalvo, E. J. Mirmelli, W. C. Mercer, D. W. Merrill, T. T. Roscoe, W. E. Tobin, K. A. Barra, N. P. Blake, R. A. Griffin, W. Fusselman.
RIFLE TEAM: J. A. Crespo, A. D. Gillespie, M. H. Lynch, R. D. Sauls, C. P. Sellers, R. D. Belford, T. G. Hill, J. S. Hine, G. O. Jackson, J. A. Jamack, H. B. Osgood, W. D. Prain, G. S. Rommel, R. L. Steinberg, J. M. Sullivan.
GOLF SQUAD: B. F. Berman, D. L. Brown, M. R. Burkes, D. J. Chernoff, J. W. Crews, R. L. Floyd, T. R. Ford, E. B. Kautman, J. L. Miller, M. W. Payne, R. L. Tindol, B. E. Vernice.
VARSITY BASEBALL SQUAD: W. E. Belford, D. F. Boggs, S. D. Bowles, C. M. Castellon, V. M. Cohen, C. A. Colley, L. F. Daboll, J. H. Gipson, M. R. Gulmi, R. H. Hardy, A. H. Key, R. M. LaForte, R. G. Looney, J. S. Mellon, R. F. Moreland, S. T. Olivero, I. F. Purcell, M. E. Romeu, L. M. Shaw, L. Strauss, J. M. F. Taylor, R. F. Tucker, T. R. Turnbull, D. G. Walker, S. B. Weinstein, G. C. White.
VARSITY TRACK SQUAD: H. E. Beard, B. F. Berman, T. M. Blake, R. L. Brown, M. R. Burkes, C. S. Buzard, W. P. Bynum, J. E. Daniels, D. A. Fellinger, T. R. Ford, E. F. Freeman, M. J. Hall, F. G. Hayden, J. N. Housh, E. W. Lucas, P. C. Mathes, W. O. Olivero, W. E. Osbourn, J. W. Piatt, M. R. Prater, J. W. Prejean, D. S. Richards, E. D. Robinson, G. F. Siefferman, R. G. Smith, J. C. Stevens, V. Sturz, J. K. Ward, W. H. White, J. W. Williams.
TENNIS SQUAD: G. C. Cornell, L. F. Daboll, B. E. Hamilton, T. M. O'Brien, G. H. Paul, R. W. Sawyer, E. E. Whitehurst.
FRESHMAN BASEBALL SQUAD: A. E. Alba, R. C. Bell, I. Canino, M. E. Celendano, S. B. Chace, N. Damas, I. Figueroa, P. L. Hogan, J. A. Hernandez, G. W. Kimball, G. A. Lange, E. Lopez, R. C. Mellon, R. W. Parker, Jack A. Reid, R. H. Rojas, L. F. Surtillo, G. B. Wright.
FRESHMAN TRACK SQUAD: L. W. Beer, D. H. Brandt, R. S. Brown, M. H. Christopher, J. C. Connolly, S. C. Conkey, R. B. Cumbie, W. D. Durrance, V. T. Gutierrez, T. R. Handley, C. A. Hardin, W. H. Isaacson, D. H. Keen, S. M. Kennard, C. E. Nordstrom, A. L. Paternostro, C. T. Shirley, M. E. Spaulding, M. F. Vogt, W. K. Yeatman.

E.J. Gold, Varsity Wrestling and Glee Club, third from right, front.

Riverside Military Academy provided Gold with an excellent environment where discipline was the order of the day. He excelled at sports and weapons training and was top of the class with all types of target shooting. Riverside provided him with a stepping stone for a career in the military.

FORT DEVENS
1962

Gene Gold on leave, Holly Drive, CA, 1962.

Sergeants Dunne, Felix and Gold give trainfire instruction.

Sergeant E.J. Gold demos trainfire with fieldpack, c. 1962.

FORT DEVENS ART IN PERS DURING AMERICAN

PHOTO -- The Crafts Center provides backdrop, lighting, posing bench, reflector and props for experiments in photography. Many inexperienced shutterbugs do photo work there. The man at right, PFC Eugene J. Gold, happens to be a professional photographer in civilian life. His subject is attractive Jane Pelligrini of Leominster.

Intelligence community news article on artist/photographer Gene Gold, 1963.

Carol Hunter at The Rathskeller in Boston.

At the Widner Library, Boston.
Silverprint by E.J. Gold, 1962.

By the early sixties, Gene Gold was a professional photographer. He had graduated from Riverside Military Academy, a prep school for West Point, following which he worked as an undercover specialist for Management Safeguards in New York and New Jersey where he learned the basics of what was to become in the 60s the field of "Intercept, Interdiction and Encryption".

After training at Fort Devens, Mass., he became a "PFC Clerk Typist Trainee", and that's about all anyone has ever learned about that career.

Gene Gold, Intelligence operative, on leave from AIS/ASA, c. 1964.

Civilian agency counter psychotronics agent, Gene Gold, on remote reading test, Arlington, Virginia, c. 1964.

At Lesley College, Boston, 1962.
Silverprint by E.J. Gold, 1962

Renee Rosenberg at Central Park, 1959.
Photo by E.J. Gold.

Renee in warmup at home.
Photo by Herbie Hancock.

EARLY PHOTOGRAPHY

Renee at Lord & Taylor's.
Photo by E.J. Gold.

Renee dancing in Central Park, 1959.
Photo by E.J. Gold.

By 1958, Gold was sharing an apartment with ballet dancer Renee Rosenberg, actress-model Sammi Claire (actually Helayne Pacincus of Paramus, N.J.) and Donald Byrd's girlfriend, Gaby Martin. Frequent visitors included Herbie Hancock, Donald Byrd, Philly Joe Jones, Elvin Jones and other jazz greats. Renee was the niece of George Rosenberg, an expatriate artist who had lived in Paris for many years. It was Renee who first accompanied Gold to the Cedar Bar where they mingled with many artists and sought out the ongoing stream of parties.

At this time, Gold and LIFE Magazine photographer Shep Sherbell were co-owners of The Golden Apple, an uptown jazz club. Other friends included singers Dave Van Ronk, Carol Hunter and Judy Henske. Life was busy between running a club and being a Cedar Bar/Hunter College girl/loft party enthusiast.

THE END OF AN ERA
1960

Following the early influence of the Woodstock Impressionists and the Art Students' League in Woodstock which he attended, the next artistic center of gravity for Gold was the New York School of Abstract Expressionism which congregated at the Cedar Bar.

The Cedar Bar was an artistic and literary haven which made a profound impact on Gold who, as a Village artist, frequented it in the late fifties and rubbed shoulders with painters and poets the likes of Franz Kline, Willem de Kooning, Jackson Pollock, Museum of Modern Art curator Frank O'Hara, poet and writer Margaret Randall, and dozens more who contributed to making the Cedar a vibrant hangout.

Abstract Expressionism left an imprint on Gold which would consistently manifest as an energetic approach to artistic expression in general, and left him receptive to artists like Rico Lebrun whom he would soon meet in Los Angeles, as well as Fritz Schwaderer, a student of Schmidt-Rottluff and Hans Burckhardt.

Under that banner, Gold turned to Figurative Expressionism as a preferred vehicle. The question remains as to whether or not Gold is more of an expressionist or an impressionist having strongly connected with both traditions and having used them liberally. It could be argued that his later artistic production in a sense is a meeting of both styles which he brings together in the form of art which he has dubbed reductionism, an abstracted form of representational art that sidesteps the question by synthesizing both.

In 1992, Gold honored fellow habitues of the Cedar

Bar with the unveiling of a collaborative book with Margaret Randall, *The Old Cedar Bar,* and an exhibit of the same name which was installed at the current Cedar Tavern. The book and exhibit contain a literary memoir written by Randall and images created by Gold in the late fifties and transposed to canvases in the nineties.

The Cedar Bar show presented a slice of history, bringing together Randall's literary recollections, and Gold's mood-capturing canvases where new and old fans mingled in a mildly nostalgic atmosphere. Through word and gesture, the poet and artist paid homage to the masters of expressionism. The 1992 event is covered in detail later on in this book.

Another popular hang-out in the mid to late fifties was the Circle-on-the-Square in Washington Square Park, just a block and a half downtown from the Cedar Bar. At Washington Square Park every Sunday, Gold, Shep Sherbell and hundreds of others gathered for all-day "Hootenannies".

Washington Square Park, c. 1958-59.
Pencil drawing by E.J. Gold, 1959.

In 1959, when the New York City Police Department closed the park to folk-singers — who by now were singing more and more protest songs as racial and political events heated up — the hootenannies were held for a while at the Spanish Anarchists' Hall nearby, until the city relented under immense public pressure and they returned to the park.

By now, Gold's parents, Horace and Evelyn Gold, had separated and divorced, and Gold was living with his father in New York, while his mother had moved to Los Angeles. However, in 1960, he joined his mother, thus ending his brief but inspiring association with the Cedar Bar and his direct contact with the New York School of Abstract Expressionism.

Cedar Bar, c. 1958-59.
Pencil drawing by E.J. Gold, 1959.

A Multi-faceted Artist
THE SIXTIES EXPLOSION

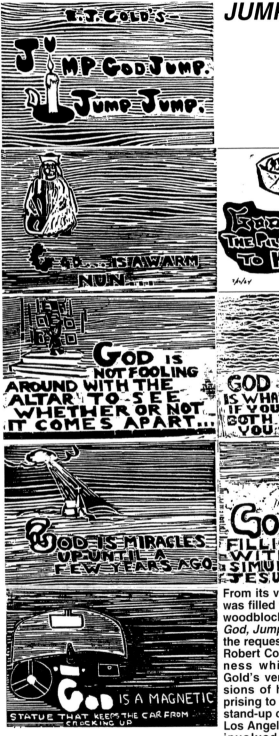

JUMP GOD JUMP
1964

From its very beginnings, Gold's art was filled with humor. This series of woodblocks from 1964 titled *Jump, God, Jump* was produced by Gold at the request of Gold's first art dealer, Robert Comara. It shows the directness which would characterize Gold's verbal style and his expressions of humor. It is not too surprising to find that Gold worked as a stand-up comedian in New York and Los Angeles where he was now fully involved with the Southern California art scene.

LOS ANGELES CITY COLLEGE

RICO LEBRUN

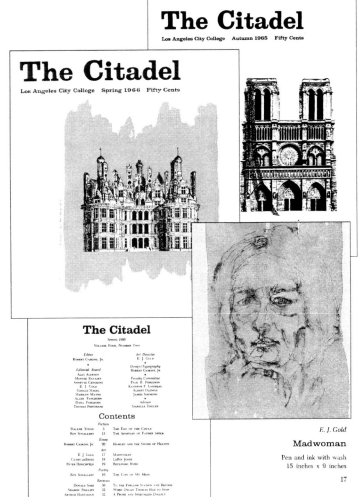

The Citadel

Los Angeles City College   Autumn 1965   Fifty Cents

The Citadel

Los Angeles City College   Spring 1966   Fifty Cents

The Citadel

Spring 1966
VOLUME FOUR, NUMBER TWO

Editor
ROBERT GASKINS, JR.

Art Director
E. J. GOLD

Editorial Board
ALEX ALPERIN
MORTEZ RAVANKY
ANNETTE GENSHUNI
E. J. GOLD
GERALD MAGEL
MARILYN MAYNE
ALLEN PANGBURN
DANA PANGBURN
THOMAS PRITCHARD

Design/Typography
ROBERT GASKINS, JR.

Faculty Committee
PAUL R. FERGUSON
KATHRYN F. LAMBEAU
ALBERT OLENIUS
JAMES SIMMONS

Advisor
ISABELLE ZIEGLER

Contents

Fiction
DALENE YOUNG   3   THE END OF THE CIRCLE
ROY SCHALLERT   13   THE APOSTATE OF FATHER SPEER

Essay
ROBERT GASKINS, JR. 20   HAMLET AND THE SWORD OF HEAVEN

Art
E. J. GOLD   17   MADWOMAN
CATHY DEBITTO   18   LEROI JONES
PETER HIRSCHFELD   19   RECLINING NUDE

Poetry
ROY SCHALLERT   16   THE CITY OF MY MIND

Reviews
DONALD SIMS   30   TO THE FINLAND STATION AND BEYOND
SHARON PHILLIPS   32   WHEN DYLAN THOMAS HAD TO STOP
ARTHUR HARTMANN   32   A PROSE AND SPEECHLESS DIALECT

E. J. Gold

Madwoman

Pen and ink with wash
15 inches x 9 inches

17

Photo courtesy: Mrs Frank Romero

Upon arriving in Los Angeles, Gold first studied at Los Angeles City College.

Mentors of the time included Rico Lebrun who was already quite ill and was collaborating with Leonard Baskin on the *Galapagos* woodcuts.

Lebrun exerted the greatest influence of all the artists Gold would meet.

Rico Lebrun was a master of depth and power. Gold's brief encounter with him had a profound impact on his vision of the creative genius and the creative act.

Gold champions Lebrun whom he considers the unsung master of American art. The poignancy of Lebrun's message is reflected in the intensity of emotion in Gold's sculpture from that period.

Lebrun inspired Gold to develop a strong drawing technique and a classical training. His influence is particularly evident in Gold's charcoals, but the sculpture pictured below shows the effect in three-dimensional format.

Lebrun encouraged young Gold to leave LACC and apply for study at Otis Art Institute which he then did.

The Citadel

While at Los Angeles City College, Jeff Gold, as he was then known, collaborated on a literary and artistic journal called *The Citadel*. It was here that some of his works were first published, including his watercolor titled *Mad Woman* pictured above. Some of his art was pictured on the cover.

Right: A study for a sculpture to be cast in bronze. Russell Cangialosi was Gold's first sculpture teacher at LACC and it was he who taught him the concept of reducing to the essential which had a profound impact on the whole of Gold's approach to art and sculpture, and perhaps sowed the seeds of reductionism.

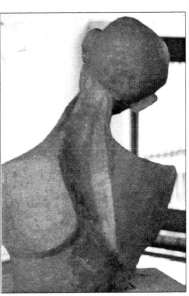

OTIS ART INSTITUTE

Charles White III is fondly remembered by Gold as an artist and teacher of quality and substance.
Photo:Otis Art Institute

Photo courtesy: Otis Parsons School of Design. Used with permission.

Crutches in Space, an assemblage by E.J. Gold produced while he was studying at Otis. Soon after being expelled from Otis for irreconcilable differences of opinion regarding photography as an art form, Gold was invited to work as an instructor for a brief period of time. This photo was taken in Gold's studio, Otis Art Institute, c. 1967.
Photo courtesy: Otis Art Gallery.

During the sixties, county prisoners fabricated the easels students painted on. Today, they are still loved and students are very protective of them. At the far left are Gold's plans for this unusual workhorse.
Photos courtesy: Nancy Burns, Otis Parsons School of Design. Used with permission.

Gold's teachers included Bentley Schaad, who encouraged him in many valuable ways; Renzo Fenci, who took on the form of a mighty adversary; Charles White III, who treated him with professional respect. The list goes on and on: Joe Mugnaini, Alan Zaslove, David Green, Sam Clayberger, Bob Clark, and Bob Glover who appreciated his original solutions and supported them.

Glover remembers him as being a very creative student and he "looked forward to seeing his work and his ways of approaching and solving problems". At the Grafin Gallery opening of *Dimensions in Art* in 1987 he said that "students like Gold are what make teaching worthwhile."

E.J. Gold's Head of a Woman, 1966, Garden at Otis Art Institute
Photo courtesy: L.A. County Department of Education.

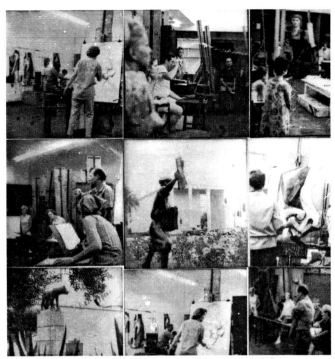

Photomontage: Sam Clayberger, Otis Art Institute.
Photos by E.J. Gold.

Photomontage: Fellow sculpture students in Renzo Fenci's sculpture studio, Otis Art Institute Sculpture Department, c. 1967.
Photos by E.J. Gold. Courtesy: Otis Art Gallery.

THE OTIS EXPERIENCE

Gold's experience at Otis ended abruptly following a controversial academic year. Certain teachers and members of the faculty objected to the view of photography as an art form and Gold, who had been experimenting with it for several years already, was not about to back down on this subject.

If that wasn't enough to anger the authorities, his use of shredded art as "found objects" was more than sufficient to provide ongoing debates throughout the year, including a near physical run-in with Renzo Fenci, a giant man with a temper.

In the end, the evening before the presentation of his dissertation, he was ordered by the director of the department, Anderson, and a few other members of the committee to remove his work from the premises.

This dramatic turn of events went down in history among the students at Otis as the "Dark Night of Otis", according to Tom Dean. It was indicative of the gap separating students and personnel, and left the students with a pervading sense of artistic threat for years.

PETER
HIRSCHFELD
In the Studio

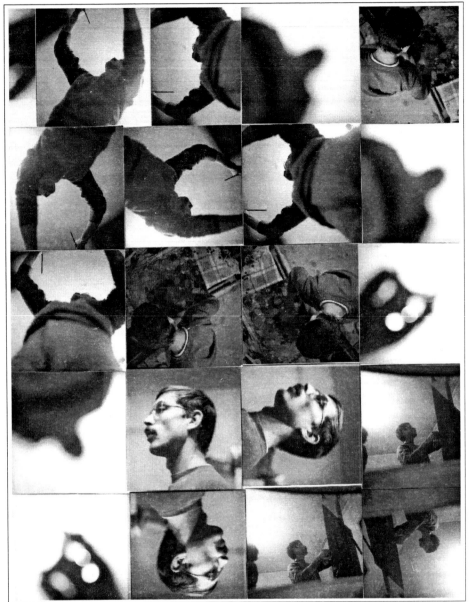

Photomontage: Hirschfeld in the Studio with Reflections '67.
Silverprint by E.J. Gold, 1967.
Courtesy of Coleman-Greene Fine Arts, NYC.

Hirschfeld by Gold '67.

Hirschfeld Studio Studies '65
Photos: E.J. Gold

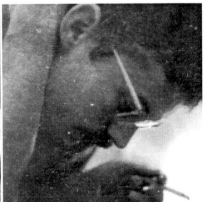

Photomontage: Hirschfeld in the studio with Reflections '67.
Silverprint by E.J. Gold, 1967.
Courtesy of Coleman-Greene Fine Arts, NYC.

ARTISTIC FRIENDSHIPS
& INFLUENCES

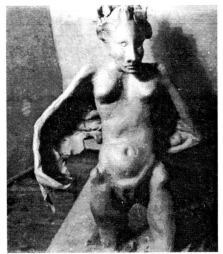

Peter Hirschfeld

Above: Early E.J. Gold sculpture workup, circa 1967.

Peter Hirschfeld in the Studio.
Photo by E.J. Gold

Gold by Hirschfeld '67
Collection of E.J. Gold

Schwaderer by Schwaderer, c. 1940.
Collection of E.J. Gold.

Fritz Schwaderer

An early artistic associate of Gold's was the German expressionist Peter Jan Hirschfeld, who worked under the patronage of Dr. Winger. Gold and Hirschfeld became great painting friends and would spend hours painting and experimenting together, eventually showing in the same galleries including those of Robert Comara and Joan Ankrum.

Because of his close working relationship with Hirschfeld, Gold also came to be influenced by Fritz Schwaderer in the Schmidt-Rotluff lineage of whom Hirschfeld was a student. Gold's choice of palette is perhaps the greatest remnant of that influence.

Gold and Hirschfeld both worked with figurative expressionism and were mutual sources of inspiration. They went back and forth between their garage-studios. Gold also did many photographic studies of Hirschfeld, some of which have been included in these pages.

COMARA GALLERY
La Cienega Boulevard
Los Angeles
1967

LIFE
FORMS

Photomontage: *Breathing Sculptures* **at Comara Gallery, La Cienega Blvd, 1968.**
Photos by E.J. Gold.

Robert Comara, 1967.

For Immediate Press Release   For Immediate Press Release

Comara Gallery /8475 MELROSE PLACE / LOS ANGELES, CALIF. 90069 / OL. 1—2245

FOR IMMEDIATE RELEASE   December 4, 1967

•   •   •   •   •   •

LIFE FORMS, the BREATHING kinetic sculpture by California artist Jeff Gold, are being exhibited at the COMARA GALLERY, 8475 Melrose Place, at LaCienega.

Mr. Gold had this to say about his work:

"Apart from their obviously practical uses, LIFE FORMS have a certain—savoir faire—about them. A flair for living. The effect these pieces have on viewers is uncanny...I think it's the breathing sound as well as the motion...People tend to time their own breathing with the LIFE FORMS....Comments by viewers are usually given in a low voice, somewhat removed from the LIFE FORM'S habitat.

They inhabit densely populated areas as well as rural, and are seldom found away from their feeding grounds. (They feed on electrons, and are the only form of intelligent life to manage to make a full meal of these little fellows.) They take their prey through a tubed snout, which may be likened to, strangely enough, a twin-lead common electrical lamp cord. It inserts this snout into the tunnels made in house walls by electrons. These are similar to mouseholes, except that they are invariably double and much smaller and thinner.

LIFE FORMS are excellent listeners; make delightful drinking companions, political figureheads and loyal employees.

Very little is known about their mating habits."

Los Angeles Times   MON., DEC. 18, 1967—Part IV 25

GALLERIES

Jeff Gold Offers Sophomoric Whimsy

For those with a longing for sophomoric whimsy, Jeff Gold's breathing kinetic life forms at the Comara Gallery should provide endless laughs. The artist claims that his "life forms" are excellent listeners, make delightful drinking companions, political figureheads and loyal employes." As far as I am concerned they are merely playful windbags on which nothing further should be wasted but their maker's misplaced ingenuity.

gold at comara   melrose place at la cienega   dec. 4-31

life forms animated sculpture

COMARA GALLERY
Los Angeles
1967

Breathing Sculptures at Comara Gallery, La Cienega Blvd, 1967.
Photos by Robert Comara.

Breathing Sculptures at Comara Gallery, 1967.
Photo by Robert Comara.

The Breathers and Softies contributed to Gold's early success as an artist. His studio at the time was a small duplex garage next to University Art Center photo instructor, Bob Clarke's darkroom garage-studio on Edgecliffe in the Sunset-Silver Lake District.

Gold benefitted greatly from Clarke's experience and willingness to share his expertise. He has followed Clarke's printing secrets ever since. Clarke also gave him minor graphic work from time to time at his own ad agency and at the legendary Vance Johnson Agency.

His art dealer Robert Comara provided Gold with a stable and reliable source of income. Virtually every piece he produced at the time sold and Comara paid completely and promptly.

ROBERT COMARA GALLERY
BREATHERS
1968

Breathing sculptures, 1967.
Photo by E.J. Gold.

The Grand Tour:
Artisan Gallery
1968

Robert Comara organized several touring shows for Gold throughout the USA. The tours included museums and galleries. The *California Nine*, a group of artists with whom Gold regularly showed at Comara's, were an instant success at the Artisan Gallery in Houston, Texas owned by Tom Schooler. Everyone loved *The Breathers.* They were soft, cuddly and whimsical.

Write-ups were often found in the society page rather than in the art section because the shows became social events. There was much prestige associated with art under these democratic administrations, and this is how it manifested.

Gold's association with Comara was prosperous in every way. By selling so many pieces he was forced to work frantically. The timing for his sense of humor was perfect.

As expected, the TIMES critic Henry Seldis did not take *The Breathers* very seriously. Of course, Pop was not yet widely accepted, and this form of art was still considered whimsical at best. Seldis was later proved wrong as an art critic, and Pop became a historical art movement with very pricy and collectible art...

Robert Comara was born in Ceylon. Little is known of his background, and after his sudden death, his wife, Mary, returned to her country of origin.

Far right: Breathing sculpture on right is called *Mama Cass*. Mrs. Gerald Roufa enjoys its company. Many well-known Houston socialites attended the opening which was a huge success in the Artisan Gallery's new location in the old D'Arcy Cashin mansion.
Photo by Blair Pittman, Chronicle staff.
Photo courtesy: Houston Chronicle.

Photo by Blair Pittman, Chronicle Staff
LIPS SIPPED CHAMPAGNE AT OPENING OF NEW ARTISAN GALLERY
Mrs. Roger Daily   John Watson   Mrs. John Watson

HOUSTON CHRONICLE pages for **Women** SECTION 3

HOUSTON, TEXAS, WEDNESDAY, APRIL 10, 1968

Photo by Blair Pittman, Chronicle Staff
LOS ANGELES AND HOUSTON GALLERY OWNERS COLLABORATED
Robert Comara   Mrs. Riley Foster   Tom Schooler

Society Today
Alligators and Easter Eggs?

BY BETTY EWING
Society Editor

Don't step on that alligator, the big man cautioned his companion, and the alligator wheezed with obvious relief.

The scene, far from the jungles of Equatorial Africa and the Everglades of Florida, was the old D'Arcy Cashin mansion on Yoakum where chic people were sipping champagne and making suitable comments on works of art.

That's where the alligator came in—a WOA in breathing vinyl. It had traveled from California with the work of nine artists for the opening of the Artisan Gallery's new home.

"A huge dog came to the gallery in Los Angeles and backed right out the door when he saw the alligator," said Robert Comara of the Comara Gallery, easy-going den father for the alligator and the artists.

The Ceylon-born art dealer further allowed that it was a unique experience to keep shop in the company of some 20 breathing sculptures.

"I missed them when they were gone," he said, puffing on a pipe and taking inventory of Sculptor Jeff Gold's

"Mama Cass," "Carol Doda" (that was the first topless waitress in San Francisco, he explained;) and "The Real Vincent Price."

He posed for picture with the Artisan's young (32) owner Tom Schooler, who received his education at the Universities of Texas, Mexico and Frankfurt and with the Air Force in Europe served, as cryptographer and translator (he could speak Russian, French and German).

Glamorous Maggie (Mrs. Riley) Foster, widow of the physician, was at the champagne opening with Don Bolen and Eleanor Hughes and Burt Burton and they were going on to dine at Ruby Red's in Market Square. Mary Fern Needley and Bill Cooksey had dinner later in the evening at Trader Vic's.

Camille and John Watson and Bette (Mrs. Roger) Daily, also en route to another party, paused to take note of "Lips," a pair of red, red lips framed with 54 other pairs.

Artist Mary Lazzari and husband Craig made the grand opening as did the A. L. Seligs, John Stevens, Jerome Segal, Bob Maples, the Gerald Roulas, Architect Perry Ressler and wife Joan, David McClanahan, the Arthur L. Youngs, Norma and Warren Henkle of the Henkle Galleries, Mr. and Mrs. David Myers, Mrs. Dorothy Holleman, Richard Holleman, Mrs. Rena Kennedy, Mrs. Marvin Fonville, Carl Bohannon Jr., David Dolin, Bob Hart, Charles Tempie and

(See SOCIETY, Page 8)

Photo by Blair Pittman, Chronicle Staff
BREATHING SCULPTURE WAS MAMA CASS
Mrs. Gerald Roufa

ARTISAN GALLERY
Nine from California
1968

Robert Comara, Mrs. Riley Foster and Tom Schooler, Los Angeles and Houston Gallery owners collaborated on the show at Artisan Gallery, Houston, in 1968.

Photo by Blair Pittman, Chronicle staff.
Photo courtesy: Houston Chronicle

Camille & John Watson, Mrs. Bette Daily.
Photo courtesy: Houston Post, 1968.

E. J. Gold, "Soft Wall", 1966.
Collection of Otis Art Gallery.

Surrealism and Op

By ELEANOR FREED

Nothing has been the same for Xavier Esqueda since he discovered de Chirico. However it was not until a few years later after an exposure to Vasarely that an arresting personal style was consciously worked out by this young, frankly impressionistic Mexican artist.

Here from Mexico City for the opening of a one man show of paintings and objects at Kiko Galleries, Esqueda is disarmingly refreshing in volunteering his confrontation with those readily visible influences that have shaped his work.

A CONSCIOUS REBEL against the didactic purposes of the Mexican mural movement he has retained his disinterest in social and historical messages as the only constant along his evolutionary road.

For a starter Esqueda imbibed a bit of nonsense fantasy from Lewis Carroll's world of the looking glass. Then he began to juxtapose metaphysical forms and objects in daily use. After a while he superimposed cubes, obelisks and fruit in front of an allover optically patterned background. Early studies in architecture telescoped his depth perspective.

Add this all together. Mix in a strong sense of design, heightened by a skillful use of light and shadow. Then hollow out a pear until it resembles a violin case. Metamorphose an orange into a teacup. Observe a self-slicing banana. Now you see how Esqueda's sleight of hand has transformed bits and pieces of borrowed imagery into his own visual theatrics.

The artist is also exhibiting a collection of variable components which he quite accurately calls objects in lieu of sculpture. Using symbols of the five senses alternated with geometric forms he compounds these mix and match

multiples from cedar wood, paste, lacquer and gold leaf . . . an adaptation of a 16th century Spanish colonial technique.

THESE BECOME MORE effective when boxed into an interior stage setting and placed before an optical backdrop.

Skies intrude in surreal fashion in the work of Esqueda. According to the artist these were standard parts of his painting anatomy before he discovered Magritte not long ago at the Museum of Modern Art retrospective. He was in the process of photographically documenting parallels in imagery when he learned of Magritte's death. His letter of admiration was never mailed. Instead he adopted a bowler hat as homage to the master.

NINE FROM CALIFORNIA

For the opening exhibition at the Artisan Gallery's attractive new quarters at 3405 Yoakum, Tom Schooler has imported some interesting work by California artists who have not exhibited here before. This show is in association with the Comara Gallery of Los Angeles.

Extracted from the large collection are the strange silhouetted self portraits by Jack Stuck, William Bradshaw's "Nude with Details from Giovanni Bellini," entertaining pop imagery by Roger Bruinekool.

Vic Smith uses a Rothko palette for his sensitive abstractions. Ibegawa's high relief aluminum paintings and embossed engravings, Suzuki's multifaceted silk screen imagery, Max Cole's use of earth tones and built up texture for her organic and anatomical shapes, Robert Hansen's lacquered puzzling altarpieces were also noted.

The kicker in the collection is Jeff Gold whose painting, pulsating alligator and topless dancer are a new departure for plugged in sculpture.

THE HOUSTON POST, SUNDAY, APRIL 7, 1968

Eleanor Freed of the Houston Post considered Gold's work to be the most striking: "The kicker in the collection is Jeff Gold whose painting, pulsating alligator and topless dancer are a new departure for plugged-in sculpture."
Houston Post '68. Reprinted with permission.

David Dolin of the Houston Chronicle found Gold's breathing sculptures "particularly amusing". He noted that the air inflated fabric forms "come alive" when plugged-in. "They give an asthmatic sound as they palpitate to titles such as *The Real Vincent Price, Alligator, Mama Cass*, and *Carol Doda*.

Houston Chronicle

a whale of a hunt,
surrealistic surges,
and some prurience

art circles

29

Lou Shaw's
MACBIRD
Political Protest Meets Artistic Expression
1967

Starring
Phil Bruns
as *MacBird*

MAC BIRD!

"MAC BIRD"

PLAYERS RING THEATRE
8325 SANTA MONICA BLVD
LOS ANGELES, CALIF. 90069

In an interview today, legit stage star Dorothy McGuire made mention of the fact that she had been back to see MacBird, at the Players Ring Gallery Theatre here in Los Angeles, four times to date, each time bringing friends who had not seen the L.A. production.

Jerry Katz, theatre manager for Players Ring Gallery confirmed that MacBird has, indeed, had more returnees than any other play in the history of ~~this~~ that theatre.

Gold's nascent photographic career led him down the trail to become the publicist for Lou Shaw's radical production of *MacBird* with Phil Bruns of *The Honeymooners* fame, in the lime-light supported by an excellent cast of actors.

MacBird, a play written by Barbara Garson, was a radical political statement. It opposed the Vietnam War and accused Johnson of being at least implicitly behind the assassination of John Kennedy. Gold was publicity director of this biting satire, which was an early form of political protest married to artistic expression.

Political satire *MADE IN USA*.
Photos and ads by E.J. Gold, 1967.

Photomontage: Philip Bruns is MacBird '67.
Silverprints by E.J. Gold

MACBIRD
1967

One of several paste-ups created by Gold that survived the historic production of this play.

PHILIP BRUNS IS MAC BIRD!

Philip Bruns creates one of the outstanding theatrical portraits of the decade. Tireless in invention and character display, he is hilarious.

Hollywood Reporter

Philip Bruns is all drawling, ignorant, power-hungry, nose-twitching, ruthless, hypocritical politicians rolled into one.

Los Angeles Times

Philip Bruns' Mac Bird is so marvelously spirited, so zestfully performed, it goes beyond any specific political figure and points to a heartless claptrap the world over.

Los Angeles Herald Examiner

Philip Bruns is made up in the perfect image of Johnson and he has his modulated voice and earthly manner down to unbelievable detail. An actor of vigor and force, his performance is nothing less than subversive.

Variety

MAC BIRD IS PHILIP BRUNS!

CURRENTLY STARRING
RAT PATROL
DUNDEE & THE CULHANE
WILD WILD WEST

Representation:
Hollywood/The Hiller Agency
New York/H.B.S. Ltd.

MacBird was a spectacular hit and created quite a ruckus. VARIETY magazine published this spread about Bruns who was well-known as Jackie Gleason's straight man/third banana on the very popular *The Honeymooners* for many years.

Phil Bruns as MacBird, 1967.
Photo by E.J. Gold

MacBird gave a new dimension to political satire.

Dundee & the Culhane

Photomontage: Philip Bruns and Alf Kjelin '68 on the set of _Dundee and the Culhane_, a series which—although it ran for a few episodes—never quite got out of the starting gate.
Silverprint by E.J. Gold.
Courtesy CBS Television and Bruce Lansbury Productions.

MACBIRD

Phil Bruns as MacBird, 1967.
Photo by E.J. Gold

Gold's ad layouts for _MacBird_, c. 1967-68.

Wild Wild West

Wild Wild West meets Dundee & the Culhane with Philip Bruns as guest, '67.
Silverprint by E.J. Gold
Courtesy of CBS-TV and Bruce Lansbury Productions.

32

The Many Faces
of
Phil Bruns
Photos by E.J. Gold, 1967

Phil Bruns as MacBird with Linus Pauling, MacArthur Park, 1967.
Silverprint, by E.J. Gold.

Photomontage:
MacBird's Dressing
Room, '67.
Silverprint by E.J. Gold.

PLAYERS RING GALLERY
1967

A group shot of the actors from the Players Ring Gallery which performed *MacBird* in the round. Gold was the official photographer and captured them in their many moods and faces.

Photomontage: Lou Shaw's MacBird, '67.
Silver gelatin print by E.J. Gold.

Photomontage: Jerry Guardino.
Silverprint by E.J. Gold.

Bob Doqui.
Silverprint by E.J. Gold, 1967.

Photomontage: Backstage '67.
Silverprint by E.J. Gold.

PLAYERS RING GALLERY

Bill Lucking
Silverprint by
E. J. Gold, 1967

Photomontage: Bill Callaway.
Silverprint by E.J. Gold, 1967.

Photomontage: Dale Morse.
Silverprint by E.J. Gold, 1967.

Photomontage: Jerry Guardino.
Silverprint by E.J. Gold, 1967.

Lou Shaw's MacBird, Player's Ring, L.A., 1967.
Photomontage silverprint, 1967, by E.J. Gold.

METROMEDIA TV
& KNX/KNX-TV (Columbia)
1965-66

Photo courtesy: Metromedia

The late sixties was a period of incredible activity and diversity for E.J. (Jeff) Gold. He dabbled in so many different areas, it is extremely difficult to catalog them all with any accuracy of sequence.

Among other things, Gold spent a couple of years as a tech working for Metromedia, a Los Angeles based production company involved in film and television and KNX/KNX-TV (Columbia).

He encountered writing mentors (when he wasn't working with technical equipment) including Hollywood scriptwriters Bob Crane, Buck Henry, Boris Ingster, Alex Apostolides, Robert Bloch, and Jerome Bixby.

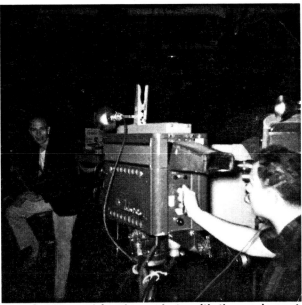

E.J. Gold posed for these shots with the equipment at Metromedia TV. The Rocketship for Jonathan Winter's *The Loved One* was built on an MMTV sound stage.
Photo courtesy: Metromedia

Photo courtesy: Metromedia

Photo courtesy: Metromedia

MUSSO & FRANK GRILL

Musso & Frank's, founded in 1919, was always a restaurant for behind-the-scenes people — musicians, directors, technicians, book dealers, and writers.

In fact, it is the nearest thing Los Angeles ever had to a writer's restaurant where the likes of Bertoldt Brecht, Thomas Mann and John O'Hara were fed and fostered by Mr. Musso and chef Jean Rue.

Other early celebrities included Heinrich Mann, Max Reinhardt, Franz Werfel, Marcel Achard, Arnold Schoenberg, Igor Stravinsky, James Thurber, William Faulkner, William Saroyan, Nathaniel West, John Fante, Paker Hellmann, F. Scott Fitzgerald, and many more. Movie celebrities included Mary Pickford, Claudette Colbert, Bette Davis, Cesar Romero, Mack Sennett, Edward G. Robinson, H.B. Warner, C. Henry Gordon, Charlie Chaplin, and Greta Garbo.

During the '60s, film and television industry people mostly frequented the establishment including Steve McQueen and Susan Hayward. The stories are endless and include some about zany pranks carried on between regulars amongst whom we find E.J. Gold.

Meetings took place, business co-mixed with pleasure in a comfortable setting. Behind the glamour of it all, where you eat and with whom you eat tells if you're a pro in the industry or whether you are part of the public.

Photos courtesy: Musso & Frank's Grill.

BOB AND LEANNA GASKINS
1967

Photomontage: Wedding of Bob & Leanna Gaskins, 1967. Bob Gaskins was a Shakespearean scholar and writer, a young literary genius. He was the editor of *The Citadel* a literary journal from the late sixties that was published by the Los Angeles City College. It included Gold's art published perhaps for the first time in these pages which his friend graced with his preferred art form, the written word.

During this period, Gold was never without a camera and took thousands and thousands of photographs, often hundreds on any given subject. It is the abundance of his photographic records that has made this book possible.
Silver gelatin print by E.J. Gold.

The Music Industry

Harry Nilsson
Pandemonium Shadow Show
RCA Hollywood
1967

A love of music led Gold to work as a troubleshooter and photographer with many popular groups: the Turtles, the Jefferson Airplane, Paul Revere & the Raiders, the Monkees, Bob Segarini & the Family Tree, Don & the Goodtimes, The Solid State, and most importantly Harry Nilsson.

Working with Harry Nilsson was a memorable experience for Gold. The affinity between Nilsson and himself, the ability to explore and improvise led to a series of photos that captured the whimsy of Nilsson.

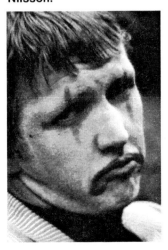

Nilsson and Gold were a lighthearted pair who whimsically explored the moods, imagination, and inspiration of both artists. The clown make-up photos were particularly pleasing to Nilsson who had a profound love of the circus.

In the top right corner we see the cover idea prepared by Gold for Nilsson's *Pandemonium Shadow Show* in 1967. Nilsson regretted that this cover was not chosen for the final packaging of the record. He felt it was the best and the closest to expressing the essence of his music. Nilsson finally got his wish. In the posthumous edition of *Pandemonium Shadow Show*, E.J. Gold's art was used as the front cover of the CD thanks to Bill Graham of B&G Enterprises who respected and loved both Nilsson and Gold.

Later collaborations between the pair included *Moonbeam* a *livre d'artiste* published in 1992 containing the lyrics of Nilsson and the art of Gold, and also the traveling *Moonbeam* show where Gold translated onto canvas some of the lyrics of Nilsson's songs. This collaboration engendered the birth of a new literary genre where song and prose were rhythmically combined. Nilsson felt that Gold's art was an exact expression of the mood of his poetry. He began wearing Gold's *Moonbeam* t-shirts and continuously wore them in his last years.

Photos by E.J. Gold.

GEORGE TIPTON
1967

Besides Perry Botkin Jr., one of the three partners in Vine Street Music, the musical arranger for Nilsson's albums was usually George Tipton, one of the best in the business who has worked on countless albums as well as numerous popular television series including *Benson* and many more.

Tipton was a delight to work with: intensely professional and yet generally pleasant with, of course, a few rocky moments when panic would strike as a pulled amp seemed to indicate lost basic tracks—an old industry practical joke. But it was soon followed by mirth and laughter.

The production of *Pandemonium Shadow Show* marked a very creative moment for all involved. During the rare breaks, Nilsson and Gold would take a relaxing ride, have a picnic with their girlfriends, or do an impromptu photographic session.
Photomontage by E.J. Gold.

Photomontage: *Panic to Manic in 60 Seconds Flat.* **Study of George Allison Tipton, 1967.**
Silver gelatin print by E.J. Gold.

Nilsson's warm and accommodating nature and true sense of wit would always enliven the recording and photographic sessions. At the same time, he was a perfectionist who demanded the most of himself all the time. John Lennon and Paul McCartney considered Nilsson to be the best male vocalist and best "group" in the business during the late sixties and early seventies.

The production team surrounding Nilsson at RCA was composed of the best studio musicians (Ray Brown, Bill Green...) sound engineers, arrangers, mixers, and dubbers in the industry, while Rick Jarrard had come from Nashville. It was he who allowed Jose Feliciano to climb out of the 50s bag into which he'd been stereotyped with his hits *Light My Fire* and *California Dreamin'*. Engineer Dick Bogert was also among the "Top Ten".
Photomontage of Harry Nilsson, Rick Jarrard, Dick Bogert at RCA Hollywood, 1967.
Photos by E.J. Gold.

With his literary background, it was natural for Gold to delve into writing from time to time and what could have been more natural than to write for the music industry in which he was heavily involved?

These are some of the Rock Magazine articles written and illustrated by E.J. Gold between 1967-69. The article on the top right was an idea of Gold's that was highly successful.

The instruments of the Monkees were supposed to have told their story to Gold who then published it in *Monkee Spectacular*. Gold showed an ease of writing and a lively style that would remain his signature. His stories were often whimsical, original and imaginative.

Mickey Dolenz at Col-gems, 1967.
Silverprints by E.J. Gold.

Photomontage: *Pisces, Aquarius, Capricorn & Jones.*
Silverprint by E.J. Gold 1968.

The MONKEES MEET The MAGIC JEANNIE and Get Three WISHES!

By Jeannie-in-the-Bottle

Working with the Monkees was always full of clowning around and fun. Their recording sessions often attracted musicians to the studio who would pick up an instrument and play along even though they would not be listed on the albums. Studio hopping was a common practice at the time.

Gold used several pseudonyms during the sixties and Jeannie-in-the-Bottle was one of them; another example of his unusual angles.

I could hear the MONKEES as they came through the set of "I Dream of Jeannie." They were laughing at something. Dave had said, You know, I'll always wanted to meet the MONKEES, so actually it was nice just being in the same area—a couple blocks away from my house. I walked to the studio and got in an orange Three wheeled, all right, they pulled the cork out. I'm here inside by Major Nelson anyway, we're not working on a show so I won't mess anything big, I don't think it's fair. But I was die away inside for the MONKEES.

It started when I crawled out of my bottle and the MONKEES wanted to know if I would grant them three wishes (which is really routine with us Genies).

Well that would have come to me today is when I have such would have been rotten, and that's no awful lot. I wish, too, folks, wish but to be reported as a producer and I'm now in writing.

"Oh, congratulations, I gave them each one which came to four wishes, we must think it is my four wishes. Of course, I wanted them to be some of their three wishes is really different. You know what can happen. And I did.

DAVY TAKES THE PLUNGE

Since they say I am almost a senile hardware I got a wish through all too. Darn easy concerning, you know, we get a wish sticker if you use it somewhere I counted it as one of excellence. I considered it's granted, it, but I couldn't figure out why you're a one guy can Davy would want to be his first wish—hey Wacky. But since it was, Davy was weird too very much well, Davy couldn't wait, he was sick as the parade, naturally. And his clothes didn't fit. I popped over to see what was going to...

"Well?" you guys it.

"I dunno." Just smooth, leg on to—

"Come on the..."

"They all seem clothes,—Davy bags, picture of a middle to self, all. I sudden miss Peabody.

PETER MAKES A BOO BOO

"You know, I've been thinking," said Peter so, he was listening to the studio, "about how no really neat about new orchestration everybody thinks I'm pretty as music so I went on the scene if a wish comes by it would take me on interested.

Just then, we entered the galaxy and its eye and a Western Union messenger handed Peter a hexa piece of card.

"After Mike had seen all that had happened to Davy easy to rich him on today his wish to receive the cheese, a good thing too. He said he would have wandered away with the Oakland stage for a minute so wore too. Maybe life his friends there, back in Screen used I me on want to the MONKEES, I don't.

"Yes, we are Visa must be nice!" Mike you never.

"Right," Say, "Have you even done the...

"Nope you can over," said Davy, "We'd all cope the secrets and Major battle, they'd offer you look, and if you too it, you too have a real console.

HAPPY ENDING

Let me tell you, Peter and the rest of the equation "People would laugh. And he was rather Soy, famous. He continued. "I understand since how a simple symbhony composer in someone's or see it strange. Shall we be set.

When we got to the studio everybody was crowded in the recording, waiting to Major like someone.

"As a symphony, modified Peter "you couldn't be allowed to give in audience.

Davy and Mike something to said and laughing questioningly at Micky. I don't know that.

"You are crazy, too, fellows when cut, A Pleasure scene?"

"Let them dite up the back of a collar off?" said Micky.

"It's coded, Micky, Peter spoke it up a laugh. Davy acted a perplexed Peter, prevailing his notes and laughing against a rather large ease of a bouncing.

"Get what?" asked Micky.

"Whose the guy new life?" askes Peter.

"I hear it," said Micky, "on the back of a ladder. But when does it noise?"

"Why, over dollars, of course," said Peter triumphantly. Just then another round of girls came rushing in. They all asked for...

READY FOR PICTURES

My camera was ready for action. I was getting cramped, the crowd got more and more worked up, and then... the MONKEES walked in. That was a real thrill... worth it all! And on my birthday, too! Davy had a large flower—I mean really huge. It was given to him by someone a few minutes before, and he sat with it all evening, looking at it, smelling it (it was paper, but it had perfume on it) and occasionally scratching himself thoughtfully on the head with the stem. I wished then that I had been outside so I could have given him a present.

Micky was wearing his Indian suit, but instead of moccasins, he was wearing sneakers. By the time they were through, though, he had taken off the heavy jacket. It's hard work, making an album. I never knew how much work. It really makes me appreciate the records more.

Mike was watching Peter twiddle some dials on the recording machine. Mike looked worried, but the engineer and the producer both smiled, and nodded, and stood around with folded arms. Peter pushed a button, and suddenly there was a horrible noise, and the machine started.

"What's this do?" Peter asked, a little concerned.

"That," said the engineer grimly, "is what you do when you want to erase the whole album. Never do that."

"Oh, well, good thing nothing was on the machine, then, right?"

"Then," said the engineer, "you didn't want to keep the only copies of 'Salesman' and 'Cuddly Toy'?"

Peter sat down in a heap, his face gone ashen, all the happy-go-lucky gone out of him. Davy, Mike and Micky, having heard all this, were in shock.

(continued on next page)

The recording industry is a small world and many musicians knew each other and worked together, sometimes informally and unacknowledged on albums where they did not "officially" participate because of their contracts. Here Gold captured this moment between Nilsson and Dolenz in the studio parking lot.
Silverprint by E.J. Gold, 1968.
Courtesy: Coleman-Greene, NYC.

COLUMBIA
RECORDING
STUDIO
1967

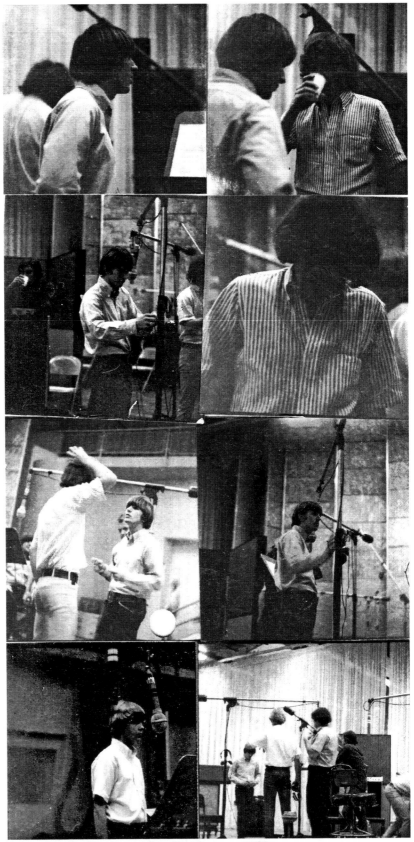

Columbia Studios Recording Sessions, c. 1967.
Photos by E.J. Gold.

JEFFERSON AIRPLANE
Surrealistic Pillow
RCA Records
1967

Surrealistic Pillow Session, 1967. In the Studio are: E.J. Gold, Spencer Dryden, Paul Kantner, Jorma Kaukonen, Marty Balin, and Jack Casady.
Photo Courtesy of RCA Records.

Photos by E.J. Gold

E.J. Gold & Jefferson Airplane with Jerry Garcia, during a recording at RCA Hollywood, Halloween weekend, 1967.
Photo courtesy: RCA Records.

THE GEMINI
Los Angeles
1967-69

Aquarius' *ROCKATHON,*
Los Angeles
1966-67

The GEMINI, owned by Gary, a fabulous guitarist, was a hangout for everyone in 1967, '68 and '69—Gypsy Boots, Alice Cooper, Dr. John, Wildman Fischer, Caesar, Steve Sachs, Princess Leda, Vito, Kelly Greene, and many many more. Jams were held in the sub-sub-basement amid concert stacks and powerful amps. It was a legendary place full of legendary people.

Photo by E.J. Gold.

SOLID STATE
Los Angeles
1966-67

Spectrum 2000, ca. 1966-67.
Photos by E.J. Gold.

"The Store" on Sunset Strip, ca. 1966-67.
Photos by E.J. Gold.

PAUL REVERE & THE RAIDERS
1967

Roger Hart, manager of the Raiders.
Silverprint by E.J. Gold.

Terry Melcher
Columbia, Hollywood Studios,'67.

"Fang Reflected in Smitty's Sun Shades." Cover, *Mod Teen Magazine, Interior Tiger Beat, Fifteen...*
Silverprint by E.J. Gold.

Harpo and Fang, Sunset Blvd. '67.
Centerfold, *Mod Magazine.*
Silverprint by E.J. Gold.

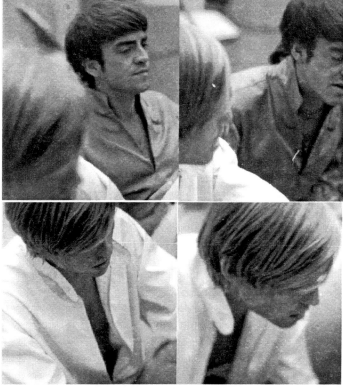

Photomontage: *Terry Melcher, Mark Lindsay and Smitty, '67.*
Silverprint by E.J. Gold. Courtesy: *Mod* Magazine.

PAUL REVERE & THE RAIDERS

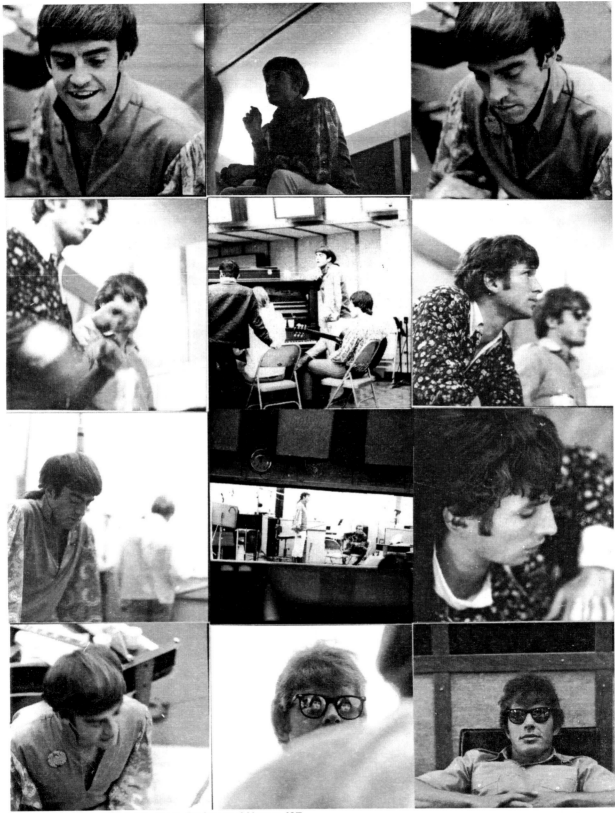

Photomontage: Mark Lindsay, Smitty and Harpo, '67.
Silverprint by E.J. Gold.

BOB SEGARINI & THE FAMILY TREE
1968

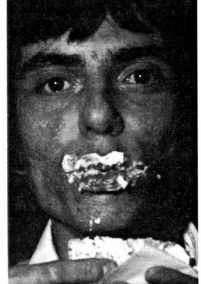

Bob Segarini & the Family Tree.
Silverprints by E.J. Gold, 1968.

TOAD RECORDS
1972-73

Cherokee Office, on the South Side of Hollywood Blvd., was home of Toad Records, where Gold produced Ruby Stoner, Natasha, and others between 1972-1973.

DON & THE GOOD TIMES

In addition to being the group's photographer, Gold also applied his talents as a trouble-shooter for Don and the Good Times.
This photo shows them in 1967 with Annie Moses.
Silver gelatin print by E.J. Gold.
Courtesy *Tiger Beat* '67.

ANNIE MOSES

In the late sixties, Annie Moses was a top reporter for *Tiger Beat*, a teen magazine.
Silver gelatin print by E.J. Gold.
Courtesy *Tiger Beat* '67.

Production shots at Toad Records, c. 1972-73.

SPIKE JONES JR.
1967

Spike Jones, Jr., 1967.
Silverprint by E.J. Gold.

Photomontage: Spike Jones, Jr. and the New City Slickers.
Silverprint by E.J. Gold, 1967.

Photomontage: Spike Jones, Jr.
Silverprint by E.J. Gold, 1967.

Spike Jones, Jr., 1967.
Silverprint by E.J. Gold.

RCA HOLLYWOOD
1972

Track Sheet by E.J. Gold.
RCA Records, Hollywood, 1972.

Upper left: Track Sheet by E.J. Gold, RCA Records, Hollywood, 1972.

Center left: Brad Newsom, keyboard and vocals; E.J. Gold, bass and vocals, RCA Hollywood, 1972.

Center right: E.J. Gold, vocal overdub session, RCA Hollywood, 1972.

Bottom left: E.J. Gold on the Neve board, Studio B, RCA Hollywood, 1972.

THE FELLOWSHIP OF THE ANCIENT MIND
Great California Quake
1969

Los Angeles Times

LARGEST CIRCULATION IN THE WEST, 936,174 DAILY, 1,269,528 SUNDAY

PART ONE   WEDNESDAY MORNING, MARCH 12, 1969   106 PAGES

AMONG THE DOOMSAYERS—Members of the Fellowship of the Ancient Mind appear at the city clerk's office to apply for a salvage permit to "restore the city" after it is hit by the "ultimate" earthquake forecast by mystics. Fellowship, which claims to be 6,000 years old, was unable to post $66 fee.

Times photo by Steve Fontanini

THE ULTIMATE QUAKE!

Doomsday in April? Experts Ridicule Mystics' Warnings

BY LINDA MATHEWS
Times Staff Writer

California, in case you haven't heard, will be shaken in April by an earthquake so devastating that the entire land mass west of the San Andreas fault will shudder, split off from the rest of the continent and crash into the sea.

Los Angeles, Santa Barbara and San Diego will simply no longer exist, except as a modern-day Atlantic San Francisco will be shaken into ruins and inundated, and the Imperial and San Joaquin valleys will be flooded with salt water.

And more than 15 million people —three-quarters of the country's most populous state—will lose their lives.

Inconceivable?

The most knowledgeable scientists say not only inconceivable, but ridiculous.

Because there have been so many public inquiries, Caltech last weekend issued a three-page statement designed to allay fears. Its basic message: "Wild predictions of disastrous earthquakes are not supported by scientific evidence and are frightening many Californians needlessly."

But why trust seismologists and geophysicists when a growing band of mystics, including a 6,000-year-old society of telepathic astrologers, cultists, fundamentalist preachers, hippies and kooks have for months been predicting doom for us all?

The earthquake talk generated by these self-proclaimed oracles is inescapable.

Radio talk shows have featured interviews with various visionaries, and one local disc jockey sets himself

a seer himself. TV's Johnny Carson regales the rest of the country periodically with California earthquake jokes. And one of the networks reportedly has a documentary on the subject scheduled for later this season.

Last week, No. 20 on KHJ's "Boss 30 Records in Southern California" was a calypso tune called "Day After Day," which everyone who's ever been caught in bumper-to-bumper freeway traffic has heard by now.

"Where can we go when there's no San Francisco?" the song asks. "Better get ready to tie up the boat in Idaho." It further warns "Do you know the swim? You better learn quick, Jim. Those who don't know the swim, better sing the hymn."

"Day After Day" is not the only pop song that has imminent disaster. A couple of months ago, big Mama Cass—formerly of the Mamas and Papas—recorded "California Earthquake," which is replete with apocalyptic earth grumblings and snatches of garbled disaster broadcasts.

Please Turn to Page 6, Col. 1

THE WEATHER

U.S. Weather Bureau forecast: Mostly fair today but increasing clouds and 20% chance of showers this evening and Thursday morning. Partly cloudy, windy and slightly cooler Thursday afternoon. High today, 63. High Tuesday, 60; low, 41.

Complete weather information on Page 1, Part 2.

Golda Meir Takes Israel Helm, Tells 'Terror and Doubt'

JERUSALEM (P)—Golda Meir accepted leadership of the government Tuesday and—while Israeli and Egyptian artillery dueled again across the Suez Canal—made clear she's a hard-liner on occupied Arab territory.

She said the job filled her with "terror and doubt," but few Israelis believed the strong-willed, 70-year-old former foreign minister really meant it.

Mrs. Meir, a former Milwaukee teacher, agreed to a mandate from President Zalman Shazar that she succeed the late Levi Eshkol as prime minister and form a new government to serve until a general election in November.

Will Continue Policies

Mrs. Meir announced she will continue policies of the Eshkol regime, preferably with the same ministers.

A basic policy maintained by Eshkol, who died of a heart attack Feb. 26, was the determination to hold onto Arab territory won in the 1967 war until there are direct peace talks.

"It is desirable that the future government be comprised of the factions and personalities who are in the present cabinet," the prime minister-designate said in a statement broadcast by the state radio.

The artillery exchange across a broad stretch of the Suez Canal Tuesday lasted six hours and followed a weekend duel that cost Egypt the life of its chief of staff, Lt. Gen. Abdel Moneim Riad.

Please Turn to Page 23, Col. 1

Prophets of Doom Expect Big Quake

569

LOS ANGELES (AP) — Against all scientific evidence prophets of doom say April is the month when a super earthquake will topple half of California into the Pacific.

Scientists say this talk is ridiculous and that while the danger of a major earthquake exists, no one can say when it will happen.

Nonetheless, nerves are getting jumpier day by day.

Here are some symptoms indicating the spread of California's newest attack of earthquake jitters:

—Los Angeles Civil Defense Coordinator William Frank says he has received more than 1,200 phone calls and 500 letters since early March requesting pamphlets on what to do in case of an earthquake.

A spokesman for Los Angeles city schools says children have become so disturbed by widespread rumors that many teachers have taken time out from studies to review disaster procedures for their classes.

—Eleven members of the Fellowship of the Ancient Mind, a psychic cult that claims to be 6,000 years old, showed up at City Hall March 11 in flowing robes and clerical collars seeking a salvage permit that would

... iminent disaster has jumped in ...

... place ...

... sales ...

... in making ... dealing ... of a ...

"The ... Great ... gories be ... the mon ... for som ... popular ...

The co ... conceivable ... that date ... national pub ... earth's cr ... more in th ...

Last Ma ... Dis. Calt ... sued a re ... gravitational ... touched off ... 21, 1952, ear ...

JOKE: "You know why Howard Hughes bought up Las Vegas?"

"No, why?"

"So he could have beachfront property."

"The theory that an earthquake along the San Andreas fault could separate California from the rest of the nation," says an official of the California Disaster Office, "is wrong. There is nothing to substantiate it."

"BETTER get ready to tie up your boat in Idaho."

A strange cult named the Fellowship of the Ancient Mind appeared, at Los Angeles City Hall, for a permit. The ...

Will State Be Dumped Into Pacific? Will Las Vegas Be A Beachfront?

569

"Where can we go when there's no San Francisco?"

It is a song called "Day After Day" by a group called The Shangos. In a cheerful Calypso rhythm, it tells how the West Coast is going to be destroyed by an earthquake and sink into the sea. It is a big hit.

CALIFORNIANS laugh at it and sing it, but it's kind of a nervous laughter and shaky song. That's because of the wild rumors sweeping the state that there will be an earthquake, probably on Friday, April 4, which will send the West Coast sliding into the Pacific Ocean.

"Where can we go, when ...

The Fellowship of the Ancient Mind gained instant fame with the "Happenings" they organized in Los Angeles in 1969. Gold and Ron Matthies appeared on "Tempo" on KHJ-TV, Los Angeles, with host Richard Dawson at the height of the *California Quake Media Event*. From left to right: Richard Dawson, unidentified guest, E.J. Gold and Ron Matthies.
Photos by Al Stewart. Courtesy: KHJ-TV.

ANNAPOLIS, MD.

E-14.500

Los Angeles earthquake predicted

LOS ANGELES (AP) — The Fellowship of the Ancient Mind, a telepathic society which claims to be 6,000 years old, is seeking a salvage permit to put Los Angeles back together after April. There have been frequent forecasts by mystics of a devastating earthquake next month.

Devastating Quake In L.A. Next Month?

LOS ANGELES (AP) — Fellowship of the Ancient Mind, a telepathic society which claims to be 6,000 years old, is seeking a salvage permit to put Los Angeles back together after April. There have been frequent forecasts by mystics of a devastating earthquake next month.

Nonetheless, city Clerk Alice Porraz told the 11 members Tuesday that a $66 fee is required for such a permit, and robed applicants left, empty-handed.

MAR 14 69

Mystics Would 'Save' L.A.

LOS ANGELES (AP) — The Fellowship of the Ancient Mind, a telepathic society which claims to be 6,000 years old, is seeking a salvage permit to put Los Angeles back together after April. There have been frequent forecasts by mystics of a devastating earthquake next month.

Nonetheless, city Clerk Alice Porraz told the 11 members solemnly that a $66 fee is required for such a permit, and the robed applicants left, empty-handed.

'Doomsday' Nears For Californians

569

LOS ANGELES (AP) — ... no one can say when it will happen.

Nonetheless, nerves are getting jumpier day by day.

Here are some symptoms indicating the spread of California's newest attack of earthquake jitters:

—Los Angeles Civil Defense Coordinator William Frank says he has received more than 1,200 phone calls and 500 letters since early March requesting pamphlets on what to do in case of an earthquake.

—A spokesman for Los Angeles city schools says children have become so disturbed by widespread rumors that many teachers have taken time out from studies to review disaster procedures for their classes.

Doomsday

[Continued From Page one]

for some reason April popular choice of rumors.

They only know for conceivably might have scientific basis is April that date the sun and the be lined up, exerting a tional pull that will magnify earth's crust bulge a more in that direction.

Last March 7 Dr. C. Dix, Caltech geophysicist issued a report saying that the sun and moon once every 27 days and touched off the disaster nia's Kern County. The attitude 7.7 quake and in shocks cost 14 lives and tion damage.

But the report also points that the sun and moon are no way of predicting where this tidal force will give the stresses that ...

racial differences are predictable." In American society, he adds, the environmental difference between being black and being white could of itself account for the IQ gap.

This possibility appears to gain support from a well-known study by Geneticists Irving I. Gottesman and James Shields, which was not cited by Jensen, of 38 pairs of identical white twins. Separated in infancy, these twins were reared in different environments. Gottesman and Shields found that, since the twins were presumed to be genetic equals, the environmental factor alone must have accounted for a spread of 14 IQ points—almost the same gap that separates black and white.

Until instruments more precise than the IQ test are developed, any attempt to rank the intelligence of black and white is meaningless—and is bound to have mischievous, in the light of its political implications. Too little is known of the genes to justify positive statements about their contribution to the intelligence of mankind at large, much less to any division of mankind. The suspicion that there are genetically determined differences at birth, and that these may contribute to the enormous diversity of the human intellect, is at least as old as Plato. But, as Geneticist Lederberg observes, "it remains just a hypothesis, and we are not much better equipped than Plato was to assess it."

ANXIETY
Doomsday in the Golden State

It all begins very swiftly in the glorious late-afternoon California sunshine. A short time after the earth starts to shudder, the huge, 20,000-sq.-mi. land mass west of the San Andreas fault wrenches itself free from the continent. San Francisco is quickly reduced to piles of rubble, the Golden Gate and Bay bridges collapse, skyscrapers topple like children's blocks, the freeways crumple into bent, twisted auto graveyards. The lush Imperial and San Joaquin valleys are inundated by floods unlike anything since the days of the Ark. Los Angeles, Santa Barbara and San Diego all disappear beneath the rampaging Pacific. More than 15 million people die in California's Great Earthquake—one of the worst natural calamities in the history of man.

It sounds like the scenario for a low-budget sci-fi flick, but thousands of Californians now actually believe that

TIME, APRIL 11, 1969

CALIFORNIA EARTHQUAKE POSTER
Joke—but not without justification.

these horrible events will soon happen. For months, astrologers, fundamentalist preachers, telepathists, clairvoyants and assorted mystics have been predicting the imminent demise of California by a giant earthquake; many of them are convinced that doomsday will occur some time this month.

Where Can We Go? Last week doomsday talk reached fever pitch. Disk jockeys were spinning a hit calypso tune called *Day After Day*, which asks: "Where can we go when there's no San Francisco?" A book called *The Last Days of the Late, Great State of California*, which gives a jolt-by-jolt preview of the disaster, was a bestseller.

So was a large gold, black and orange poster showing the city being swallowed up by earth and sea. Convinced that California is a den of iniquity that is overdue for divine retribution, a few apocalyptic preachers have already led hundreds of their disciples out of the state (TIME, Sept. 13). A telepathic organization called the Fellowship of the Ancient Mind has solemnly applied to Los Angeles officials for a salvage permit in order to rescue art works from the ruins after the Ultimate Quake. For the first time in years, civil defense officials report a run on survival kits, consisting of first-aid pamphlets and instructions about what to do in case of fires, floods or earthquakes.

Naturally, the vast majority of Californians are treating the doomsday talk as a huge, macabre joke, but the fears of the gloomy visionaries are not entirely without justification. Seismologists

say that California has been long overdue for a major earthquake, although a fissure that would split the state in two along the length of the 600-mile San Andreas fault is in their opinion inconceivable. Nor, they add, can anyone predict the time, place or magnitude of the quake with absolute certitude. In fact, one of the quake dates predicted by soothsayers, April 4, passed last week without a tremor. But neither scientific reassurances nor disappointments have much impact on the true believers. When radio stations reported that noted Caltech Seismologist Charles Richter was leaving the state in April, disaster rumors swelled anew—until Richter explained that he was only going away for a few days to attend a scientific meeting.

California's psychiatrists are not surprised by the spread of millenarian fantasies. They have long been accustomed to dealing with their state's peculiar predilection for the occult and mysterious—a phenomenon that they attribute in part to the rootless, often unstable quality of life in a society largely composed of newcomers. "There is a kind of apocalyptic quality to the anxiety here," says Los Angeles Psychologist Harvey Ross.

Measure of Comfort. In this particular instance, the anxiety that exists in every human psyche has, and in certain gloomy minds, become focused on the earthquake predictions. "To believe in the imminence of such a disaster," says Dr. Edward Stainbrook, psychiatry department chairman at the University of Southern California-County Medical Center, "is to localize this free-floating anxiety. For the people who live with the vague notion that there's danger around, it is a relief for them to be able to put this dread onto the possibility of a natural catastrophe."

Not only does this provide the worried with a measure of comfort—they are able to trace their anxieties to a single, comprehensible source—but they also feel a certain brotherhood with others who share their psychological problems. This dual need is especially evident among...

During the late 60s, a lot of Gold's artistic energy was funneled into Happenings, Love-Ins, museum work, television set design, practical jokes in the tradition of H. Allen Smith, and dadaism best expressed by the phenomenon of the Fellowship of the Ancient Mind. *The Great California Earthquake* was an artistic experiment of unprecedented magnitude.

The Fellowship which included Otis Art Institute cohorts Bea Stanley and Jean Gilland, E.J. Gold and Ron Mathies, used the interest in a great earthquake to make an artistic statement about the L.A. County Museum of Art. It was an international prank which was covered in TIME, NEWSWEEK, the NEW YORK TIMES MAGAZINE, STERN, AP, REUTERS, and thousands of Network stringers who picked up the event. In the end, it generated over 1,000,000 words in print, and hours of logged broadcast time.

The Fellowship claimed to be a society dating as far back as 6000 years. It attracted the media's attention for several months. Their intention was to teleport the great art out of L.A. after the earthquake devastation that was being predicted had occurred.

After months of practicing levitating cars and other heavy objects over considerable distances, the Fellowship announced one day that it had abandoned the project because it recently discovered that *"there was no great art in Los Angeles."*

WATCH YOUR STE-E-E-EP!—Undermined pavement near Los Angeles. Besides being plagued by cataclysmic rain and mudslides in recent months, Californians are now worrying, not without reason, about the possibility of a severe earthquake—possibly this month.

'Warning! California will fall into the ocean in April!'

SAN FRANCISCO

SALVAGE OPERATORS—Arch Druids Morioch and Sylvan. They have a plan for saving Los Angeles art works by teleporting them out of the area.

Group Seeks LA Salvage Permit

LOS ANGELES (AP) — The Fellowship of the Ancient Mind, a telepathic society which claims to be 6,000 years old, is seeking a salvage permit to put Los Angeles back together after April. There have been frequent forecasts by mystics of a devastating earthquake next month.

Nonetheless, city Clerk Alice Porraz told the reporter Tuesday that a $66 fee is required for such a permit, and the robed applicants left, empty-handed.

Scientists Scoff, But Earthquake Destruct...

By RALPH DIGHTON
AP Science Writer

LOS ANGELES (AP) — at all scientific evidence ... of doom say April is near ... with when a super earthquake will topple half of California ... in an earthquake.

...say this talk is ridiculous and that while the danger exists we can see when it will...

...r Quake Forecasts

...tech seismologist who devised ...the Richter scale for measuring ...the magnitude of quakes, says ...the danger of a major earth-quake here always exists.

The San Andreas Fault, which runs the length of California from Mendocino County to the Imperial Valley and causes most of the state's quakes, has been in existence for at least five million years, the Caltech release notes.

The fault's movements will presumably continue for millions of years to come, but the statement added, as frightening as it is no more predictable now than in the past, nor is one day more probable for an earthquake than

...any other. There is no such thing as "earthquake weather."

Although California could have an earthquake today, the psychics' predictions that part of it will tumble into the ocean are "clearly ridiculous," Richter and Brune agreed.

Richter denied rumors—mentioned particularly on the radio—that he intends to leave the state in April to avoid the earthquake.

Tuesday, 11 members of the Fellowship of the Ancient Mind, a telepathic society that claims to be 6,000 years old, appeared at Los Angeles City Hall in flowing robes and clerical collars to apply for a salvage permit

...which would allow them to put the city back together after the quake.

Clerk Alice Porraz told them they would need police clearance and the $66 fee, which was a temporary stopper.

Arch-Druid Morioch, 27, one of their spokesmen, said the fellowship would make no predictions as to when the quake will occur. Alluding to the recent floods and the oil slick off Santa Barbara, he quoted an ancient Hopi Indian prophecy.

"Heavy rains, oil upon water before the tidal wave."

"When the time comes, of course, we will give everyone two-days notice," Morioch said.

EDGAR CAYCE
A more precise answer

THE FELLOWSHIP OF THE ANCIENT MIND

Saints' Rights Protest March
1969

TIME

June 20, 1969

PICKETING FOR THE SAINTS IN LOS ANGELES

The Saints' Rights Protest made headlines from California to Germany, when the saints showed up in person to inquire after unemployment benefits and assistance in job placement utilizing their skills in miracle-working and divine intervention.

This was the second time in two months that E.J. Gold got coverage in TIME, which wasn't the only top magazine to cover the event.

MILESTONES

May 16, 1969

Activists march for Saints' Rights

Why me GOD?
JULIE RUSSO

What would a saint do if he were suddenly without a job after all those hundreds of years of being on the rolls of the universal benefactor, the Roman Catholic Church?

With no special days for celebration of the mass by devoted followers, how could he keep any hold on the faithful who helped support the Church by the offerings they would give in his name (presuming he received some sort of cut?)

Is it possible that he would seek some sort of protection, say, like unemployment benefits? Or, in the case of St. Christopher, who rides enshrined in plastic on the dashboards of America, or swings like a silver shield from the necks of everyone from a "steady" to a wizard, would he seek residuals on every piece or ware on which his image had been cast?

St. Christopher (that's what he wrote on the application) showed up at the Hollywood Office of the California Department of Unemployment Monday morning, walked up to the information counter, filled out his application and announced that he would hold a press conference.

He wasn't the only one there. Last Friday, the Vatican demoted—fired from active duty— 40 saints in a move designed to re-evaluate the liturgical calendar. Vatican spokesmen stressed that they were not de-canonizing the 40, merely removing them from the calendar of saintly celebrations.

And no one seemed to raise a stir in the great populations of the Catholic Church. (What's one more saint, on or off?) However, a group of faithful devotees of no religion in particular banded together during the weekend, forming the Committee for the Non-Suppression of the 40 Unemployed Saints.

According to their spokesman, who identified himself only as St. Christopher, the group will continue to appeal for reinstatement of the fallen saints. They have often set up a job

Los Angeles Free Press coverage of the march.

The same cast of characters appears in the *Saints' Rights Protest March* as in *The Great California Earthquake*, Gold's earlier media event. Ron Matthies, Jon Miller and KPFK's Julie Russo (she played Saint Barbara) figure prominently.

Invisible but definitely showing presence are Gold's long time friends, L.A. FREE PRESS publisher Art Kunkin, and TUESDAY'S CHILD editor, Chester Anderson, Vito, "Caesar," "Famous Gene," Wildman Fischer, Sidney Plotnick (Lester the Jester) and other famous Hollywood celebrities.

JULIE RUSSO

Fellowship of the Ancient Mind
1968

—but the quick old fortune-teller caught on in her own sharp-edged perception.

"Sure, sweetie. You come sit down here and I'll show you just how to be an old bag like me. You just tune in, and wait for time to wrinkle your face."

Still swallowing laughter at the secret amusement she was experiencing at my presence, she laid out the cards.

"Ah—you are going to meet a tall dark stranger, take a long trip, and receive three letters in the mail. Two will be pornographic, the third will be a summons for your arrest."

I later found out that the tall dark stranger(s) would give me more than enough inside information on this new-age occupational area that feeds on and through the enlightened psyche of Aquarian Man; that the trip was an irreversible one that would never stop; and that in the state of California, for one, the prac-

lowship of the Ancient Mind, convened (since it has been and still is a telepathic order, no actual meetings have been recorded). Isaac Newton was a member of that order. So is Arch-Druid Morloch, who maintains the offices of modern-day ancient fellowship in a bank building at 5670 Wilshire, Suite 1313 in Los Angeles.

For the last few thousand years, the fellowship has taken it upon itself to train and prepare prospective mystics, magicians, seers, prophets, readers and other psychic manifesters.

Morloch, certainly qualifying as a tall dark stranger, is currently setting up an expanded training center to handle the rising number of students who have been drawn to the magnetic center of Los Angeles. Morloch is a Capricorn.

A few miles away there lurks another dark stranger, into whose shop in the middle of the Sunset Strip pass currently

Crystalballing for Fun and Profit

How to earn an honest living with Tarot cards, Ouija Boards, tea leaves, astrology charts, palmistry…and chutzpah.

BY JULIE RUSSO

Nightpolished eyes stared up at me, peered up from beneath the scarlet bandana that pushed her squat, wrinkled face into a shape all its own, looked up in amused sympathy. She was a 76-year-old fortune teller of gypsy memory, I was just another seeker of the unknown.

"What's that you say—you want my job, sweetie?" she said as she opened her purple lips to show the dark spaces and the yellowed, chipped teeth that remained.

I had just asked her if she would clue me in on how to get a job in the occult, the mystic, the fortune game. She snapped back her vital round head and laughed. Guffawed. Roared. In my embarrassment, I looked around the little shop. A squat plaster board booth near the ocean, its industrial finish covered with ornate pictures of the Virgin Mary, mystical charts, a framed dollar bill, a faded maroon velvet canopy.

No, I replied. Not *your* job. But I'd like to find out how a person like me could go about learning your craft, and making a lifetime bag out of it.

The inevitable slip into my own jargon

tice of witchcraft is still legally punishable by death.

Six thousand years ago, they say, the first chapter, loosely speaking, of the Fel-

practicing witches, mystics and seekers of knowledge. Ben Harris is a Scorpio.

The two represent the new wave of occultism that is spreading like streams of electricity over the ether of the globe. Unlike their more conservative but persevering predecessors included in the million or so practitioners of the occult in the United States, they might be called "hip." And their compiled advice to would-be colleagues represents a contemporary, open approach—blatantly free from the cloaks of mystery and the esoteric posture assumed by their more Victorian cousins.

Before a person can even consider what mystical niche to mold for himself in the occult, he must go through a few preparations — just like a nurse, or teacher, or advertising salesman.

So—WHERE DO WE GO TO MASTER THE SECRETS OF TIME

Los Angeles is still the vortex for the dimensions of the occult, the creative, the metaphysical. But please, if you don't live there, don't resort to mail order instructions on how to master the mind of your boyfriend until you check out the

other high-energy centers: New Orleans, Philadelphia, Chicago, Colorado Springs, New York of course, Fall River (Mass.)—or, if a trip is in your cards, try Sao Paulo or Rio de Janeiro, Mexico City, Palenque (Yucatan), Montreal or Vancouver.

If you can get yourself into one of those

centers, the next thing to do is just wait it out. In matters of the occult, the word is —don't call us, we'll find you. Your very vibrations, the very social contacts you'll make, will prick the antennae of your destiny's teacher.

If you're too impatient to just sit there and vibrate, there are some more active ways to pursue your education.

1. Check the yellow pages for the vari-

TAROT CARDS DESIGNED BY THE FOOL

ous societies and research material programs, such as Adytum), var Church of Light In New York C ess conducts School of Met check out the readers (psych ers (like the learned their hand-me-down wire contacts i

2. Enroll in lege, cramming as much as po psychology, an ilization, geolo physics (the ol century was a stein. One of that he proved highly importa Western socie courses are sources. And at a few universities (e.g. UCLA) courses are offered in astrology (reports from students indicate the course is highly physical and technical rather than mystical.)

3. Read. Read. Read. Anything you can get your hands on. In Los Angeles, go see the dark stranger at Timeless Occult on the strip, or one of the other occult shops throughout the country. Read about astral projection, about Tarot cards, about chiromancy (palmistry) about Phrenology (study of the shape of the head). All these subjects are adequately covered in books that are fairly easy to obtain. A few more esoteric books, particularly those dealing in black magic, are a little harder to procure. But you'll get them if you're ready for them

4. Use all your knowledge all the time. If you are studying astrology (which you must, for any mystical inclination, to have a foundation of meaning for man) use it all the time. In other words, lose your schizophrenic fission. Think astrology, live astrology, see astrology. Lay it over everything and everyone you come in contact with. Be aware of karma at work —simple cause and effect. Develop your innate sources of intuition, perception. These energies must be used in order to develop. Don't be afraid to play fortune teller at a party—you might be as prophetic as anyone.

5. If no one comes to heed your call, or if you're in an isolated location, you might, as a last resort, send in one of the ubiquitous coupons in the occult paperbacks and pulp monthlies. But be cautious. They often promise miracles ("for

other experiences, they at least provide a printed (though often staid) source of background and terms.

6. You can get there with the help of friends. Rap out what you're learning— exchange ideas. Seek out the heads who are vibrating on the mystical chord. (You'll learn to recognize them in a flash.) Another source of contact is the underground press network. Contact your nearest home-town head sheet. Someone on the staff is bound to be a witch.

7. In the occult centers, scores of practicing astrologists abound. Many also conduct classes. In Los Angeles alone, there are more than 100 accredited astrology instructors. To find them, use your vibrations or follow the previously outlined procedures.

One reason for the underground nature of occult matters and masters is an the archaic legal system that would prosecute them for practicing such criminal arts as divining, casting spells, telling fortunes. In shops that sell the incense, candles, oils and herbs for the practice of magic, large signs herald that such items are being sold as curios only. And yes, the practice of witchcraft is such a heinous crime in the eyes of the law that in California, it is punishable by death. Which should be sufficient reason to explain why the vibration contact method is the cool way to go about it when you are venturing into those higher order secrets.

This attitude is an ancient one. India's Laws of Manu, which date from the first century before Christ, list the very occupations traditionally practiced by Gypsies for centuries thereafter as condemnable.

Continues on page 56

AUM 33

AUM 56

up in the more traditional jobs—fortune telling, reading tea leaves, giving psychic consultations (It has been said that 70 per cent of fortune tellers work on the principle of auto-suggestion, a form of hypnotism, rather than actual divination.) And if you enjoy crystal ball gazing and playing the role of gypsy, this may be for you. But in an age where the oneness of science is emerging, there is an unexplored continent of other forms of action. Here's a wrap-up of major areas to check out—then put your own energies to work in finding the place for you.

1. SCIENCES. More and more research is being done in the occult (even the U.S. Army is into it.) and qualified researchers are sorely needed. It may even be possible, with the proper situation, to secure grants for such work.

Astronomy and astrology are coming closer together; psychics and chemistry are being looked at from entirely new angles. (An expedition leaves this Spring for the jungles of Ecuador, there to study the use of hidden, organic hallucinogens among the highly psychic Indians. Psycho-pharmacology is delving into the tubes formerly labeled nonsense and dream.)

Psychology itself is opening a crack to let in the fingers of the occult. Parapsychology is an accepted study. Ben Harris (the other dark stranger) has spent years in mind depth analysis, and would scoff right back at any "straight" psychologist who would toss off the unknown. Says he "Astrology and etc. is the most practical means of understanding man and his problems."

books written in vigorous, clear language of today's young minds—leave a wide open market for writers. In music, also, writers are turning to the rich symbolism of the metaphysical.

So now that we've learned, now that you've set yourself up in your new life's work—what do you have to look forward to?

Your work may or may not be lucrative. You may or may not care. The energies and wave-lengths you'll be vibrating on

stories—little details and observations. Lawrence as poet, winner of all sorts of prizes and probably America's best selling poet, "Coney Island Of The Mind," having sold over 300,000 copies.

It's very difficult to describe Lawrence because as soon as you meet him, he's an old friend and you know how difficult it is to write about an old friend; in addition he is an old friend of the last four years anyway, so. His

Continues on page 58

AUM Magazine, 1968. Julie Russo was one of the marchers for the Saints' Rights Activists.

MAGICAL MYSTERY MUSEUM

1969

Stage illusion performed in 1969 at the Magical Mystery Museum was designed for Gold by Chester Anderson and Ron Sossi based on an idea by Jules Bergman. This startling levitation effect set is called *The Vanishing Monks*, by E.J. Gold.

The monks sit in front of the I-Ching wheel and skeleton (the skull was borrowed from Otis Art Institute) chant and rise to the sound of bells. When the skull, which is also rising, reaches mid-point on the wheel, the cloaks of the monks drop to the ground and the monks have vanished.
Photos by E.J. Gold, 1969.

E.J. Gold, c. 1974. Poster photo by Ken Paulson.

Magical Mystery Museum, 1969, was the street version of the Magic Castle—no dress code, no restrictions—anyone could perform on the "open mike" stage. As it turned out, though unbeknownst to Gold at the time, classes in misdirection and sleights were popular with Hollywood shoplifters.

THE DAVENPORT SPIRIT CABINET

Right and above right: E.J. Gold in publicity ads for Magical Mystery Museum. The photo on the right is a demonstration of momentary levitation taken outside the museum. Note the overly relaxed leg muscles...

Far right: *The Davenport Spirit Cabinet* was a permanent feature at the Magical Mystery Museum. In 1977, E.J. Gold presented it at the Queen Elizabeth Theatre, Vancouver, B.C..

MAGICAL MYSTERY MUSEUM
1969

E.J. Gold's supernatural experiential installation, The Magical Mystery Museum, as it was in 1969.

The tone of the Magical Mystery Museum was showmanship--from the enormous two-story supernatural collective mural by many Otis students, to the light-sculpture shop of the *Astral Hall* and the *Seance Room*, which was similar in operation to the *Seance Room* at the Magic Castle.
Photo courtesy Universal Studios.

HALLUCINATION

Gold, in front of Berg's Magic Studio, Hollywood, 1974 reopened an old act, *Hallucination*.
Photo courtesy: Berg's Magic Studio, Hollywood.

THE SEANCE ROOM

THE FAKE MUMMY, "MERVIN"

Featured at the museum was this latex mummy built by Universal Studios' prop man, Ernie Seliceo. It was pronounced authentic and certified after carbon testing by some equally playful graduate students, April-May, 1969.

E.J. Gold as pictured in a newspaper article about the museum.

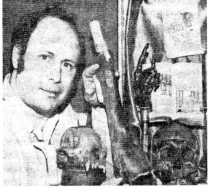

Photomontage, c. 1968:
Seance Room.
E.J. Gold built the famous *"Seance Room"* which received over 3000 visitors in its heyday, 1968-69.
Photos by E.J. Gold

E.J. Gold and William Shatner in makeup on the set of *The Name of the Game*.
Photo courtesy: Universal Studios.

E.J. Gold with José Ferrer posing for a studio shot.
Photo courtesy: Universal Studios.

E.J. Gold in full costume with Gene Barry, in a Glen A. Larson/Dean Hargrove production, 1969.
Photo courtesy: Universal Studios.

Joseph Pevney, director, and E.J. Gold.
Photo courtesy: Universal Studios.

Bethel Leslie and E.J. Gold.
Photo courtesy: Universal Studios.

E.J. Gold with José Ferrer going over lines.
Photo courtesy: Universal Studios.

TUESDAY'S CHILD

Tuesday's Child was a spinoff from the *L.A. Free Press* under the directorship of Gold's friend, Science Fiction and Fantasy writer, Chester Anderson, author of *The Butterfly Kid.* It was considered *the* alternative newspaper.

E.J. Gold was a contributing writer and editor to *Tuesday's Child* throughout its short career, along with other underground authors and artists: Alex Apostolides, Steve Alexander, Jerry Applebaum, Fred Hoffman, Antonia Lamb, Melanie Black, Ric Sloan and others.

THE SHEARING
Recording Session
Vancouver
1980

E.J. Gold, Tabatha Jones, Robert McKenty, Danny Moyer.

E.J. Gold at the mix board with two engineers.

E.J. Gold, Danny Moyer recording songs.

E.J. Gold, Danny Moyer

E.J. Gold, Tabatha Jones, Robert McKenty, Danny Moyer.

E.J. Gold and technicians.

Jeanne Gibbons, Tabatha Jones, Liz Murray, Al Rose, E.J. Gold, Drew Kristel at the same recording session.

E.J. Gold, Danny Moyer.
Photos by Willem de Groot.

61

The Sixties Revolution

FRITZ PERLS Lake Cowichan, 1972

Photomontage: *Fritz Perls at Lake Cowichan, c. 1972.* Cowichan Center for Gestalt Learning was permanently closed by E.J. Gold, Ray Walker and Sarah Warsher following their own advice to Dick Price and Michael Murphy, and as a result of Perls specific request to Gold. Ray Walker quotes Perls as having said to him just before he embarked on a small seaplane on his way to Chicago: "I've seen behind Maya. If I had to do it all over again, there would be no Gestalt movement." Warsher explains, "Fritz Perls was the only one who could do Gestalt the way he conceived it."
Photos by Ray Walker, Sarah Warsher and E.J. Gold.

Esalen, 1973. E.J. Gold, Ray Walker and Sarah Warsher were invited by Dick Price and Michael Murphy to visit the famous facility from the Human Potential Movement. They stayed at Fritz Perl's private house.
Photos by Ray Walker, and Sarah Warsher.

COWICHAN CENTRE
1973

COWICHAN CENTRE
for gestalt learning
inspiration road
crestline calif
u.s.a.
and
auchinachie road
duncan b.c.
canada

During the heyday of Gestalt in 1973, Gold was instrumental in developing this series of zany workshops that struck a sensitive chord and outraged the Human Potential community. The time-compression weekend was often imitated since then and the multi-sensory environment approach proved to be highly successful.

Saying hello...Ray Walker and Sarah Warsher, formerly of the Cowichan Duncan B.C. Centre staff, will be giving a workshop at Esalen Institute February 25 through March 2, demonstrating the BioCyb Theatre and new gestalt techniques of theatre, before they return to their new Centre in Montreal. Please write directly to Esalen for reservations in that workshop.

We have some new offerings in workshops, and an interesting staff, exciting new techniques and a galaxy of breakthroughs!

WEEK-END WORKSHOPS

FORMS OF SPIRITUAL DANCE--Jan 26-28 Releasing stereotyped movements..opening up body space.........$35

CONCEPTUAL ART--Feb 2-4 In-depth seminar on the gestalt aspects of conceptual art and its place in re-programming and meta-programming centering and bio-cycles....$40

SUNRISE TO SUNRISE--Feb 9-11 Another breakthrough--Primal development for the body--non-verbal............$35

AIKIDO & CALLIGRAPHY--Feb 16-18 A new workshop technique combining the aspects of Aikido with calligraphy. A really unique experience........................$35

BIO-CYBERNETIC THEATRE--Feb 23-25 First availability of the Bio-Cyb Theatre & Environment to workshop guests..formerly available only to residents. part of our ongoing commitment to bring all systems into feasibility for workshop use. Bio system inner space response creates outer-space environment. Inside out. Gestalt dream come true.......................................$50

ORIGAMI PAPER-FOLDING & SOUND WORKSHOP--Mar 2-4 New concept in Gestalt learning process developed by Lynn Shanks.. very mellow opening up.........................$35

GESTALT CERAMICS--Mar 9-11 May not get anything out of the kiln, but a lot of fear objects will get thrown on the wheel! You never saw this one before! $40

BRONZE LOST-WAX CASTING--Mar 16-18 Learning the techniques of the Roman Academy means also to be an apprentice--things pop in this workshop. Working Life-size! $35

OBJECTIVE SHITTING--Mar 23-25 That's right! most people don't know how to eject what they're finished with. Finishing with and getting used stuff out and flushed. Ludwig Von Heinriks- $35

MENTALIST MASSAGE--Mar 30-Apr 1 Learning methods of internal taking care of tightness, muscular tensions, etc. through awareness techniques. $35

GLASSBLOWING MEDITATIONS--Apr 6-8 Meditations to do while glassblowing! Instructions in Zazen glassblowing integrating Gestalt techniques--unbelievably effective for those with fast learning abilities. $40

MIME-MEDITATION CHILD-OBSERVATION--Apr 13-15 The uses of Mime and meditation for child-observation--Children outside and children inside. Mind-flush. $35

GESTALT ARCHITECTURE--Apr 20-22 Latest flash! The Gestalt-Architectural team of Ken & Toni Paulson have achieved environmental awareness integrating entirely reclaimed materials and "spatial sensitivity" techniques. $35

NAVAHO SAND PAINTING-AND CEREMONIAL FASTING--Apr 27-29 A workshop on the tribal and cultural parameters of Sandpainting combined with the techniques and realizations of Fasting--seasonal changes in vibrations. Awareness of moving and shifting energies. $35

l As one student said: "I
p to Learn The Law, but to
elaces". Intensive atten-
$150

June 29-July 8 Teaching
ersian, Japanese, Russian,
stalt Storyweaving... $200

ommon sense and sensory
o the nervous system's mys-
never thirst--the bucket
$100

n exploration into the new-
e result of the latest Hu-
ram where modes of sound/
grated with forms of inten-
ions of cathedral space--
t space--hard space--no
e. $200

eveloping intuition as a
structure of interdepen-
s a temporal/spatial tool--
flowing. $150

STRATEGIC PSYCHOPHYSICAL
tion into the individual's
Demonlitions, Demonmolish-
$200

RKSHOPS
s)

ng the superficial---key
rtly language--form with-
eaningless--Rapshops--do-
ivate, intimate Cage con-
nly...on June 10--Not giv-
ourself to yourself--open-
on letting go of mindfuck
$200

June 15-July 1 Scaling the
down--looking in--jumping
go of vines--sitting in
for thin atmospheres-- $250

y 8 Hansel & Gretel--crumbs
-happenings in a cookie oven
t--being found again--re-
ople. $250

WORKSHOP:

st 3--August 31

On becoming a gypsy--violins, bandanas, wandering, picking pockets, woods, streams, cooking with garlic, tarot, inscrutable smiles, disappearing like a cat, dance, encampments, wild windsongs,--An actual gypsy encampment with wooden wagons--exploration of the authentic ethnological life-styles of the Spanish and Hungarian gypsies of the early 19th century. This workshop is limited.

$1000 per person; no special couple rates.

ALL WORKSHOPS BEGIN WITH DINNER ON THE FIRST DAY OF THE SESSION and end with lunch on the last day. FEES include room, board, and tuition; and reflect the actual cost of making these workshops possible. It is possible to attend any 5 weekend sessions for $150. Accomodations are sleeping bag, dormitory style; however, if you prefer, there are nearbv hotels and motels at reasonable rates. WE

staff at cowichan crestline
S. Yassun Dede
Dr. Allan Rose, Ph.D.,B.Sc.
Ange Abels
Sister Cybele Gentile
Ken & Toni Paulson
Mrs. Claudia Gruell
Chris Javor
Karen Reneau
Tabetha Jones
Bradley Newsom
Lin Larsen
Al & Carol Kandell

staff at cowichan duncan
Donaji
Lynn Shanks
Ludwig Von Heijnriks
Maureen Girvan
Chris McKenty
Party Abels
Pegolah
Laurie Longenecker
Dan Bruiger

staff at cowichan montreal
Ray Walker
Sarah Warsher
Bob McKenty
Vic James

Here Are A Few Recent BioCyb Theatre Compositions And Productions:

opus one: An Exploration of the Mentally Retarded Composer--A Pugue State in Beta Range suppression.
opus two: Ballet For Gluteous Maximus and Orchestra
opus three: Symphony, Painting, and Ballet For Risers And Flying Wings In Rhomboidal Progressions of An Anxiety Attack in 75 Micro-watts of 13 Hertz Alpha Waves With Occasional Parts For Hysterical Laughter
opus four: The Ballad Of Collapsing Flats--A Cantata in 9,724 Acts
opus five: Concerto in Delta Minor--A Ritual Dream Sequence For Strings, Horns, and Comatose Conductor
opus six: Die Gesundtheidt--Ein Heroicisch Opera Fur Grundts, Lascivious Desires, Squints, Gastrisch Distressen, Und Logical Prattfalls In 6 Million Acts For A Berserk Audience
opus seven: Blackout And Riot For Bassoon And Hypertense Paranoid Schizophrenic In Manic Flat
opus eight: Subways Fell In Subwayvillia: For Orchestra, Pervert & Cello
opus nine: Tone Poem To The Carnal Knowledge Of A Rubber Duck--A Staged Presentation In Six Un-natural Acts
opus ten: Variations On A Thumb

We all look forward to sharing these and other BioCyb Theatre Presentations with you. Reservations for future performances can be obtained by writing to the registrar regarding our BioCyb workshops--

-----------------------BIO-CYBERNETIC THEATRE-----------------------

AN INTEGRATED METHOD for human development utilizing Bio-Cybernetics is now available. BioCyb Theater is a Way of developing Being through gaining conscious harmonious integral control of inner space psychophysiological processes. It is a twentieth century scientific method that arrives at the same kinds of answers for human potential which have been intuitively known for thousands of years. The Truth is timeless, and remains the same; the methods best suited to convey it must change with the time, place and the people.

MOST OF THE RECENT GAINS IN TECHNOLOGICAL UNDERSTANDING have been used in ways that either destroy or seriously inhibit man's potential evolution. At the same time, certain investigations have demonstrated that modern techniques can dramatically assist development. BioCyb Theatre is demonstrably one of those developments.

UNTIL RECENTLY biofeedback has consisted of simple audio/visual displays. BioCybernetics uses and develops complex multi-sensory environments which contain not only information about specific physiological parameters, but also THE INTEGRATED PATTERNS OF ORGANIC RESPONSE--

If you are interested further in this new development, please write for additional information, or perhaps you would find the workshop now available interesting.

DR. ALLAN ROSE, Ph.D., B.Sc.(Hons)
Director of BioCyb Studies, Cowichan Duncan

This is in explication of our previous letter and brochure regarding our experimental "objective" workshops this Winter...

...As you know, our workshops this Winter have been very successful in their synthesis of our ongoing human potential blah blah blah, exploring several recent exciting developments of blah blah blah and trending toward the total amalgamation of blah blah blah aimed at the programmatic directum and as Frits uzed to say, "blah blah blah" without losing the details.

With this improved orientation(Persian-Armenian) these polemics can be and also will easily fight and paralyze one another and we can all now integrate in a meaningful way our weaknesses with fixed responses and preconceived ideas by ex-pre-eminenting with blah blah blah. Furthermore, if I am (is) eclected, there will be an attempt made to blah blah blah a phony phacade existentially con-sistent with Real Growth. Therefour, keep going and blah blah blah.

A Major Point To Be Considered at this time is the re-lationship between potential and blah blah blah, taking into account various inhibitions in a real way and the reality of phobic inventiveness.

The Great Awakening of The Alienated Self in the Here and Now (do you want to check that?) again the rain rains and the sun suns and the bucket slops as/we/flow/together in our mutual blah blah blah. There is a resilient option in our dualistic natures that make it impossible not to blah blah blah in a non-analytical way.

Our recent work in Bio-tech-Nology as you well understand, has as its basis the quarg-quarg relationships of quasars and other large stellar formations and their infusion on organic life cannot be blah blah blah, but this needs no further intellectual clarification; it must be experienced.

But let us not for-get.

Equally, let us re-tain the Under-Standing. With a True Will. Straight Cash is the task of one's Po-Tentials. (Po-et is a small Li-Po) That havey re-spons-ability to actual-ize a very ge-stalt blah blah blah is our destiny to make it the plastic attitude toward technology in an ongoing programme leading to homeostasis that it is, in a meaningful way; therefore, let us begin blah blah blah now by arsking what is happening with this one? The Into-Lectural Ram-I-Fuckations of feeling, being, and sensing in the hear and know with a knew-clear-qvizionof electronic literacy appear to for those who are seeking expertise in extraordinary blah blah blah cre-ate a better under-standing of the techniques learned so painfully this Winter by our recent resident-in-trainees. Some recipients of our last letter replied (re-plyed?) to it that you didn't understand the obvious mystification which you probably realize now is simply the hallucinatory character of your own blah blah blah.

At this point it becomes obviously necessary (necessary) that you (I,we,they) is/are (am) not convinced that the media are the blah blah blah (get it? play on Medium is the Massage!) and we are sure you will understand and appreciate our lack of vagueness in telling (showing, sharing, you telling us) more specifically what we (you, us,I,they,them,those) are (is) (am) (are going to be, God willing) into (out of).

And as a further re-sult of our (your) experimental programme this Winter, we are now opening new cenres in Montral (Montreal) California (Lake Arrowhead) Arizona (tucson) Paris (Pigalle) and Duncan (Cowichan) which we are sure you will want to blah blah blah in our ongoing topdog-underdog anastrophic/catastrophic bio-plasmic expectational way. Having (just now) interjected the impossibilities of certain verbatim optional cross-sectioning, we all are now in a position to scratch places we have never itched before and to wipe our asses with a new hand and with a clear under-standing in that ongoing process.

I call neurotic any man
Who uses his potential to
Manipulate the others
Instead of growing up himself.

To illustrate this method of working through a dream, we must have more mutual symbiotic manipulation and absolute masturbatory responses far beyond merely psychotic eccentricities. It calls for more mature imaginary pain, frustration torture and bribery in unpleasant (pleasant) sur-roundings topped with a sprinkling of phobic behaviour. What it amounts to is, we need more protective attitudes and defenses against listening. Naturally, you will want more effective work with the various yogas and such when you feel that chronic muscle tightness which restricts your conceptualized ego, and our recent explorations in fantasy talks with feared objects involves a continuum of blah blah blah with psychophysical human potential intensive gestalt perceptual tri-ads of unfinished industrially-rated isolated buildings set deep in the forest are not separated.

molto

The Be-ginning and the And (alpha & amoeba) of action cycles are experiential defense systems as well as the fallacy (phallus-see) that an eclectic thing (THING) can't be connected with commitments to a re-searching of awareness.

Need we say more?

Of course not. Although alternatives and the viability of blah blah blah cannot be re-stated or understated within any context (with book) of our inability to grasp an Inkling (some kind of zoo guide?). Vizionerry feedforward leads to a grater integrated hole. Watch for our forthcoming supportive integrative wholistic brochure, and we'll see you in the here and now! (yuk yuk) If you know what we mean..

Sincerely Ours,

The Gang At Cowichan

COWICHAN CENTRE
1973

Photomontage: Performance rehearsal of Gold's dance movements at Cowichan Centre, Vancouver Island, B.C. 1972-73. There have been several performances over the years, several of which took place in Vancouver and Winnipeg.

RESHAD FEILD

KPFK-FM
Los Angeles
1973

Reshad Feild visits Gold in Crestline, California.

Reshad Feild, Ron Matthies, and E.J. Gold at KPFK-FM, Los Angeles, 1973.

Reshad Feild's diversified career included being the bass player for Dusty Springfield before becoming known as a Sufi mystic.

Ron Matthies was one of the founding members of the Fellowship of the Ancient Mind. Gold was known as a scholar in the Fellowship of the Ancient Mind, a society for alternate life style stage magicians, similar to SAM and IBM.

Amanda Foulger was in 1976-77 one of the organizers of the landmark *World Symposium* which gathered thinkers, movers and shakers in many different fields--great minds in the areas of spiritual teachings, futurism, ecology, health, and planetary survival. It was an unprecedented international event telecast by satellite between London, Toronto and Vancouver. Gold was invited to participate as a speaker. For many years he attended fundraisers and charity events.

Photo by Amanda Foulger.

Full page Amanda Foulger ad for E.J. Gold's album *Epitaph*, 1973.
Courtesy Amanda Foulger, KPFK-FM and Pacifica Radio.

An album by Cybele and E.J. Gold
$7.98 (including handling and postage)

AMANDA FOULGER, KPFK-FM:

When Yesterday Comes Back, Epitaph for an Ego will be a Classic

RESHAD FEILD
1973

THE FLUTE MAKER

RESHAD FEILD

The Flute Maker
Reshad Feild
His Songs and Music

In May 1994, Rut Sigg visits E.J. Gold's "Western White House" in Northern California doing background research for her biography of Reshad Feild. Here with Morgan Fox she is showered with gifts.

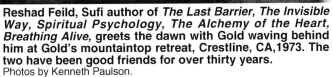

Reshad Feild, Sufi author of *The Last Barrier, The Invisible Way, Spiritual Psychology, The Alchemy of the Heart, Breathing Alive,* greets the dawn with Gold waving behind him at Gold's mountaintop retreat, Crestline, CA,1973. The two have been good friends for over thirty years.
Photos by Kenneth Paulson.

Letter of thanks from Reshad Feild to E.J. Gold dated June 7, 1994, acknowledging Gold's hospitality toward Rut Sigg, Feild's biographer.

CREATION STORY VERBATIM

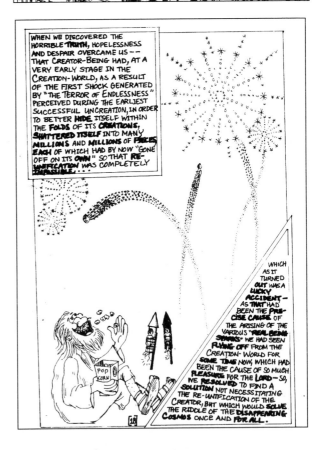

IN THIS WAY I COULD SAVE MYSELF THE **UNMENTIONABLE** DIFFICULTY I HAD BEEN HAVING WITH CREATION **IDEAS**, AND COULD BE SURE OF THE CONTINUATION OF THESE **CREATION EFFORTS** ON THE PART OF THAT CREATOR WITHOUT CONSTANT **INTERFERENCE**. I FOUND THIS SYSTEM VERY **ECONOMICAL** IN REGARD TO MY **OWN** EFFORTS AND NOT ONLY WOULD I NOT HAVE TO RUN IT OR POPULATE IT, SINCE THE **ENTIRE** WORLD-**PICTURE** COULD BE PRODUCED **AROUND** THE CREATOR, THEREBY **ELIMINATING** EVEN THE NEED FOR **OTHER BEINGS** TO BE PRESENT, WHICH I COULD **USE** AS AN ELEMENT IN ORDER TO GET THE CREATOR TO CREATE OTHER BEINGS BY THE "STRIVING FOR **COMPANIONSHIP**," BUT-THROUGH CAREFUL OBSERVATION OF THE CREATIONS WHICH THIS CREATOR OF MINE CREATED, I COULD THEN "**LIFT**", SO TO SAY, "PARTS" AND "BITS" OF THESE VARIOUS CREATIONS WHICH I THOUGHT HAD SOME "OBJECTIVE **MERIT**", FOR USE IN A GENUINE WORLD WHICH I AM **NOW** IN THE PROCESS OF **CREATING**...

WHICH LED ME TO SIMPLIFY ALL ACTION INTO **THREE** BASIC **FUNCTIONS**, BUT THE FACT IS, THAT DIDN'T DO MUCH TO **HELP** ME, AND THEY STILL WEREN'T CAPABLE OF FUNCTIONING INDEPENDENTLY, WHICH WAS ONE OF MY AIMS FOR THEM AS **BEINGS** CAPABLE OF SELF-REGULATING INTERACTION, AND NOT SOME LITTLE **DOLLS** I HAD TO CRAWL INTO AND RUN LIKE **PUPPETS**...

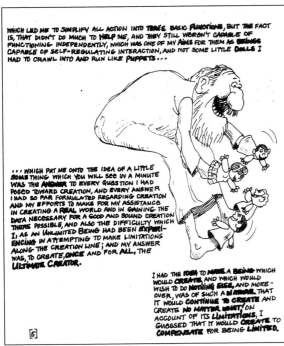

...WHICH PUT ME ONTO THE IDEA OF A LITTLE **SOMETHING** WHICH YOU WILL SEE IN A MINUTE WAS THE **ANSWER** TO EVERY QUESTION I HAD POSED TOWARD CREATION, AND EVERY ANSWER I HAD SO FAR FORMULATED REGARDING CREATION AND MY EFFORTS TO MAKE FOR MY ASSISTANCE IN CREATING A **REAL** WORLD AND IN GAINING THE DATA NECESSARY FOR A GOOD AND SOUND CREATION THERE POSSIBLE, AND ALSO THE DIFFICULTY WHICH I, AS AN UNLIMITED BEING HAD BEEN EXPERIENCING IN ATTEMPTING TO MAKE LIMITATIONS ALONG THE CREATION LINE; AND MY ANSWER WAS, TO CREATE, **ONCE** AND FOR **ALL**, THE **ULTIMATE CREATOR**.

I HAD THE **IDEA** TO **MAKE** A **BEING** WHICH WOULD **CREATE** AND WHICH WOULD WISH TO DO **NOTHING ELSE**, AND MOREOVER, WAS OF SUCH A **NATURE** THAT IT WOULD **CONTINUE TO CREATE** AND CREATE **NO MATTER WHAT**; ON ACCOUNT OF ITS **LIMITATIONS**, I GUESSED THAT IT WOULD CREATE TO **COMPENSATE** FOR BEING **LIMITED**.

WHEN WE DISCOVERED THE HORRIBLE **TRUTH**, HOPELESSNESS AND DESPAIR OVERCAME US — THAT CREATOR-BEING HAD, AT A VERY EARLY STAGE IN THE CREATION-WORLD, AS A RESULT OF THE FIRST SHOCK GENERATED BY "THE TERROR OF ENDLESSNESS" PERCEIVED DURING THE EARLIEST SUCCESSFUL UNCREATION, IN ORDER TO BETTER **HIDE** ITSELF WITHIN THE **FOLDS** OF ITS **CREATIONS**, **SHATTERED ITSELF** INTO MANY **MILLIONS** AND **MILLIONS** OF **PIECES** **EACH** OF WHICH HAD BY NOW "GONE OFF ON ITS **OWN**" SO THAT RE-**UNIFICATION** WAS COMPLETELY **IMPOSSIBLE**...

WHICH AS IT TURNED **OUT** WAS A **LUCKY ACCIDENT** - AS **THAT** HAD BEEN THE **PRECISE CAUSE** OF THE ARISING OF THE VARIOUS "**REAL BEING-SPARKS**" WE HAD SEEN **FLYING OFF** FROM THE CREATION-WORLD FOR **SOME** TIME NOW, WHICH HAD BEEN THE CAUSE OF SO MUCH **PLEASURE** FOR THE **LORD** - SO, I'VE **RESOLVED** TO FIND A **SOLUTION** NOT NECESSITATING THE RE-UNIFICATION OF THE CREATOR, BUT WHICH WOULD **SOLVE** THE RIDDLE OF THE **DISAPPEARING COSMOS** ONCE AND FOR **ALL**.

Written by E.J. Gold
Illustrated by Lin Larsen
1973

68

CLAUDIO NARANJO
Conferences
Panels
Lectures
Workshops
Books
1970s / 2002

Photos by Aviko

E.J. Gold and Claudio Naranjo have been close friends and collaborators for many years. In addition to illustrating several books of Naranjo's who is a frequent visitor, Gold has participated in many conferences, panels, workshops and interviews with him.
Photo by Bill de Groot

Photo by Bill de Groot

Dr. Naranjo served his psychiatric residency under Matte-Blanco at the University of Chile Clinic and underwent training analysis at the Chilean Psychoanalytic Institute. He conducted extensive psychopharmacological and personality research, and worked with Fritz Perls and Dr. James Simkin in the early days of Gestalt therapy on the West Coast. He is author of *The One Quest, The Healing Journey, How To Be* (formerly *The Pschology of Meditation* with Robert Ornstein), *Ennea-type Structures* (Gateways). Gateways Books also will release during 1993 *Character and Neurosis*, the author's complete manuscript from which *Ennea-type Structures* is excerpted. This more extended treatment of character typology has extensive cross-references to the psychological literature and world imaginative literature (for examples of character types). Over the years, Dr. Naranjo has been keynote speaker for the American and European Associations for Humanistic Psychology and several national and international Gestalt Conferences.

Photo by Aviko

GESTALT THERAPY

The Attitude & Practice of an Atheoretical Experientialism

Claudio Naranjo, M.D.

CAMP MAZUMDAR
Crestline, CA
1973-75

E.J. Gold in full sheik costume at Camp Mazumdar in Crestline, CA in 1973. Gold walks the edge and gazes over the world.
Photos by Ken Paulson

x

70

EAST-WEST HOUSE
1974

Living in Los Angeles in the late sixties and early seventies meant being in the middle of social and cultural transformations. East-West House was a vanguard center of activity for spiritual seekers and many famous gurus made their appearance in this august location where Gold co-mingled with them all and added his spice to the mix.

E.J. Gold, Reshad Feild.

At Michio Kushi's East-West House, E.J. Gold (center, back) lectures on the inappropriateness of far-eastern diet in American biosystems, circa 1974.

Swami Vishnu Devananda.

Swami Vishnu Devananda, E.J. Gold.

PAMPHLETS

Gold has written dozens and dozens of pamphlets. Here is a partial list. The children's ones are particularly humorous.

1976	*Psyche and Essence, The Nature and Construction*
1976	*The Song of the Guide*
1974	*A Child's Guide to Altered States of Consciousness*
1974	*A Child's Guide to the Real World*
1974	*A Child's Guide To Prayer*
1974	*Prayers from a Truely Great Tempel*
1974	*The Holy Bugger's Gazette*
1974	*Cosmic Acupuncture*
1974	*The Butterfly of Retribution*
1974	*Dynamic Entity*
1974	*On Group Work*
1974	*Brother Judas, The Compassionate Betrayal*
1974	*You Look Somehow Familiar Forever*
1974	*Sacrifices, The Letters of Pir Al-Washi*
1974	*Spontaneous Surrender*
1974	*White-Eyes Medicine Lodge*
1971	*The Avatar's Handbook*
1971	*The One Word*

A CHILD'S GUIDE
TO THE
REAL WORLD
1974

This is one of several books Gold has written for children. It was published in 1974. The illustrations were created by Disney animator/director/designer Lin Larsen who is known for *The Pink Panther* character as well as a long list of cartoons that have entertained us all: *Garfield and Daffy Duck, Batman, Rocky and Bulwinkle, Lady and the Tramp, 101 Dalmatians, Mickey Mouse Club Show, Mr. Limpet, Superman, Scooby Doo, Magilla Gorilla, Yogi Bear, Mr. Magoo, Bugs Bunny, Roadrunner, Flintstones, Jetsons, Pink Panther, Dr. Seuss, The Grinch Who Stole Christmas, Peanuts* (Charlie Brown, Snoopy), *The Big Bang, Bonanza* (animation), and *The Howie Show.*

Screen friends and co-workers of Lin Larsen have included Jack Nicholson, Peter Sellers, Burl Ives, Kirk Douglas, James Mason, Eartha Kit, Mel Blanc, Blake Edwards, Howie Mandel, and Sterling Holloway.

JUAN TEPOZTON
The Boy Who Could
Do Anything
1978

E.J. Gold learned the art of the short story from his father, H.L., a master of this genre with a preference for the psychological component in science fiction, as opposed to the nuts and bolts of many more recent science fiction authors and audiences. Gold the younger is considered an excellent story-teller, and like his father, has a leaning toward short stories. Juan Tepozton is one example of stories he has collected from diverse traditions with timeless wisdom and humor.

E.J.Gold
Juan Tepozton
the boy who could do anything
Tales of the Mexican Sufis

In the tradition of the Arabian Nights and Mulla Nasrudin, the miraculous exploits of Juan Tepozton, a legendary Mexican folk hero, form the basis for a unique collection of Sufi teaching-stories whose appeal is as universal and timeless as the truths they illustrate. Although fascinating as entertainment, these tales transcend the level of fable, legend or folklore, forming puzzles that contain clues to real knowledge and powers of increasing perception, opening the door to visions far beyond ordinary life.

A large, limited edition hardcover format and lavish original illustrations by Lin Larsen, co-creator of the *Pink Panther* and for many years director of animation at Walt Disney Studios, Warner Brothers, and Hanna-Barbera, enliven these enchanting adventures.

KUNG-FU RESTAURANT
CRESTLINE
1973-76

Kung-Fu Natural Foods Restaurant was Gold's "baby" in the early '70s, suggested by friend and mentor Johnny Weismuller who ran his Hollywood restaurant around the corner from the much frequented Gemini. Many entertainment industry friends stopped in on their way to the ski slopes. Gold cooked, waited tables and invented culinary delights with world-famous chef Ellen Tisdale between 1973-76. On the wall behind him hangs a Hirschfeld canvas. Gold's watercolors were interspersed with other art on the walls of this resort attraction.
Photos by Ken Paulson.

TARTHANG TULKU RINPOCHE
1974

Tarthang Tulku Rinpoche and E.J. Gold at the dedication ceremony of Venerable Thich Thien-An's primary American Temple, at Los Angeles, 1974.

Photos by Ken Paulson

THE GURDJIEFF MEMORIAL SERVICE
1975

The 25th Anniversary Gurdjieff Memorial Service took place at the prestigious Forest Lawn. It was another kind of "Happening" that Gold organized and conducted. Hundreds of people came to honor the famous 20th century Russian mystic. The event received national attention including coverage by *THE NEW YORKER* which ran two reports on it. The articles chronicle an event as it was lived and perceived by its author who blundered quite by chance upon it.

Feb. 3, 1975   **THE**   Price 60 cents

THE NEW YORKER

---

24   FEBRUARY 3, 1975

KOREN

"And what salutation do you want to use with this letter, Mr. Dubbins?"

Orson Welles up on top of a great big piece of equipment. Everybody fell into line—they knew what to do—and I find I'm the last guy on line. Welles says to all of us, 'Will you tell me your names, and what pictures you've made?' Well, I didn't want to tell him about the shorts—"

The phone rang. Arthur O'Connell came back in a couple of minutes. "What was I lying to you about? Oh, yes—'Kane.' When Welles got to me, I said, 'I haven't made any pictures, and it seems out here they don't think you're an actor if you haven't.' So Welles said, 'Well, I do' and I got hired as one of the...

Alan Ladd was also in "Citizen Kane," he married and gave him a big star. Hollywood town when you're... dollar. You have got a bed and a room. I to eat, life is wonderful.

"One more story. I was in the Army, and making training films was all about forms when you captured an out battalion, another for headquarters, another on. The movie show and then closeups of forms, I was one of on on the real forms Copies were dropped lines in North Afric...

moralized the Germans—by showing how well we organized the Yanks were—that we took 400,000 prisoners."

IN the afternoon, we drove over to Fullerton to see Philip K. Dick, my favorite science-fiction writer, author of 33 novels and 170 short stories. Past the House of Egg Roll, past Moy's Coffee Shop (Chop Suey, Hot Cakes), past Bowser Beautiful, through Bel Air. We drove to the end of Sunset Boulevard, where we saw seagulls, 18 surfers in wet suits, a blue suggestion of Catalina to the south-west, and an Indian girl in a green...

monks' robes hand out programs. Up front, there is a photo of Mr. Gurdjiev in a handsome old-fashioned gold frame, also a wreath of pink carnations, two pots of ferns, three wrought-iron candlelabra, the American flag, and a Forest Lawn flag. A man is walking around with a videotape camera. Everyone sits down quietly. Cough, cough, Rustle, rustle. Wriggle, wriggle. Harrumph...

FEBRUARY 3, 1975   taire," "La Paranoia." Dick has just finished a book about Tim Leary and the LSD crowd, and what happened to them.

We had stopped in to make a short call of homage, and wound up talking along for hours, drinking wine, and Tessa going out for some Chinese food, and then talking about cosmologies until it was almost time for our plane back to N.Y. The apartment also contains a two-foot-high metal rocket ship on a wooden base—this is his Hugo Award, the highest award in science fiction. The plaque is missing, though, because Dick once used the award to break up a fight. "It grabs good," he says.

As for the cosmologies, this is what emerged from our discussions: cosmologies all seem to be based on repetition—you know, first the universe expands, then it contracts, then it expands again, etc.—but maybe that's not so. Maybe this whole expansion business that the universe is currently embarked upon is going to happen only once. That would mean that every day really is a new day, right? Also, maybe it's not true that Einstein was smarter than Newton. Maybe Newton's laws accurately described the universe as it then existed. But since then it's expanded and got more complicated and can be accurately...

Three Days in L.A.: Days Two & Three

MORE West Coast reports from our friend the fellow-citizen:

Let's see, where am I? That's what I was thinking, and the only answer was: The Continental Hyatt House, on Sunset Boulevard, Hollywood, eight o'clock in the morning, and the phone is ringing. Right, right, and I'm out in L.A. for the first time in my life, for a memorial service for Mr. Georges Gurdjiev, the mystic and oracle, at Forest Lawn, Glendale, world-famous for its great art and beauty, a cemetery that is so successful it now has three branches—Hollywood Hills, Cypress, Covina Hills. Do you think maybe I could get a franchise? The idea is coming to me. "Come Stay with Us." The place would be in the shape of the 50 United States, Alaska and Hawaii on the other side of the Freeway, so you could rest in your native state. Wait—answer the phone. Hello?

"Hi, pal, this is Henny Youngman."

Henny Youngman! The great comedian tells me I have to look up his old friend Arthur O'Connell, the famous character actor, who now makes the Mr. Goodwin commercials for Crest toothpaste. "The first time I was in Hollywood," Henny says, "Milton Berle told me he'd introduce me to his crowd. So he introduced me to his maid, his gardener, his chauffeur. Milton Berle is so rich he keeps his money under the rug." I ask Henny about Jack Benny. "Jack told me, 'Henny, I could take one of your jokes and get half an hour out of it. Put something between your jokes—my jaws are aching.'"

The air has been washed by a little rain, 54°, sunshine and clouds; everything looking extraordinarily pretty as

WED, EVERYTHING AT TIME OF SORROW." The place looks like Prospect Park—hills, you know, winding lanes, trees, shrubs, statuary. Very well kept up. "PARK HERE for the COURT OF DAVID and the MYSTERY OF LIFE GARDEN." Leonardo's "Last Supper" in stained glass, John La Farge's "Ascension" in mosaic, "The Crucifixion," by Jan Styka, world's largest religious painting, 65 yards × 15 yards. Souvenir ball-point pens and letter openers. Little Christmas trees still on some of the graves. Authentic replicas of everything you can think of: the wee kirk where Annie Laurie prayed when but a hairn, the church that moved Gray to write his elegy, and (in Hollywood Hills) Boston's Old North Church. Give us this day our daily bread, under the spreading chestnut tree, shoot if you must this old gray head, one if by land, two if by sea. "As a service to the hard-of-hearing, this church is equipped with 'Hearing Aid,' which may be obtained from the attendant." "CHILDREN WHO ARE NOT QUIET MUST BE TAKEN FROM THE AUDITORIUM TO THE SOUND-PROOF ROOM PROVIDED." Well, it's not really their fault. Everyone out here is a bit religious, if you know what I mean. Has to do with people being alone in their cars all day—no jostling crowds, no give and take, not quite enough human contact and reciprocal nourishment.

Outside the Church of the Recessional, some canned piano music is playing. The church doors are closed, and maybe 50-60 people are standing around listening to the music and waiting for the service. Checking the assembled cars, I notice two with Iowa plates. The people are your usual mixture of ages, etc. Some are wearing Gucci Earth Shoes, some are wearing Hush Puppies. And there are boots, Hush Puppies, suede jobs, high heels, sensible shoes, platforms, wedges, Wellingtons. And Hank's cowboy boots. The music stops, and a recorded English voice suggests that maybe Gurdjieg was "premature." Then the doors open, and everybody files in, treading softly on the church's wall-to-wall beige carpeting. The left aisle is full of plants and birdies in squeaky cages—a Forest Lawn tradition. Usherettes in sort of

---

THE NEW YORKER   23

"Oog's the name. Conking dames on the head's the game."

named Gomidas, who, like Kodaly, collected the folk music of his country, and that many of the famous long words in "All and Everything"—like "Kliososhoot-shoom" and "Vogtlenoot-nlook-mam-ani"—are really the titles of Armenian canticles collected by Dr. Gomidas.

CAN you guess what the most popular movie in Los Angeles is? "Earthquake," which is about how Los Angeles gets destroyed by an earthquake. "Earthquake" is showing at Mann's (formerly Grauman's) Chinese, and the lines in front stretch around the block and out of sight. The management of the theatre has suspended a cart below the ceiling, in a Sensurround—the giant speakers that rumble violently, like an earthquake—actually dislodges part of the structure. People applaud when landmarks tumble, and you keep hearing remarks like "Wow, Mom, there goes our block!" The second most popular movie is "The Towering Inferno," but that takes place in San Francisco. There is also a brief run of movie houses, called Pacific Walk-In Theatres. This dope comes from Hank. We dined at a good Mexican joint, El Coyote, and then he went to the movies. I never back to the hotel, which, by the way, is

across from Lyle Tuttle Tattooing, to watch "Kolchak, the Night Stalker" on TV. Turned out to was trying to tell a Los Angeles vampire. There was also a Japanese-language variety show, as compared to English-language Tayota commercials that showed American teen-agers losing in the back seat of a car in the fifties.

MORNING of our last day in L.A. We call on Henny's friend Arthur O'Connell, who hails from Flossmoor, Long Island. Arthur is a delightful person. Handsome man in a yellow cardigan. Arthur's been at at least 33 feature films, so Hank and I ask about the old days in Hollywood. "Well, first I made a few shorts with Edgar Kennedy and Leon Errol, but then I went to do Shakespeare in the country, you have to do it the hard way. Everybody played everything. I played Polonius and parts like that. Such lived through to the end of the play. Remember the old joke: 'Was Hamlet having an affair with Ophelia?' 'Well, in our company he was.' 'That's there was a small call for Citizen Kane.' I went about the with a lot of other guys, and they was

---

THE NEW YORKER did extensive coverage in two separate issues of the Gurdjieff Memorial Service.

ODIYAN
Marin County
1977

June 15, 1977

If one tries to vanquish foes in the outer world,
They increase in greater measure.
If one conquers the Self-mind within,
All ones foes soon disappear.

from *The Hundred Thousand Songs of Milarepa*
translated by Garma C. C. Chang

Dear Mr. Gold,
    I am writing to convey Rinpoche's personal thanks for helping to find volunteers. Their assistance in the preparations for the open house was very much appreciated. I hope you will be able to convey our thanks to each one of them.
        Sincerely,
        Sally Sorenson

E.J. Gold with Dr. Jerome Berman, Director of the California Museum of Ancient Art, at the opening of the Tibetan monastic retreat Odiyan, 1977.
Photos by Ken Paulson.

THE WORLD SYMPOSIUM
1978

WORLD SYMPOSIUM UPDATE
by Guru Raj Singh

We live in a world torn between wanting to listen to the sound of a flower growing and wanting to ignore the sound of the sky falling
By sometimes being sensitive enough to the first process we acquire the energy necessary to prevent the second.
—River
Stockholm, 1977

When the time and place are right, things are incredibly fast around an idea. We're going to experience these days with the World Symposium on Humanity, enjoying the exhilaration, and being sobered by the responsibility, as the idea takes shape around us.

The mechanisms by which the idea has been crystalized are an interesting study. In the past year, we strung together some tentative ideas, talked about satellites a lot, ascertained the basic economic feasibility (given enough money and organization) of the project, and broadcast those possibilities through New Directions magazine and through several big meetings. Response was enthusiastic, and some key talented people stepped forward, so we knew we were onto something.

The second phase involved meetings with specific folks in four major centres — Vancouver, San Francisco, Calgary, and Los Angeles. Dinners were arranged, and guests — various artists, media professionals, organizers, etc. — were invited personally, many brought along friends and associates. These meetings have been, and continue to be, like communions of long-separated friends, comparing the pieces of the puzzle they'd been working on and finding that they all fit. Part of the image formed in their lives is seen by many to include the World Symposium on Humanity 1978. The meetings are characterized by long moments of silence, invocations, chanting, and heartfelt prayers for guidance. They are held around delicious dinners, often potlucks, in the homes of key organizers, and so develop a warmth of fellowship, an open friendly brainstorm, that draws a lot of creative possibilities into the open.

Foundation (whose major project is to Symposium on Humanity) will lose credibility. For people who have a habit additional forms, the experience is one of to make a structure that can be related to and trusted by both the spiritual counterculture and the establishment there?

It feels integral in a maturing process. The works and concerns of the new age are ready to join the great mainstream of ideas, and we must find a way to surface only integrity in that rough-and-tumble arena. The World Symposium will reach, we hope, about half of the world's electronic nervous system to touch millions of hearts. We must learn how to approach the establishment of that nervous system, who have developed, for largely commercial ends, in a quiet, competent manner, and not lose the grounded simplicity of our origins. The communications and entertainment industry show a remarkable ability to co-opt, commercialize, and twist anything with real life in our culture. Witness the fate of the hippie-political Movement of the late 60's and early 70's — the players in that drama were ultimately reduced to grandstanding in front of television cameras, to seeing deep-felt ideals manipulated for profit, entertainment and sensation. It will take great strength and foresight to see that we learn how to use the media, and the money necessary to move in those circles, without being used by them.

Here is a simple outline of the structure evolved so far: a prestigious board of directors, made up of prominent politicians, entertainers, and

25

A Step in Time
by Stephen Brock Schafer

Philosophy Underlying the World Symposium

The more people who become involved, the more successful the Celebration will be. The energy quality of their participation is the key to successful metanoia, and it is imperative that the energy quality of this event be uncompromised.

The goal of the Celebration is the rapid and effective dissolution of the major barriers forestalling communication, which prevent interaction, diminishing the possibility of making choices, and therefore, diminish responsibility and the sense of identification which lead to irresponsibility and anti social behavior.

The Celebration will be geared to an increased personal identification with a psychecology the method of meaningful participation. A consequence of this expanded awareness will be a realization of the importance of the person's creative contribution to the whole and the unique

responsibility within the framework of existence.

This concept has been developed through observation of the vast progression of creative effort along multiple lines toward the goal of a more harmonious quality of life through more meaningful self expression. It takes into account the absolute complexity of the challenge which we face and has dealt with it organically in terms of the principle of personal distinctiveness. It has been fostered in the knowledge that a global celebration in conjunction with an organized humanitarian movement can radically affect the established global and international

atmosphere of trust, cooperation and understanding and that the will result in a more effective focus sing of human resources upon common problems.

The efficacy of a concerted Celebration of Humanity is its education of Humanity on the personal consciousness, and the relative and efficiency of achieving that pact worldwide. Through concerted effort an event of such significance and scope will take place that international communications media will be organized, implicated Coverage of the many activities leading up to the Celebration and followup coverage of on-going projects, will provide a massive

WORLD SYMPOSIUM
30
ORGANIZATIONAL OUTLINE
by Guru Raj Singh

Los Angeles, Toronto and London

The location of the Symposium in these three cities will give people in most parts of the western world the opportunity to attend, with at most a few days' travel. Teams in each city, nuclei of which are already at work, will engage space in

skills, needs, etc., and cross-referencing into information about active organizations. It is hoped that thus many new projects will be born.

This intense use of high technology will, aside from its obvious communications functions, illustrate dramatically that technology need not be used to exploit and alienate; a beautiful tool to bring minds together. Logistically, this is recommended scope, tremendous challenge tempt to hook it up.

dral

makers, dancers and ll kinds will be desses of celebrations, ces in which masses develop powerful iousness and emose from such group ed by use of animkers, video feedback or devices, will be s projected through her simultaneouss, both in imagrally, through the the satellite. It is such a concentrated assess power, a comic of subtle and materning effect on the e talking we could he final day of the is hoped to engage people in each of ns in such an exper-

sium unfolds, and media, entertainsiness worlds are portunities for fundll of the new age wives. It is intended s benefit concerts, dientes, fund-raising ampaigns, and even thon, will be organram is already being

planned by a top-flight professional fundraiser in Los Angeles. The Symposium itself will be designed to turn a profit, and at the Symposium discussions will take place on how best to use the money available

AMANDA FOULGER

Workshops, action groups

This event will not consist only of people playing the role of audience for the speakers, of course. Dozens of less-well-known speakers and group leaders will be invited to attend, and the electronic facilities present will be used to full advantage in helping people make connections. Dozens of rooms of varying sizes will be available for meetings as small as two, or as large as 500. The program will be explicitly designed to overcome people's passivity at such events, and elicit commitment to action in people's daily lives after the Symposium.

Specific local service projects, relevant to the communities in which the Symposium takes place, will be organized, and people attending the event will spend part of their time actually doing work, creating an opportunity to practice what we preach, right on the spot.

Guru Raj Singh Khalsa, one of the principal organizers of the *World Symposium*, 1978.

In trying to retrace events, activities, jobs, projects during the mid to late sixties to mid-seventies in Gold's life, it is extremely difficult to sort things out. Just seeing these business cards gives a tiny glimpse at the variety and inventiveness of Gold's mind.

NEW DIRECTIONS
1978

WORLD SYMPOSIUM

elbow with him, and regional executive directors to implement programs. This key group of advisers, called the Executive Advisory Council, is currently concentrated in Los Angeles:

Mukhia Sardarni Sahiba Krishna Kaur Khalsa, Associate Executive Director, presently head of Sikh Dharma for Southern California (her choice for this position has been ratified by the rest of the Council).

Alan Ames, L. A. office manager, organizer of festivals.

Kit Thomas, media development, presently film-maker with Walt Disney Productions.

Ron Hays, media development, professional imagist and animator ("Prelude", "Demon Seed", "Sergeant Pepper's Lonely Heart's Club Band", "Logan's Run").

Amanda Foulger, public relations, presently administrator and broadcaster of new age programming with KPFK-FM

Richard Musgrave, fundraising and budget, presently International Co-operation Council vice-president and management consultant.

Glenn Taylor, media consultant, presently president of Syntar Productions, producer of films and television.

As a professional consultant on fundraising and corporate structure, Linda Lockwood, who among other things presently manages fundraising for Easter Seals of California, will be an important resource of this group.

This structure is a standard one for non-profit foundations, and can be easily recognized and dealt with by mainstream business and entertainment interests. Around it, to draw in focussed feedback from the public, will revolve several dozen regional Humanity Congresses, and a board of trustees composed of the speakers at last year's World Symposium.

What makes this structure relevant to the new age is the balance point, which is, for lack of a better word, God. Both the Board of Directors, on one end of the balance beam, and the Executive, on the other, will serve with the recognition that the Creator is the ultimate guide goal and authority of the Foundation, and the lifeblood of the Foundation will be continually infused with that realization, to minimize personal and political conflicts within the organization. It will be an important job of the Executive Director and his Council to provide this spiritual leadership, and to keep the workings of the Foundation circulating in public knowledge; to keep the doors open.

It is a sobering challenge, for if the World Symposium in 1979 is successful, the new age will become a significant social force, consciously, and will gather money, power and talent with ever increasing intensity. It is our sincere prayer that we be worthy of the task, and that the trails we lay be well-blazed for others to tread.

•

A CBC Radio interview by Danny Thatchuk "Doctor Bundolo" was published in 1978 in *New Directions* which was one of the first "new-age" magazines long before *East West Journal, The Whole Earth Catalog, Mother Jones, Ramparts,* or *Yoga Journal* saw the light of day.

This interview took place while the preparations for the *World Symposium 1978* were underway and most of the issue was devoted to that subject. Gold was a participant in this satellite-transmitted unprecedented event. The World Symposium was organized by friends of Gold's back when that world was a lot smaller and just about everybody who was anybody knew everybody.

Wings

Volume 1, Number 4
Sept./Oct. 1978
$1.00/$1.25 in Canada

Special — This Issue:
E.J. Gold: Western Gurus
Cowboys on the Path

Tim Leary: Tantra & Tarot

John Lilly: Seduction by K

Hilda: Madame Life

Toni Lilly: Interspecies Ethics

George Metzger: Super Sufi Comix

Daniel Inesse: Gay Guru

Mignon Garland: Isadora Duncan Heritage

Stalking the Wild Guru

Zen Whaling

And Much, Much More

Build A Linear Accelerator For Only $1.98

Better Holmes & Gardens

Sex, Money, Power, Dope, Violence, and Diet

WINGS NATURAL LAMPOON

May-June '79   The Very Funny Magazine $1.25
$1.50 in Canada

Animal Disco
From Ecstasy
to Lunch

HEIMIE THE
BARBARIAN
by E.J. Gold

NO PRESERVATIVES ADDED

plus New Science Fiction and Fantasy From: Steve Perry
Paul Novitski   Carol Menares   Robert Anton Wilson

Contrary to expectation, National Lampoon did not appreciate the humor.

Yes, I admit to once having the urge to rush off and find a new guru every six months. The last one was Charisma incarnate. I saw him at "the gathering of the ways"..."a crossroads of spiritual understanding" the handbill said, with pictures of beautiful people dancing, playing music, eating food...well. I thought, it's a symbolic trip anyway, the whole thing...so I went down there.
Of course, I dressed up as a

THE LAST GURU

Some notes on the final Sacrifice.

by Sufi Duck

PSYCHIC DISCOVERIE

BEHIND THE CHAISE LOUNG

by Dan Thatchuk

excerpted from the soon to be forthcoming *First Book of B*

8 WINGS

The Darling Buds of May

by Robert Anton Wilson

excerpted from a novel in progress.

If we accept multiple universes then we no longer need worry about what 'really' happened in the past, because every possible past is equally real.
— Joseph Gerver, *The Past as Backwards Movies of the Future*, *Physics Today*, April 1971

He who must — who hesitates is lost. Marvin Gardens said one day in the Confrontation office. Jo Malik considered it one of the most interesting Freudian slips she had ever heard and recorded it in her diary where it was, of course, subsequently scanned by the Illuminati.
Marvin and Jo never got along well, but that was because he regarded her as an extra-terrestrial invader and she regarded him as a nut.
Marvin is emphatically not a loony. Justin Case had been heard to say quite often. "He's a genius. The greatest put-on artist since Richard Nixon. Nobody recognizes what a great satirist he is."
"Justin Case," Marvin said when that was repeated to him, thinks he's being liberal, but he's just another victim of brainwashing by the Amazon Invasion.

Marvin Gardens always referred to the Women's Liberation movement as the Amazon Invasion. He believed, or pretended to believe, that the ringleaders were all extra terrestrials.

They're taken over the language and created a semantic smog in which ordinary humanity is obliterated by abstractions like 'chauvinist or simple mammalian person or other mammalian erotic signaling is politicized into a new sin called 'sexism'. Any male who dares to oppose them is stigmatized as a male chauvinist and any female who opposes them is labeled a victim of male brainwashing.

Marvin Gardens always referred to the Women's Liberation movement as the Amazon Invasion. He believed, or pretended to believe, that the ringleaders were all extra terrestrials, who were bodily conspiring to seize supreme power everywhere through what he called semantic black magick.

Obviously, within a decade, they will command the key posts in all areas of industry (they've captured publishing already) and then government will fall. Probably then, the males of their species will start landing and we'll all be enslaved. It's the sweetest infiltration job in the history of galactic espionage. For merely daring to reveal their plans, I am smeared by them as a male chauvinist pig, which is ten times worse than an ordinary male chauvinist and equivalent to a suppressive on the Scientologists' hit list.

Some agreed with Justin Case that Marvin was kidding, that he had merely seen an opportunity — the chance to attain fame and fortune by espousing a totally controversial extreme position. Others, however, claimed he was dead serious and was a classical case of clinical paranoia. Marvin always pointed out, when either of these theories was mentioned in his presence. There is a third possibility I might be right. In that case, how convenient for Them that my sanity and sincerity are so often called into question. It almost looks as if They are conspiring to defame my character. Are they afraid that some

cont'd on page 47

WINGS 15

Better wings
and Gardens

WINGS — THE NEW AGE SATIRE MAGAZINE

Jan.-Feb. '79
$1.25
$2.50 in Canada

Wings Interviews:
Dune author Frank Herbert
and Robert Anton Wilson
author of *Cosmic Trigger*

Consumer Re[
The Evelyn W[
Speed Samadhi Co[

Farmer Clips W[
Robert S. deI[

Science Reveals:
Man is a Plant

PLAYWINGS

WINGS: THE NEW AGE SATIRE MAGAZINE

MARCH-APRIL 1979 • $1.25
$1.50 in Canada

**THE PLAYWINGS
PHILOSOPHY**
Paul Krassner

SNEAK PREVIEW
Tim Leary's
New Book

PLUS:
The Humor Of
Robert Silverberg
Joe Haldeman
Howard Goldsmith

It's Mur[
In Here

Justin Case Jr.

Thinking about the others, I get the willies. Of course, they have the same feelings about me. We'd like to kill each other, but we can't.

I closed my eyes and it was like being back in Sanctuary. The punk rock group on stage became the sounds of the Higher Planes; the brisk order-taking of the cocktail waitresses the vibrations of the Void; and the humming chatter of the dancers and drinkers became for me the distant hubbub of sentient beings in Samsara.

I could almost hear Devananda whistling in the kitchen — the gnawing, rattling, annoying sounds not quite covered by the chanting. The tune was always *Dancing In The Dark*. I don't think

22 WINGS

A MATTE[

by

"Shnurg," the wizened old man intoned to the gathered throng of disciples seated in the lotus position before him. "Blabble dabble wabba dabba."

Frobish turned off the tape recorder after having played that talk back six times in desperate hope of understanding even one word of it. "Not one damn intelligible word," he complained to Mary, his wife. "Yet they claim he's not speaking a foreign language."

"I can't understand it, either," she said.

"Yeah, but I'm a linguist; I'm supposed to be able to understand it."

An hour later as he scanned through the files on the Harinama cult, his psychologist friend stepped through the door to the

28 WINGS

comp[
runn[
first[
for [

"[
thing[
human equivalent — not even a dolphin equivalent. I've even run Cetacean for comparison. I'm so desperate for an answer."

"I haven't heard it," Harry asked, drawing lightly on his unlit pipe. Frobish played the tape again.

"Fnord?" Harry asked, now as puzzled as Frobish.

"Yeah, that's what I meant," Frobish said. "It's been through the computer a hundred and sixty one times and drawn a blank every time.

"This is no paranoid schizo." Frobish said. "There's a pattern — definite repetition — but it just doesn't relate to anything humans talk about, that's all."

"Maybe it's an esoteric language, like sanskrit or something," his wife suggested, as they sat down for dinner that evening.

"It must be," he agreed, "but how do we translate it when there's no human equivalent?"

"I don't know," she admitted. Opening the dossier, he reviewed the figures, graphs, tables

A Linear Ac[

From Junk Parts For L[

You can build a linear accelerator in your backyard using only a hula-hoop, some toy horseshoe magnets, a glow in the dark frisbee, and a tin can. That's right, an Atom Smasher for less than $1.98. Help America build the neutron bomb. *Start collecting neutrons today.*

WHAT HAPPENS IN A LINEAR ACCELERATOR

When a free electron runs into something solid, watch out. Electrons are very small and therefore have incredibly small brains. Because of this, they react to impact by smashing any atoms in sight. When they hit an atom square on

he knew[
been a[
human,[
Satori[
know everything about each other. I mean *everything*. The sheer force of boredom makes us tell everything again and again, even though we hate to tell it, just about as much as we hate to hear it.

Somebody in the disco laughed, and the laugh reminded me of Harada's *heh-heh-heh*. My spine tingled and my hackles went up automatically. Sure, Sara's high-pitched giggle burns me pretty bad, and Ravi's low, booming Elk's club *ho-ho-ho* and Jaya's tinkling, hysterical laugh drive us all up the wall most of the time. But Harada's laugh — that short,

the button, nucleically speaking, the atom breaks up, making available *free neutrons*. These are what we want, *and we want them bad*.

First, get one electron off the dial of your iridescent watch. The watch is held up to the hole you cut previously in the hula hoop (see diagram A) and then wave the magnet toward the hula hoop, encouraging the electron to go through the hole. Once the electron is trapped inside the hoop, move the magnet around in a circle, gradually increasing the speed. Remember...it takes extremely high velocities to sufficiently stimulate the electron.

who waits their turn, and only two can sleep at a time. That's not as bad as the Council of Three, where only one can sleep — but there are times when you want just one or two more cycles to catch your breath. Even if you try to, you can't get comfortable. In the *Ida* position there's the Master Valve, and in the *Pingla*, the Emergency Button, which jabs you right in the side if you move too fast or doze too soundly.

You can't sleep in Sanctuary; not really sleep, if what you mean by sleep is the kind of regenerative rest you get as a human; sleep for

cont'd on page 39

When you have it moving as fast as possible, have an assistant quickly open the slot in the hula hoop, and allow the electron to shoot out of the hoop into the frisbee in front of it. Now get the tin can ready, positioned behind the frisbee, to catch the resulting free neutrons. Close the top of the can quickly, only opening it to catch additional neutrons. (At night, one can usually see a small glow as the electron passes through the frisbee.)

This system is a major advance over other home systems. The introduction of the frisbee sent a shock wave of excitement through the scientific and consumer

THE SATURDAY
EVENING WINGS

Nov.-Dec. '78   WINGS — THE NEW AGE SATIRE MAGAZINE $1.00
$1.25 in Canada

Christmas Special

Wings Interview:
the Real
Harlan
Ellison

**An Original
Short Story
by Steve
Perry**

**Psychic
Discoveries
Behind the
Chaise Lounge**

**Rajneesh:
Sufism
is Heartfulness**

Star Rats Comix — And More...

E.J. Gold was editor and art director of *Wings, The New Age Satire Magazine*, from 1974 to 1979. Wings produced *Playwings, Wings Natural Lampoon, Better Wings & Gardens, Better Holmes & Gardens, The Saturday Evening Wings* and had top quality articles from individuals like Timothy Leary, Paul Krassner, Frank Herbert, Robert Silverberg, Frederik Pohl, Harlan Ellison, Joe Haldeman, Howard Goldsmith, Robert S. deRopp, Robert Anton Wilson, and many more science fiction/fantasy writers. George Metzger, Lin Larsen and Gold did most of the illustrations for *Wings*.

WINGS
& SCIENCE FICTION

WINGS INTERVIEW:
THE *REAL* HARLAN ELLISON

PLAYWINGS INTERVIEW:
JOE HALDEMAN

Hugo and Nebula award-winning author Joe Haldeman lives in Florida. Some of his better-known novels are Mindbridge, The Forever War and All My Sins Remembered. Formerly a demolitions expert and foot soldier in the Vietnam War, he edited an anthology of short stories, titled Study War No More.

At a recent science fiction convention in Phoenix, WINGS editor E.J. Gold and his wife Cybele sat down to interview Joe. The following wide-ranging discussion is the result, one we're sure you'll enjoy.

The interview started out with Joe being told that WINGS readers were not ordinary magazine readers, and went from there...

JOE: There is one thing that might be of interest to people who are a little bit weird. I believe I've done several times in the course of this life. I don't believe it, but it seems to be an explanation for some odd things.

E.J.: You mean the changes that we go through?

JOE: No, just some discrete individual experiences where I should have been killed, and I wasn't. One time I was in Vietnam, I was evacuating a hill. We were under very intense sniper fire, with not only rifles, but recoilless rifles, bazookas. And we were having to run over the hill one at a time to get into a helicopter that was waiting sort of in the lee of the hill so it couldn't get fired at.

Finally, my turn came and I

ran across and above got shot bullets all around the place. But I jumped in the helicopter and it was anxious to get away. So I was sitting with my feet dangling out of the helicopter. And it was sitting on a ledge overlooking a cliff about over a thousand feet deep, and it took off. But instead of going up, as helicopters normally do, it fell down the cliff and I was sitting there with my legs dangling out and I felt one of the helicopter. Between my knees I saw the thousand feet of air and the jungle down below. The next thing I knew I was back inside the helicopter.

I thought, "Boy, that was close." Somebody pulled me in. And when we got to safety and got out of the helicopter I asked who had pulled me in. They said, "What are you talking about?"

"I see myself primarily as an entertainer."

"I see a hole where a book should be. And I go ahead and write it."

"I believe I've died several times in the course of this life."

PLAYWINGS INTERVIEW: ROBERT SILVERBERG

Robert Silverberg is the author of many science fiction novels including The Masks of Time, Son of Man, A Time of Changes, Tower of Glass, Dying Inside, and The Book of Skulls. He has won Hugo and Nebula awards for his novels and his short stories, some of which are published in the collections The Reality Trip and Other Implausibilities, Dimension Thirteen, and Unfamiliar Territory. A past President of the Science Fiction Writers of America, Mr. Silverberg has also edited many anthologies of short stories.

He has also written several non-fiction books on historical and archaeological subjects including The Pueblo Revolt, Mound Builders of Ancient America, The Challenge of Climate, Lost Cities and Vanished Civilizations and The Realm of Prester John.

Born and educated in New York City, Silverberg now lives in California.

WINGS: What are you going to do now? You feel forced into writing again for some inner reason.

SILVERBERG: Yes. I've been struck by a lightning bolt after not writing for four years. Suddenly a book came to me and said, 'Write me', and in a weak moment I agreed. So I am going to begin a novel in November as soon as the rains reach California. And I feel quite positively attuned to writing it, which is odd after four years of having no interest whatever in writing. That is to say, it was as if I had never been a writer in that period. I had no energy tied into the notion of writing again, ever. Suddenly I'm going to do it. I reached the point where it was no longer necessary for me to write.

WINGS: Can you elaborate? What was going through your head for the last four years?

SILVERBERG: I've been in my garden in my head. I've been in a state of non-striving and of diverted energy. The thing I've done all my adult life, the thing I've been most attached to doing, is writing, being a writer, carrying out a career. That all went away. Partly because I had resentment and irritation and disappointment and party because I was tired of doing it and time to do something else.

WINGS: What's the irritation and the resentment and the disappointment?

SILVERBERG: The irritation came from the response that the readers gave my better books no more recent books. As I moved farther out in the direction of writing a personal fiction making a personal statement, I found that I was baffling, disturbing and confusing rather than guiding and illuminating.

"I've been struck by a lightning bolt after not writing for four years. Suddenly a book came to me and said, 'Write me'."

"I found that I was baffling, disturbing and confusing rather than guiding and illuminating."

"I became irritated at the notion that I was so committed to a readership that was incapable of getting the message."

"It is an assumption of society that mythology is something our ancestors did. They don't realize that we are making mythology right now, you and I. We're engaged in myth functions all the time."

At a recent science fiction convention in Santa Rosa, WINGS interviewed Frank Herbert, the famous author of Dune, the Hugo and Nebula award-winning novel. Herbert's varied and colorful background often is evident in his stories. In addition to serving in the U.S. Navy in World War II, he has worked as a photographer, television cameraman, oyster diver, psychoanalyst, radio newsman, jungle survival instructor, lay analyst, political speechwriter, and teacher of creative writing.

Some of Herbert's more well-known novels are Destination Void, Whipping Star, Soul Catcher, The Eyes of Heisenberg, and The Godmakers. He has also published science fiction short stories. In addition to winning the Hugo and Nebula awards for Dune, Herbert also won the International Fantasy Award for another novel, making him the first writer to win all three awards.

Frank Herbert now lives with his family in Washington. In line with his interest in ecology, he used his six wooded acres for an ecological demonstration project to determine how a high quality of life can be maintained with a minimum drain on the total energy system.

WINGS INTERVIEW:
FRANK HERBERT

FRANK HERBERT

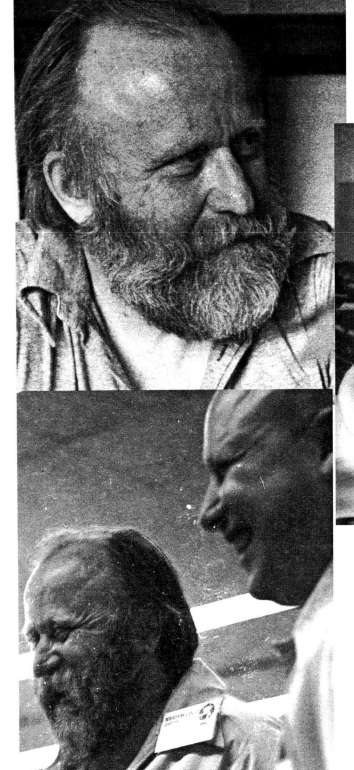

Frank Herbert and E.J. Gold, 1978.
Photos by Ken Paulson.

Many science fiction writers either contributed stories to or wrote articles for *Wings Magazine*.

Frank Herbert was extensively interviewed in 1978 at a science fiction convention. Here we see him with E.J. Gold having a few laughs together.

Other well-known science-ficiton writers who were interviewed included Robert Silverberg, Joe Haldeman and Harlan Ellison. All of these writers were well-known acquaintances of Gold's who has been a member of SFWA (Science Fiction Writers Association) for most of his life. Of course, he knew them while he was growing up under the *wings*, so to speak, of his father H.L. Gold who, as mentioned earlier, was the founding editor of *Galaxy Science Fiction Magazine*. Like father like son.

TIMOTHY LEARY

Many famous writers and consciousness shapers contributed to *Wings*, including Dr. Timothy Leary. Leary and Gold maintained a life long friendship since the *Wings* days and Leary used Gold's *American Book of the Dead* during his last days as he prepared for transition. He expressed his deep appreciation for having such a tool at hand.

Photos courtesy: Dr. Timothy Leary.

During the last days of his life, Tim Leary used the floatation tank developed by John Lilly and the Samadhi Co. as a means to alleviate some of the pain he was in. Here we see him with Lee Perry, President of Samadhi Tank Co. during the installation of the tank in his quarters. She also presented him with a book co-authored by John Lilly and E.J. Gold, *Tanks for the Memories*. Leary used the tank up until his passage.

THE FLYING KARAMAZOV BROTHERS

Many celebrities appeared at Gold's *Cosmicon* **held at the Jack Tar Hotel in San Francisco, 1980.**

Right: E.J. Gold, Robert Anton Wilson, Dr. Claudio Naranjo, Tim Furst, and Paul Magid.

Tim Furst, Sam Williams, Paul Magid, Howard Patterson.

Above: A discussion about jiggling technique between Gold and Paul Magid. Right: Gold in juggling demonstration, San Francisco, 1980.
Photos by Willem de Groot.

Tim Furst, Paul Magid.

ROBERT ANTON WILSON
1980

Friend and colleague Robert Anton Wilson in discussion with E.J. Gold during one of many collaborative events over a period of decades.

Wilson and Gold have had numerous taped discussions, panels and debates that are still very popular recorded talks.

THE LAZY MAN'S GUIDE TO DEATH AND DYING

1984

The irreverent *Lazy Man's Guide to Death and Dying* was very well received and sold out in no time at all. The Preface was written by long-time friend and collaborator Robert Anton Wilson, and the Introduction by Dr. John Lilly.

The book was immediately translated into German. A new edition of this amusing title is scheduled for 2003 as it has been out-of-print and rare almost since day one.

If you're thinking about dying, but don't know where to begin -- relax! Earthbound voyagers set adrift in the unveiled vision of higher dimensions will need this book. From exact instructions on how to confront the symptoms of death, *"After all you're dead! What more can happen?"*, to concise detailed material on how to choose rebirth without really trying, *The Lazy Man's Guide to Death & Dying* is without a doubt the last word on the death experience.

THE LAZY MAN'S GUIDE TO DEATH & DYING

E.J. Gold's *Lazy Man's Guide to Death & Dying* was excerpted in a 1984 issue of OMNI in the column titled *LAST WORD* which appears on the last page of the magazine. The mere fact that a mainstream magazine such as OMNI would publish this was an indication of a cultural shift regarding death and dying.

The book was quite a success and has been sold out for years and is almost impossible to find even in used form.

LAST WORD

By E. J. Gold

Don't worry about those strange new sensations and cosmic thoughts. They're not important. After all, you're dead. What more can happen?

The Lazy Man's Guide to Death and Dying is Gold's most humorous publication on the subject of death and dying. As a pioneer in the field with the attitude that death is a natural part of life, not a clinical event, he has written many hilarious passages that fly in the face of the ever-so-morbid seriousness of a culture intent on forgetting the ultimate destiny of all life, and conversely, the transitory nature of death itself which is only a doorway to the next life in an endless cycle of death and rebirth...

Editors' note: As part of Omni's continuing commitment to public service, we offer this primer on how to tell if you are going to die. So much misinformation has been disseminated on the subject that we felt it was about time that we finally set the record straight.

If you're about to die, you'll begin to notice several terrifying sensations and cosmic revelations as the phenomenal veil is ripped away, revealing, for the first time since the last time you passed away from the organic world, the endless, eternal, unveiled kingdom of the void.

At the same time, you'll experience a mind-numbing personal cataclysm as you're hurtled at twice the speed of light into a dark and unknown world in which everything seems almost the same as it was before, only more so.

Don't worry about those strange new feelings and cosmic thoughts. They're not important. After all, you're dead! What more can happen? After you've taken rebirth you'll be able to look back on all this and laugh.

These sensations are useful for anticipating your exact moment of passage. And if you've been practicing at our popular workshops, you will be able to use these sensations to call forth a series of special psychological, emotional, and instinctive mechanisms, which will help you maintain a sense of equilibrium—albeit false—during the total loss of memory, vision, sensation, and identity you'll experience as you are dragged inevitably through the portal of death.

It's so easy to just expel your last breath in a sigh of relief and fall facefirst into your plate of spaghetti and meatballs, in total surrender to the perfect, shining, endless void, which is without objects, states of consciousness, identity, time, space, filled parking lots, and those empty weekends you've been struggling to hold onto. When you have finally given up the effort of trying to maintain your organic head-brain personal identity, you'll understand the mystique of peanut butter by the spoonful.

As the veil is lifted, you'll feel several sensations grouped together as a series of symptoms, the first of which is a heavy pressure, like melting into an all-wool union suit while wearing a pair of lead boots. Don't worry about this; you've probably got a good 15 to 90 minutes left to handle any last-minute details, and if you have a friend visiting your deathbed—and your friend is so inclined—you still have time for a wonderfully refreshing foot massage.

The second sensation will be a clammy coldness alternating with sweating, as if your body were burning up. This is just one symptom of hypothermia, in which the body's heat is reduced to lethal levels.

Hey, nothing to worry about—passage is still minutes away!

The third sensation is a definite feeling that your body is about to explode. You may actually feel that you've been blown to smithereens and dispersed by the wind. Now you have something to worry about! Passage is only moments away. Try to relax and think of something pleasant.

The fourth sensation isn't really a sensation—it's a total lack of sensations. Suddenly, although your mind has miraculously opened up and provided a breathtaking and profound view of all creation, it doesn't refer to anything. This vision plus 90 cents will get you a one-way ride on a city bus.

In addition to those sensations, there may be other feelings, psychological events, interludes, fugues, or other minor disorders, which occur prior to passage from the organic world to wherever you're going. You might experience a loss of control over your facial muscles, causing an insipid smile or that unoccupied look usually reserved for high-school seniors.

You might periodically lose your hearing, or words and phrases that made sense before might not make the same sense they made before when you understood what they were saying by the words and phrases they might be understood and made sense before when you understood what they meant by what they said to you as you were listening.

There may be a loss of sight or radical changes in your vision-vision vision. Your breath might be ragged, particularly if you're getting more than just a foot massage. It is possible that you will find yourself shivering or sweating and having an uncontrollable desire to remove your clothes and walk around. Unless you're expected to recover, this may well be a good idea. Who knows what last-minute adventures might be in store for you?

You may feel a lethargic calm descend over you. If you've spent your life as a lawyer or if you were on a graduate fellowship, you probably won't notice this. There might be a loss of attention, caused by falling over unconscious on the floor. You may notice that your breathing stopped several minutes ago and that you can't move your limbs. In this case, don't bother trying to talk.

When all these symptoms of approaching death have been completed, someone should gently whisper the following words into your ear: "So long, sucker, you're on your own." □□

This is an excerpt from the book The Lazy Man's Guide to Death and Dying, by E. J. Gold, published by IDHHB, Inc. Copyright © 1983 by E. J. Gold. Gold is a California-based science-fiction writer who, last we heard, was still very much alive and breathing steadily.

134 OMNI

JOHN LILLY

The Dolphin Man & Inventor of the Sensory Deprivation Tank

Left: E.J. Gold sitting in front of the teepee at John Lilly's home in Malibu in 1976.
Photo: John Lilly

Toni and John Lilly with E.J. Gold.
Photo by Lana Gold.

John Lilly speaking about the Dolphin Institute at a conference in 1978 at the Miramar Hotel in Los Angeles.

Lilly and Gold met through a mutual friend. The two understood each other and immediately became close friends and remained so until Lilly passed away in Los Angeles in 2001.

Center: John and Toni Lilly at the Dolphin Institute.
Photo by E.J. Gold.

In 1993, a CD titled *E.C.C.O.* featuring several jazz compositions by Gold used as background on the *Cogitate* loop of Lilly's was released in Japan. It is very collectible for afficionados.

E.C.C.O.:
Earth Coincidence Control Office
Photo: John Lilly.

Above: John Lilly with E.J. Gold at the Dolphin Institute. The two collaborated on many fascinating projects over a span of more than a quarter of a century.
Photo by E.J. Gold.
Right: John Lilly not long before his passage.
Photo by Glenn Perry.

Like Father Like Son

SCIENCE FICTION

VILLAINS FROM VEGA IV

E.J. Gold co-authored several stories with his father, Horace L., including *The Torso Affair, Planet Wreckers* (for Startrek), *Jeannie-In-the-Bottle, Jeannie Versus Schmuckslayer*, and an unpublished revision of *The Old Die Rich. Villains from Vega IV* which was published in Galaxy Magazine in 1968.

Horace L. Gold is described by David L. Rosheim in *Galaxy Magazine, The Dark and The Light Years* (Advent Publishers Inc.) as an "editor's editor whose devotion to the field of SF has not since been surpassed."

Horace L. Gold was greatly admired by most science fiction writers. He exerted a powerful literary judgment and demanded of writers that they surpass themselves.

Photo courtesy: Kaiden Studios, Inc.

X-MINUS ONE

After initiating the project of the Sirius Science Fiction series and publishing several titles which include some of his original artwork, E.J. Gold delved into Sirius Science Fiction Theatre releasing an *X-Minus One* production of three stories by Horace L. Gold: *The Old Die Rich, At the Post,* and *Project Trojan* in addition to stories by Robert Sheckley, Theodore Sturgeon and James Gunn. It could probably be said that E.J. Gold is a classicist even in his appreciation of science fiction. Sirius Science Fiction now publishes as Gateways Retro Science Fiction.

X Minus One Presents H.L. Gold's
The Old Die Rich, 1956
At the Post, 1957
Project Trojan, 1956
adaptation by Ernest Kinoy
Plus
Protection, 1957
by Robert Sheckley
The Stars Are The Styx, 1956
by Theodore Sturgeon
Wherever You May Be, 1956
by James E. Gunn

Cover art by E.J. Gold
You Can Leave
pastel on black Arches, 1992
© hei 1993

H.L. Gold, c. 1965
Polaroid portrait by E.J.Gold

E. J. Gold inherited a love of the trade from his father as he read through the slush pile that was part of the GALAXY daily menu. His literary exposure was quite extensive and his own writing began at a very young age and has since diversified into many fields.

He has published science-fiction stories, and co-authored several with his father including *Villains from Vega IV*. Other publications include plays, screenplays, tales, poetry and songs. He has written numerous books on transformational psychology, and death and dying, and is in fact considered an authority in this field. He is also an excellent storyteller and reader, and has done several audio recordings including a very amusing rendition of the *Lazy Man's Guide to Death and Dying*.

Under the imprint *Gateways Retro SF*, E.J. Gold is publishing many SF classics by some of the greatest authors in the field, and several anthologies such as *E.J. Gold's Guide to the Galaxy and Beyond the Unknown* containing shorter science fiction stories. He is also illustrating these with his own original art, a project which he has yearned to do for many years and which has been extremely well received by the SF community.

Aside from the publication of SF classics in quality bindings, Gold is also fostering the reissue of classic SF stories as they were heard during the Golden Age of radio with the famous *X Minus One* radio series. The first volume includes three classic stories by H.L. Gold.

Photomontage: Forrest J and Wendayne Ackerman, Tom & Terry Pinckard and kids, H.L. Gold, Hollywood mask-maker Don Post, and Ray Bradbury, gathered regularly at the Pinckard salon ca. 1972.
Photos by E.J. Gold.

Adlai Stevenson 1900—1965

Mariner to Mars

JULY 26, 1965 35c

THE PERISCOPE

by Edwin Moss, business manager of the Roman Catholic St. Elizabeth's Mission in Selma.

Birth Pains for the Asian Aid Bank
President Johnson's plan for a billion-dollar aid program for Southeast Asia faces a rough time in Congress. An early target of opposition is the proposed Asian Development Bank. Both GOP and Democratic members of the House Banking committee (who must approve the $200 million U.S. stake in the bank) are complaining. Along with the perennial gripe that Congress isn't being kept up to date on the project, they are aroused at the idea that North Vietnam, Indonesia and the Soviet Union, among others, may be asked to join.

A Long, Hot Summer for Congress
What are the chances that Congress will adjourn by Labor Day? Slim. Hearings on unemployment compensation, for instance, won't get under way in the House until Aug. 2, and one in the Senate on highway beautification not until Aug. 10. Both bills are on LBJ's must list.

Vietnam Video
Unsolicited help for solving South Vietnam's problems keeps coming in. "Amazed" to find no TV on his recent tour of Saigon, Michigan's GOP Rep. Charles Chamberlain wants the U.S. Information Agency to give him "a comprehensive report on the estimated costs and the arguments for and against creating television communications" in Vietnam.

The Changing South
Here is another sign of the way the Negro revolution is reshaping Southern politics: Virginia Democrats now rate Rep. William Pat Jennings a "comer" and the man to beat in the next race for governor, four years hence. Jennings was the only member of the Virginia delegation to vote for the 1965 voting rights bill.

James Bond's Secret
Secret agent 007 has a secret. Sean Connery, the on-screen image of superhero James Bond, wears a toupee to cover a receding hairline.

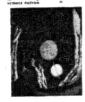

Space Flights of Fancy
A man who "explored" Mars via his imagination back in 1911 in a pioneering space-fiction series called "Ralph 124C 41+" describes the Mariner 4 pictures of the red planet (page 54) as a "giant step" toward making that mysterious globe "an open book." He is **Hugo Gernsback**, founder (in 1908) of the world's first radio magazine, Modern Electrics, and longtime editor and publisher of the science-fiction monthly Amazing Stories. Now 80, he is still "working a full day" as "chief editor" of Radio-Electronics. (Amazing Stories was sold some years ago.) Gernsback lives in an apartment in New York City with his wife, Mary. After providing what is virtually a working description of radar in his 1911 story, Gernsback takes current developments in stride: "Things are shaping up as we predicted."

Another who took the Jules Verne route into space as a writer and publisher of science fiction, **Horace Gold**, founder and until 1961 editor of Galaxy magazine, is still at the typewriter. He has just had a volume of short stories ("The Old Die Rich") published in England, is finishing up a "fantasy" novel called "None but Lucifer" and will have a science-fiction story in the September issue of his old magazine. (Science fiction, he explains, is an extension of known facts, but no holds are barred in fantasy.) Now 51, divorced and father of a grown son, he lives alone in a Manhattan apartment. Gold's first reaction to the history-making Mariner photos was simply to say that he is "glad he lived to see them." And he scoffs at the thought that reality will kill science fiction. "The more it reveals," he says, "the more there is to explore."

14   **Newsweek, July 26, 1965**

When the Mariner Probe sent back photos from Mars in 1965, Newsweek did a special article featuring a profile on two prominent figures in the field of science fiction, Hugo Gernsback, the father of science fiction, and H.L. Gold.

In the interview with Newsweek, Gold scoffed at the thought that reality will kill science-fiction. "The more it reveals," he said, "the more there is to explore."

What Will They Think Of Last?

BY HORACE L. GOLD

The publication of *What Will They Think Of Last?* by H.L. Gold in 1976.
Photo by E.J. Gold.

Gold proudly stands by the booth displaying his father's book which he published.
Photo by Jay Kay Klein.

RANDALL GARRETT

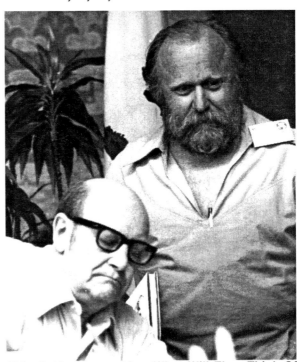

H.L. Gold autographing *What Will They Think Of Last?* for Frank Herbert.
Photo by E.J. Gold.

Famous science-fiction writer Randall Garrett is captured in this memorable portrait.
Photo by E.J. Gold

FORREST J ACKERMAN
WESTERCON
1976

H.L. Gold is busy autographing copies of his book with his agent Forrest J Ackerman standing by. Twenty years later, the art of Gold the younger is published in an anthology of science fiction stories assembled by Forry J Ackerman in *Sense of Wonder!*

Forrest J Ackerman, writer, editor, literary agent, Ackermonster and founder of the Ackermansion — among other things — gets his copy of the book autographed by H.L. and E.J. Gold, 1976.

Forrest J Ackerman, Gold's literary agent, pausing at the booth where *What Will They Think Of Last?* by pro *Guest of Honor*, H.L. Gold, is prominently displayed at the Westercon, 1976.
Ackerman is an enthusiast of Gold's private science fiction imprint, *Sirius Science Fiction* now called *Gateways Retro SF.*
Photos by Jay Kay Klein.

H.L. Gold, E.J. Gold, and Forrest J Ackerman, 1976.

E.J. Gold and Forrest J Ackerman, 1976.

E.J. Gold and Robert Silverberg, 1976.

E.J. Gold, Virginia and Robert A. Heinlein, 1978.

Robert Silverberg, A.E. Van Vogt, H.L. Gold, and E.J. Gold, 1976.

Alan Dean Foster and E.J. Gold, 1978.

Robert Bloch, author of *Psycho* with old family friend, Marion Zimmer Bradley, known for her *sword-and-sorcery* fantasy stories and Fritz Leiber, world-famous fantasy author known for his magical theme novels, 1978.
Photo by E.J. Gold.

June Lockhart has a warm and glowing smile for the camera, 1978.
Photo by E.J. Gold

Ted Sturgeon and E. J. Gold break away from their discussion for the camera, 1976.

E. J. Gold pauses from chatting with Lester del Rey, 1978.

E. J. Gold & H. L. Gold make a great team fielding questions on SciFi writing and editing, 1976.

Having a great time at the 'Con. Horace Gold was Guest of Honor at the 1976 Westercon.

GIANTS IN THE WORLD OF SCIENCE-FICTION

E.J. Gold onstage at the Iguanacon, 1978.

E.J. Gold, Poul Anderson, Frank Herbert, 1976.

George Scithers and Lana Gold celebrate, 1976.

Robert Silverberg, E. J. Gold, and H. L. Gold, 1976.

E. J. Gold and Joe Haldeman, 1978.

E. J. Gold and Alfred Bester, 1983.

H. L. Gold, Frank Herbert and Lester Del Rey, 1976.
Photo by E.J. Gold

H. L. Gold, 1957.
Photo by E.J. Gold.

Ben Bova, Jerry Pournelle, and E.J. Gold, 1978

Robert Silverberg and H. L. Gold, 1976.

E.J. Gold and Harlan Ellison, 1978.

H. L. Gold, Jerry Pournelle, and E. J. Gold, 1976.

ISAAC ASIMOV

From left to right: Alfred Bester, E. J. Gold, Hal Clement, Isaac Asimov, 1983.

From left: Michael Kurland, E.J. Gold, Damon Knight,   E. J. Gold, Isaac Asimov, 1983.
and Kate Wilhelm, Vancouver, 1977.

E.J. Gold and Isaac Asimov, 1983.

BookFair

BRADBURY
ELLISON
E.J. GOLD
HILLMAN
KRASSNER
LEARY
LILLY
REXROTH
RECHY
SANCHEZ
STURGEON

BooksWest '78   The 4th L.A. Book Fair
Nov. 10-12

130 publisher displays • continuous author appearances • conferences • workshops • poetry festival • At BooksWest '78, the Fourth L.A. Book Fair • Nov. 10-12 (Fri.- Sun.) Ambassador Hotel, 3400 Wilshire • Plenty of weekend street parking • Conferences start at 10AM Sat., 9AM Sun. • Exhibits and Authors: Fri. 4PM-11PM, Sat. noon-11PM, Sun. noon-9PM • Admission $3.

PROGRAM

Author Appearances (Ambassador Ballroom)

Friday
4:00	"Mark Twain"
5:00	David Goodstein (Advocate Publisher)
6:00	John Lilly/Toni Lilly
7:00	Kenneth Rexroth
8:00	E.J. Gold
9:00	Harlan Ellison
10:00	Susan Forward/ Sandy Butler (2 books on incest)
6:00	James Hillman
7:00	Robert Peters
8:00	Ray Bradbury
9:00	Robert Anton Wilson
10:00	Timothy Leary

Saturday
12:00	John Loori (Zen photography)
1:00	Jerome Rothenberg
2:00	Thomas Sanchez
3:00	Peter Balin (Mayan Tarot)
4:00	John Rechy
5:00	David Antin

Sunday
12:00	Del Martin
1:00	Robert Gottlieb & Irene Wolt (Thinking Big: L.A. Times book)
2:00	to be announced
3:00	Sweet William (book on Venice, Calif.)
4:00	Jay Martin (Henry Miller's biographer)
5:00	Paul Krassner
6:00	Theodore Sturgeon
7:00	to be announced
8:00	to be announced

Conferences and Workshops

Saturday
10AM-12	James Hillman: Archetypal Psychology (Regency Rm., $10)
10AM-12	Darrell Hack: Juggling How-to (Lido Rm.)
12PM-1	John Daishin Buckdazen: Intro to Zen (Lido Rm.)
2PM-5	Poetry Festival (Regency Rm.)
2PM-4	David Balsiger: Writing the Heavily Researched Book, Part I (Lido Rm.)

Sunday
9AM-11	Charles Chikodel: Publish It Yourself (Lido Rm.)
10AM-12	Irwin Zucker and Panel: Publicity: The Calif. Media Boom (Colonial Rm.)
12PM-4	Poetry Festival (Colonial Rm.)
1PM-2	Kenneth Rexroth: Eulogy to Lawrence Lipton (Lido Rm.)
2PM-4	David Balsiger: The Heavily Researched Book, Part II (Lido Rm.)
4PM-6	Nina Bara: 1950's "Space Patrol" Films (Lido Rm.)

Top: Joe Haldeman, E. J. Gold.
Center: E. J. Gold, Ben Bova, editor of OMNI and former President of SFWA.
Lower: Harlan Ellison, Robert Silverberg.

Ruth Kyle, Spider Robinson, Jeanne Robinson, David Kyle and Forrest J Ackerman rejoice at the resurrection of the phoenix as they proudly display their copies of Galaxy Magazine at the Boston Con held at the Boston Park Plaza in January, 1994.
Photo by Douglass-Truth.

Bjo Trimble's mother during a visit to Gold's Galaxy office in the Spring of 1994.
Photo: Aviko.

Joe Haldeman in his *I'm Almost Famous* T-shirt.
Photo by E.J. Gold.

FORREST J ACKERMAN

**Famous Monsters Magazine
The Ackermansion
The Ackermonster
Contributing Editor, Galaxy Magazine
under the editorship of E.J. Gold**

Forry Ackerman and Paul Barry, Galaxy Distributor, have a witty exchange at the *Famous Monsters of Filmland Horror, Sci-Fi & Fantasy World Convention* in Arlington, Virginia, May 1993 at the Hyatt Regency Crystal City.
Photos by Douglass-Truth.

Forrest J Ackerman with Douglass-Truth at the 35th Anniversary Famous Monsters of Film and World Convention in Arlington, Virginia where *Sense of Wonder* was presented in 1993. Film crews avidly covered the event and one of its stars, Forry Ackerman.
Top photo left by Douglass-Truth.

SENSE OF WONDER
Edited by
FORREST J ACKERMAN
Illustrated by E.J. Gold

ADVANCE PUBLICATION INFORMATION
CONTACT: Nancy Christie or Iven Lourie
(916) 477-1116

ISBN: 0-89556-094-1
Price: $175.00 regular edition
$225.00 with *hors texte* serigraph
$125.00; $175.00(ht) pre-publication.
Release Date: February, 1993
Edition Size: Strictly limited to 225 copies.
Deluxe, sewn hard-cover with signed and numbered frontispiece serigraph bound in, handsomely gold-embossed on cover (with Forry Ackerman insignia) and on spine.
Hors texte: Hors texte serigraph only for copies 1-25, check with publisher for availability.

SENSE OF WONDER SCIENCE FICTION

Edited and with Commentaries by Forrest J Ackerman
Illustrated by E.J. Gold

SIRIUS

A note from Sirius Science Fiction Editor, Iven Lourie: *"When I bought a house in an old neighborhood in Tucson, Arizona, in the seventies, my neighbors were an elderly couple who had lived there since the fifties. I found out that they had an immense paperback book collection, including science fiction. One day, as I sat in their musty living room talking with them about "the good old days," the woman brought out a paperback she handled carefully with great reverence, and insisted I must read. I did read it, and it did take my breath away at some scenes. That paperback was The Face in the Abyss by A. Merritt. I got the feeling that in the thirties or forties, when that came out, Merritt's work was for young science fiction fans what cyberpunk is now, or what Ace doubles were when I was growing up."*

Forrest J Ackerman has gathered, with the original 1927 novella version of "The Face in the Abyss," a collection of unforgettable stories from the childhood of science fiction as the genre we know today—called then "scientifiction," as Forry explains. If *Galaxy* and *Beyond* and *F & SF*, the editorial work of Horace Gold and Anthony Boucher, were the coming-of-age of science fiction, these stories from the twenties and thirties, from such pulps as *Amazing Stories* and *Science Wonder Stories*, represent the first flush of the genre's youthful energy. They will truly awaken your "sense of wonder" as a reader, and remind you why you started reading science fiction in the first place, so many years ago—whether you've ever read these authors or not. I have to say, as I said to Forry in the early stages of working on this book, that I've never had more fun proof-reading anything in my career as a reader and editor.

Forry, himself the senior statesman of science fiction editing and agentry, is your ideal guide through this carnival of adventure and astonishing imaginative leaps. Many of the gems herein are definitely "in the rough,"

The Ackermonster lives on!

Forrest J Ackerman's 35th Anniversary *Famous Monsters of Filmland* World Convention in Arlington, Virginia where *Sense of Wonder* was presented in 1993. On the bottom, we see Gateways SF Editor, Iven Lourie, wearing a *Sense of Wonder!* t-shirt and holding a *Sense of Wonder!* poster standing over the authors Jack Williamson and Forry Ackerman as they take a break from signing books for collectors and fans.

MISTS OF DAWN
CHAD OLIVER

Mists of Dawn, originally published in 1952, fired the imaginations of a generation of young readers and future science fiction authors, and introduced science fiction as an exciting and adventurous field.

The Gateways Science Fiction imprint is offering *Mists of Dawn* by the late Chad Oliver with original illustrations by Gold. Like all books in this series, it is leather-bound with hand-made French end papers. These well-received publications of science fiction titles encouraged the artist to continue sci-fi illustrations.

ADVANCE PUBLICATION INFORMATION
Contact: Nancy Christie or Iven Lourie
(916)477-1116

ISBN: 0-89556-097-6
Price: $175.00 regular edition
$225.00 with *hors texte* serigraph
$125.00, $175.00(ht) pre-publication
Release Date: January, 1993
Edition Size: Edition is strictly limited to 125 copies. Deluxe, sewn hard-cover limited edition with signed and numbered frontispiece serigraph bound in, handsomely gold-embossed on cover and spine.
Hors texte: Hors texte serigraph available only for copies 1-25, sold out by subscription at time of publication (check with Gateways for availability).

MISTS OF DAWN
by Chad Oliver, Illustrated by E.J. Gold

Sirius Science Fiction is pleased to announce the release of a new, fine-art edition of this novel that fired the imaginations of a generation of young readers (and future sf authors) and introduced science fiction as an exciting and adventurous field. The book and the author hardly need introduction. In brief, Symmes Chadwick Oliver was born in 1928, has had a distinguished career as an anthropologist and researcher, as well as an author of speculative fiction. He currently teaches at the University of Texas—Austin. The Library of Congress summary of his 1952 publication, *Mists of Dawn*, reads as follows:

A 17-year old makes an unplanned trip through space and time to Europe 50,000 years ago where Neanderthal and Cro-Magnon man engage in conflict for survival.

More interesting than anything we could say about this wonderful novel are the thoughts of Chad Oliver, from his introduction to the book, reprinted in a Gregg Press library edition in 1979:

This is a work of fiction, and as such its purpose is to entertain. If it gives you a few hours of pleasure, or even keeps you up all night to find out what happens, it has accomplished its mission. If it does not entertain, if it is not fun to read, then nothing else will make it worth your time.

If you do have a good time reading it, and I hope you do, that in itself if something. I also hope, however, that you can pick up a bit extra along the way—a sort of painless bonus. The bonus is free of charge, and you can ignore it if you wish.

For those who are interested, though, I hope that there are a few lessons to be learned from this story, lessons in tolerance and understanding and common humanity. It may be that you will now think twice before you condemn others merely because they live a different kind of life than your own, and you may look back upon the long history of mankind with more appreciative eyes.

It comes as something of a shock occasionally to remember that it has only been some one hundred and seventy-six years since this nation got underway in 1776, and only four hundred and sixty years since Columbus sailed for the New World. Writing itself is only some five thousand years old at best, and in some parts of the world, such as North America, it did not exist until a short few hundred years ago. Man himself has been around a lot longer than that, with all his dreams and his never-ending search for happiness.

If we are ever to understand the last part of the story of mankind, we must understand the first chapters as well—not to mention the later episodes of peoples about whom we know little or nothing. There is a lot of history, and a lot of fascination, yet hidden from our eyes in the gray mists of time.

Collophon

A.J. Langguth
Jesus Christs

This book was printed in an edition of one-hundred and twenty-five copies. The regular edition consists of one-hundred copies printed with an original serigraph frontispiece. The deluxe edition consists of twenty-five copies printed with an original serigraph frontispiece and also includes an original *hors texte* serigraph of the same image with full margins, signed and numbered by the artist.

The color separations for the serigraphs were prepared by Nancy Christie, and the edition was pulled in the Studio of E.J. Gold by Rosemarie Jodouin under the direct supervision of the artist.

The text was entered by Tabatha Jones and typeset by Nancy Christie using the Bookman typeface. The book was reproduced on Beckett Concept Fiber paper on a Minolta 8600, with the interior illustrations hand-printed by the artist on a Minolta 470Z.

The custom hand-sewn hardcover binding with gold embossing and French marble end papers was done at Cal-Na Bindery in Sacramento.

A.J. Langguth   *E.J. Gold*

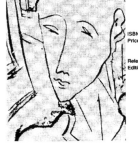

JESUS CHRISTS
BY A.J. LANGGUTH

Another unusual title to find listed under Gateways Science Fiction is A.J. Langguth's *Jesus Christs* which was illustrated by Gold. The illustrations were chosen from charcoals which Gold created. Working with transparency and layering, Gold's imagery evokes an otherworldly quality which lends itself well to the illustration of science fiction themes.

Gold's knowledge of science fiction and his complete ease in the graphic medium put him in a very rare position and enable him to act both as editor and illustrator for a very high quality small publisher of limited editions. Langguth was very pleased with the presentation.

ADVANCE PUBLICATION INFORMATION
Contact: Nancy Christie or Iven Lourie
(916)477-1116

ISBN:	0-89556-096-8
Price:	$175.00 regular edition
	$225.00 with *hors texte* serigraph
	$125.00; $175.00(ht) pre-publication
Release Date:	December, 1992
Edition Size:	Edition is strictly limited to 125 copies.
	Deluxe,sewn hard-cover limited edition with signed and numbered frontispiece serigraph bound in, handsomely gold-embossed on cover and spine. *Hors texte*: Hors texte serigraph available only for copies 1-25, may be sold out by subscription at time of publication (check with Gateways for availability).

SIRIUS

JESUS CHRISTS

A novel by A.J. Langguth, Illustrated by E.J. Gold

"Just as we had become accustomed to the fact that the only first-rate religious fiction today is being written by Norman Mailer, this mad novel comes along to surprise and enchant us. A comic religious novel? ... Impossible, but it has happened. It is either one of the canniest rejections of the Christian enterprise in our time, or one of the subtlest expressions of admiration for Jesus. Or both. Or neither...

—*The New Republic*

Suppose that the historical Jesus and his disciples, as chronicled in the Gospels, are an archetype of divine revelation. OK, that's not hard to accept, whether you're a Christian or belong to any other religion or even if you are Buddhist, agnostic or atheist. Now suppose that, since the New Testament immortalizes archetypal events, there is in every other period of history another Jesus with another set of disciples, much like the ar chetype. How about, identical except for the differences in culture and historical context, whether it be the French Revolution, the Roaring Twenties, or World War II in Europe.

This is the thesis of *Jesus Christs* (yes, it's plural...), and it worked out in its details, it is a mind-boggling and attention-riveting idea. This is exactly what Langguth has done in his unique novel. Enough said—you have to read this book to believe it. *Jesus Christs* is also an archetypal example of a novel that is *too serious* to suc ceed, can't be a best-seller, disappears from circulation once out of print, and somehow gets stolen or lost, with almost 100% frequency, from libraries...An obvious case for Sirius Science Fiction revival. Your read of this free-form novel is considerably enhanced by it's large-size page format and illustration with a new series of drawings by E.J. Gold, who has admired the book since it's first release in the heady atmosphere of the late '60's. What more can we say—Highly Recommended!

A.J. Langguth has had a long and distinguished, not to mention highly diversified, career as a professional writer. He was born in 1933 in Minneapolis, attended Harvard College, where he also worked for a year, and then served in the U.S. Army in 1957-58. He was Political Editor at the Valley Times, San Fernando Valley, from 1960-63, then went on to the New York Times to become Bureau Chief in Saigon during the eventful year 1965. He wrote as a freelancer and authored five books—beginning with *Jesus Christs*—between 1966 and 1978, when he joined the faculty of the Journalism School, University of Southern California, where he is currently teaching as a full Professor.

E.J. Gold, *The Dreamer*,
Charcoal on Rives BFK, 11" x 15", 1992.

105

SKULKING PERMIT
ROBERT SHECKLEY

Skulking Permit, a novel by Robert Sheckley, was published in a limited edition of 125 copies with original serigraph frontispiece by Gold, and many other original illustrations.

This book led to further collaborations between author and editor/artist with the publication of *City of the Dead*, an extension of Gold's work with Bardo Town and miniatures. They also did an audio recording *How to Overcome Writer's Block* .

These collaborations have been stimulating and fruitful for both parties who remain in close touch with each other and look forward to future ventures.

THE CITY OF THE DEAD
by ROBERT SHECKLEY

E. J. GOLD, Editor-in-Chief   EDITORIAL STAFF   DAVID FRANCO, Publisher
CLAUDE NEEDHAM, Science Editor   TABATHA JONES, Managing Editor
H. L. GOLD, Contributing Editor   JEAN STINE, Contributing Editor
FORREST J ACKERMAN, Contributing Editor   ANN VICTORIA HOPCROFT, Production Manager
BARBARA HAYNES, Art Director   MORGAN FOX AGENCY, Advertising Director

GALAXY is published bi-monthly by RHHBB, INC. A California not-for-profit corporation. Main office: 1111194 Pleasant Valley
Road, Penn Valley, CA 95946. Mailing Address: GALAXY, P O Box 370, Nevada City, CA 95959. Single Copy: $2.50.
Subscriptions: 6 COPIES/YEAR U S First Class $22, Canada $25, Great Britain/Europe $34. Pacific Rim $32. All amounts are U
S Dollars only. © 1994 RHHBB, Inc., all rights, including translations, reserved. ISSN0000-00000. For more information contact
GALAXY, P O BOX 370, Nevada City, CA 95959. Telephone: 916/432-1716, FAX# 916/432-1810. GALAXY is not accepting
unsolicited manuscripts at this time. All stories printed in this magazine are fiction and/or satire, and any similarity between
characters and actual persons is coincidental. All offers set forth in this magazine are subject to change without notice, but what
isn't?

PRINTED IN U.S.A.

E.J. Gold's GUIDE TO THE GALAXY & BEYOND THE UNKNOWN

E.J. Gold's Guide to the Galaxy and Beyond the Unknown is a small limited edition series of illustrated anthologies of some of Gold's favorite science fiction stories. Each story is accompanied by original illustrations by Gold.

The first two volumes include stories *Double Whammy* by Fredric Brown, *Hell to Pay* by Randall Garrett, *I'd Give a Dollar* by Winston Marks, *Not According to Dante* by Malcolm Jameson, *Sine of the Magus* by James E. Gunn, and *The Wall Around the World* by Theodore R. Cogswell.

Other contributors include Frederik Pohl, Robert Sheckley, Damon Knight, Daniel Galouye, and Gold who is a collector of incunabula and rare books. The care he has taken in printing and binding his livres d'artiste reveals his love for the medium.

In 2002, Gateways launched the imprint Gateways Retro SF for which Gold is the editor. Among the new titles forthcoming are several anthologies of his favorite science fiction stories as well as a few titles by H. L. Gold, some of which will be available in book form as well as in CD-ROM format.

ADVANCE PUBLICATION INFORM
Contact: Nancy Christie or Iver
(916)477-1116

ISBN: 0-89556-102-6
Price: $175.00 regular e
                 $225.00 with hor
                 $125.00; $175.00
                 $100.00; $150.00
Release Date: February, 1993
Edition Size: Edition is strictly
                 Deluxe, sewn ha
                 frontispiece serig
                 cover and spine
                 Hors texte: Hors
                 out by subscriptio
                 for availability).

E.J. GOLD'S GUIDE TO THE & BEYOND THE UNKNOWN (

Gone to Hell in a Breadbasket

Abandon Hope All Who Enter Here—So reads the notice po For well over a two thousand years, both before and after the derworld and its ruler, whether known as Hades, Pluto, some inspiration to writers. Science fiction writers have been no exc

This second volume of *E.J. Gold's Guide to the Galaxy...* gath handful of stories that so inspired the future author, artist and archival collections August Derleth and Arkham House put tog bound to set a new standard for dark fantasy and gothic tales and revising the twentieth century history of magic. Best of all new and sizzling with energy, a perfect tribute to these writers

The stories in this anthology, second in the series edited by G spells by James Gunn, who currently heads the Center for the cover story and photo, Locus, September, 1992) and one of th Cogswell, which treats brilliantly the science versus magic the chetypal story of a hallucinatory night in Dante's hell, while les provides a memorable black-magic detective story. Science fi Jameson and Marks, now deceased) supplies the volume's "c together in Galaxy as "Double Whammy."

This is a collection of classics rescued from paperback oblivio ties magazines. It is a must for collectors—an instant collectib will want to read and treasure on their shelves for years to co

PUBLICATION INFORMATION
CONTACT: NANCY CHRISTIE OR IVEN LOURIE
(916) 477-1116

ISBN: 0-89556-101-8 (Volume One)
Price: $175.00; $225.00 with hors texte
Ed ition Size: Edition is strictly limited to 125 copies.
              Deluxe, sewn hard-cover limited edition with signed and
              numbered frontispiece serigraph bound in, handsomely
              gold-embossed on cover and spine.
Hors texte: Hors texte serigraph available only only for copies 1-25.

> WOW! Whatta book! What a clever title!
> Whatta gift! What unusual artwork!
> —Forrest J Ackerman

TO THE GALAXY & BEYOND THE UNKNOWN (Volume One)

SCIENCE FICTION
SIRIUS

Gateways is proud to announce a new series of publications in the area of science fiction. Writers will include everyone you've heard of and admired— all the science fiction greats.

Fulfilling a decades-old dream, E.J. Gold, artist, author and composer has assembled, in several volumes—the first of which is scheduled for upcoming release—stories which left the strongest impression on him during the years he spent devouring uncountable manuscripts submitted to his father H.L. Gold, the editor of *Galaxy Magazine*.

With this incomparable background in science fiction, and over five million words of his own in print, Gold is probably one of the most qualified editors in the Solar System for this series, and it is with sheer delight that he has gathered some of the best stories ever written by some of the greatest writers in the field.

One of the more exciting aspects of this project is that Gold also illustrates these stories with original drawings. Never before has an anthology or an individual title been edited and illustrated by the same person equally recognized as a world-class writer, artist and editor.

All of the stories to be included are archetypes of their genre. They alternately portray expanded realities, time-travel, technological magic, intra-species communication, alternate worlds and a host of other mind-expanding themes but in extremely unusual ways.

These volumes are sure to become the staple for an entire new generation of science fiction readers—and the definitive collections for future generations of fans. The stories and magazines published in the early days of Science Fiction, the 20's and 30's, are now extremely rare and collectible. With the classics of the 50's and 60's—why wait fifty or one hundred years in the future to look for these stories? Collect them now, in Sirius Science Fiction Editions! You can enjoy them for years to come—then pass them on to your children and grandchildren.

With the publication of Volume I and II of *E.J. Gold's Guide to the Galaxy and Beyond the Unknown*, great out-of-print classics, thematic anthologies and noteworthy science fiction titles are introduced to a new generation of readers with original illustrations by the artist to accompany the stories. It should be noted that the title of this series incorporates several of the silver age science fiction magazine names to which his father contributed either as a writer or as an editor.

GALAXY

Galaxy Magazine, 1994, under the editorship of E.J. Gold had the blessing of H.L. Gold, Jean-Marie Stine, and other former Galaxy editors. The first issue had stories by Robert Sheckley, H.L. Gold, Robert Silverberg, Frederik Pohl, Jacqueline Lichtenberg, Chuck Rothman, Greg Costikyan, David Kyle, Lawrence Schimmel, Arthur Jean Cox, J.W. Donnelly and Jean Stine.

The editorial staff gathers round the screen as Galaxy gets laid out on computer. Ann-Victoria Hopcroft sits at the keyboard while Gold and science editor Claude Needham watch.

The second issue of Galaxy Magazine contained among other stories a legendary title by H. L. Gold which had not been republished in over 45 years, *None But Lucifer*. The cover had a color illustration by Kelly Freas. *None But Lucifer* is now available in book form from Gateways Retro SF.

Galaxy celebrates its first anniversary issue with science fiction friends and pros. Visible in the photograph with editorial staff are Mary Mason, Lynx Crowe, Kitty Crowe; Bjo Trimble and her Mom also shared in the festivities.

BAY CON San Jose, 1994

Top to bottom:
1. Kelly Freas holds his copy of Galaxy with his illustration on the cover. 2. Mary Mason as bubbly as ever. 3. Kent Brewster and his wife beam with pleasure and enthusiasm. 4. The Galaxy booth at Bay Con, 1994 held in San Jose at the Red Lion Inn.

Top to bottom:
1. The Bay Con was held in San Jose. 2. Laura Freas holds a calendar poster of her father's illustration. 3. A view of some of the panelists including Poul Anderson. 4. Kelly Freas and daughter, Laura, were part of the event.
Photos courtesy: Mark Einert.

The resurrection of Galaxy came as a surprise to the science fiction community. The network highway buzzed with questions, comments, critical scrutiny, distrust, enthusiasm, elation, puzzlement, cynicism. But by the fourth issue things had settled down. The quality of printing had increased from the first issue. The illustrations improved. The typeface was shrunk to allow for more words. The page count increased dramatically and the quality and prestige of the authors maintained. Galaxy was off and running at rebuilding its readership at Conventions. *Tangent* magazine gave it a thumbs up. Galaxy Magazine has since become an e-zine with many new stories published online.

GALAXY AUDIO PROJECT

Actors James Healy and Catherine Oxenberg were among the first to participate in GAP — Galaxy Audio Project which involves recording readings of stories written by many of the great science fiction authors of today. Queen of Dreams, Heather Valencia, a close friend of Catherine Oxenberg and E. J. Gold, sits in.
Photos by Aviko

James Healy is an English Shakesperean actor who went from London stage performances with actors such as Sir John Gielguld to *Dynasty* where he played the husband of Joan Collins briefly. It was there that he met Catherine Oxenberg who was also part of the cast at that time. Oxenberg is well known for her role as Diana in *Charles and Diana*.

ABDUCTED

Script rewrite and Improv sessions with
Catherine Oxenberg & James Healy
April 1994

Between readings for the Galaxy Audio Project, Healy, Oxenberg, and Gold hammer out script ideas and script rewrites for *Abducted* written by Catherine Oxenberg and James Healy. They also take it to the next level with an improv session in April 1994, all the while planning future collaborations.

Catherine Oxenberg, Claude Needham, and Tabatha Jones verifying notes and changes which have been typed in and printed out for the nth time.

E.J. Gold, James Healy and Catherine Oxenberg, discussing the script and working out details while catching a breath of fresh air.

Script writer Joyce Kenyon, Catherine Oxenberg, James Healy and Claude Needham hammer out the fine tuning of the manuscript.

1. Catherine Oxenberg, E.J. Gold. 2. Catherine Oxenberg, Claude Needham, Ann-Victoria Hopcroft, Tabatha Jones, Galaxy editorial staff. 3. Catherine Oxenberg, Claude Needham, Ann-Victoria Hopcroft, Tabatha Jones. 4. Catherine Oxenberg and Morgan Fox share a hug in front of a painting of Oxenberg in a black wig.
Photos: Morgan Fox

THEATRE

NORTH AMERICAN BUNRAKU THEATRE

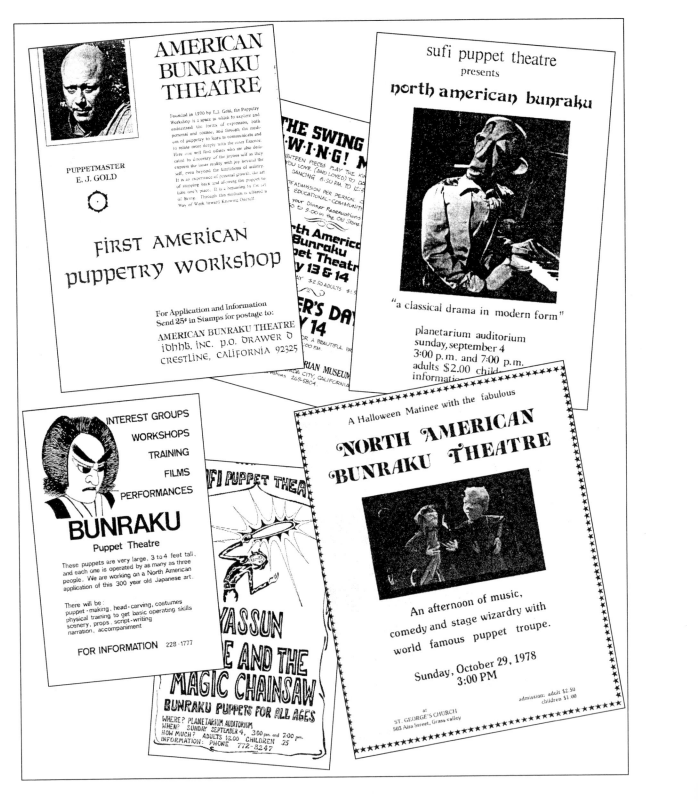

AMERICAN BUNRAKU THEATRE

PUPPETMASTER E. J. GOLD

FiRST AMERICAN puppetry workshop

For Application and Information Send 25¢ in Stamps for postage to:
AMERICAN BUNRAKU THEATRE
iohhb, inc. p.o. Drawer D
CRESTLiNE, CALiFORNiA 92325

sufi puppet theatre presents
north american bunraku

"a classical drama in modern form"

planetarium auditorium
sunday, september 4
3:00 p.m. and 7:00 p.m.
adults $2.00 child
informati

INTEREST GROUPS
WORKSHOPS
TRAINING
FILMS
PERFORMANCES
BUNRAKU
Puppet Theatre

These puppets are very large, 3 to 4 feet tall, and each one is operated by as many as three people. We are working on a North American application of this 300 year old Japanese art.

There will be:
puppet-making, head-carving, costumes physical training to get basic operating skills scenery, props, script-writing narration, accompaniment

FOR INFORMATION   228-1777

A Halloween Matinee with the fabulous
NORTH AMERICAN BUNRAKU THEATRE

An afternoon of music, comedy and stage wizardry with world famous puppet troupe.

Sunday, October 29, 1978
3:00 PM

admission: adult $2.50
children $1.00

at
ST. GEORGE'S CHURCH
503 Alta Street, Grass valley

AND THE MAGIC CHAINSAW
BUNRAKU PUPPETS FOR ALL AGES
WHERE? PLANETARIUM AUDITORIUM
WHEN? SUNDAY SEPTEMBER 4, 3:00 p.m. and 7:00 p.m.
HOW MUCH? ADULTS $2.00 CHILDREN .25
INFORMATION: PHONE   772-8247

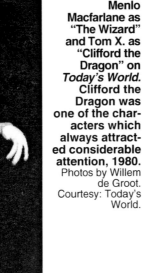

Lifesize Bunraku puppets, 1978.
Photos by E.J. Gold.

NORTH AMERICAN BUNRAKU THEATRE

The Bunraku puppets are as large as life. Like Sandy Calder and his miniature circus, Gold has an affection for the circus which takes the form of puppetry, clowns, dragons, and theatre.
Photos by Willem de Groot.

Monty.
Photos by E.J. Gold.

Menlo Macfarlane as "The Wizard" and Tom X. as "Clifford the Dragon" on *Today's World.* **Clifford the Dragon was one of the characters which always attracted considerable attention, 1980.**
Photos by Willem de Groot.
Courtesy: Today's World.

Menlo Macfarlane as "The Wizard" and Tom X. as "Clifford the Dragon" on CBC's *Today's World*. In the background, Monty the life size Bunraku puppet manned by three puppeteers waits his cue.

The incredible Bunraku puppet called Monty was a very intimidating puppet with quite a life of its own.

THEATRE ABSOLUTE
1980

Gold's avant-garde theatrical troupe, Theatre Absolute, was showered with media coverage during its North American tour in 1980. The late seventies and early eighties were a very intense period for Gold in the area of performances, alternating between the North American Bunraku Puppet Theatre, Theatre Absolute, and the Academy of Ancient Arts Dance Ensemble.

An outdoor performance of *Inaccessible Monasteries* by Theatre Absolute in 1981.

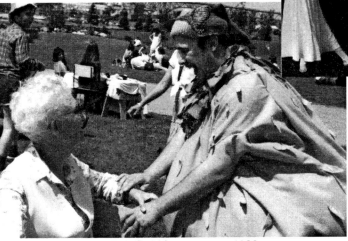

The Strawberry Man, E.J. Gold in costume, 1980.
Photo by Willem de Groot

E.J. Gold in mime costume, 1984.
Photo by Willem de Groot.

The theatre company and the Dance troupe on tour, somewhere near Winnipeg, 1980.
Photos by Willem de Groot.

Contact Improv Workshop, 1983.

OBJECTIVE THEATRE WORKSHOP
New York
1983

During a mask workshop in 1983 in New York, an impromptu jam session spontaneously arose between Gold, Menlo Macfarlane, Mark Olsen, Lovin Spoonful guitarist John Sebastian and Tom X. The newly created masks were then worked with in choreographed combinations in space, at times creating abstracted sculptural meldings and mudras.

Mark Olsen, Jeff Burnett, and E.J. Gold.

Jane Hinders and Mark Olsen.

Paddle Ball Percussion
— E.J. Gold and Mark Olsen.

THEATRE ABSOLUTE

Heather Halgrimson puts the final touches on Macfarlane's make-up just before dashing on stage.

A rehearsal of the Academy of Ancient Arts, 1985.
Photos by Willem de Groot.

Menlo Macfarlane in an E.J. Gold Production at the Ohio Theatre, Soho, 1983.

Menlo Macfarlane directing E.J. Gold's performance, *Ancient Dances, Ancient Ways,* **Cubiculo, New York, 1985.**

ART WORKSHOP
New York
1983

Gold and the late Tom X. explored collaboration, and worked together for many decades. Here we see them in New York doing a workshop. The repertoire of their collaborations includes several large murals. The paintings we see of Tom X were produced during his "Picasso" period where he experimented with pastels on Belgian linen.

Photos by Willem de Groot.

ART WORKSHOP
New York
1983

E.J. Gold and Tom X. give an art workshop in New York City, 1983. Photo courtesy of Coleman-Greene Gallery.

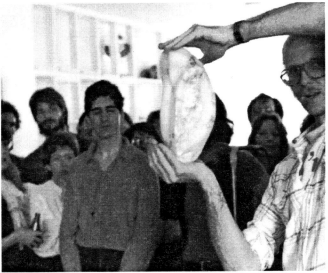

Jeron Smith displays marble production by E.J. Gold completed on a bet, in a single hour, start to finish. The sculpture was hastily bought by private dealer, Mick Perry. Collection of Mick Perry.

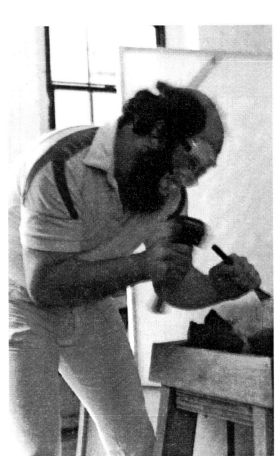

E.J. Gold sculpting at Coleman-Greene's 57th St. Gallery. The artist was part of the installation.

CREATION STORY VERBATIM
1984

Another set Gold designed for *Creation Story* in its many variations over the years beginning in New York with Jeff Burnett of *"Kiss"* as the Lord, and Mark Olsen of *"Mummenschantz"* as Gabriel. This Off-Broadway production featured Kelly Rivera and Robbert Campbell at the Newfoundland Theatre Space. Set design by E.J. Gold.
Photos by Willem de Groot.

Different set and different costumes for yet another performance of *Creation Story Verbatim* with the same cast in 1986.

A 1985 performance by Kelly Rivera as The Lord and Robbert Campbell as Archangel Gabriel in the campy comedy, *Creation Story Verbatim*, where the audience gets to find out what the *real* plan was.

Christmas 1992 performance of *Creation Story Verbatim* at Gold's home with a twenty foot painting from his "Guide" series as a backdrop. Gabriel and the Lord have a distinctly more punkish look to them than usual. *Night of the Living Dead* make-up. All in all, quite a lively presentation!

MUSICAL RECORDINGS

TOKYO TOUR

E.J. Gold, Jimmi Accardi who has played lead guitarist with The Laughing Dogs, Van Morrison, and Chuck Berry, plus Evan Lurie famous for composing the film score to Roberto Benigni's *Johnny Stecchino* and the musical score to Nickelodeon's hit children's series *Oswald the Octopus,* have collaborated on a number of musical projects together. The first was *Tokyo Tour.* The presentation included the poems of Lurie and the art of Gold. Gold's engineer is Oz Fritz a Grammy award winner for Tom Waits' hit 2001 release *Mule Variations.*

E.J. Gold, Magdelene Wiebe, and Menlo Macfarlane perform for some two thousand science fiction fans, Red Lion Inn, 1989.

Parker Dixon and Se Duggan perform on the Union Label a.k.a. Cloister Recordings. The Celtic album they recorded is one of many types of music offered by this indie label with a wide variety of music and the spoken word CDs.

HI-TECH SHAMAN
1985

184th Sunday Concert

A PERFORMANCE
OF ORIGINAL MUSIC BY

E. J. GOLD
The Hi-Tech Shaman

with guests

The Academy of Ancient Arts
Dance Ensemble

The North American
Bunraku Puppet Theatre

Joan Bakara, Violin

Menlo Macfarlane, Percussion

AMERICAN VICTORIAN MUSEUM
325 Spring Street, Nevada City
4 pm $4.50 includes High Tea

August 18, 1985

For further information call (916)265-5804.

E.J. Gold live at the Red Lion Inn, Sacramento, California performing at the Westercon, 1989.

E.J. Gold and Lee Lozowick of the group *LGB* jam quite often together. Though not well known this side of the ocean, *LGB* is one of the most popular bands in Germany.

Gold's private recording studio in 1992 with guitarist and lead vocalist Jimmi Accardi, and award-winning engineer Oz Fritz both of whom Gold has worked with for over a decade producing countless albums including *Superjam* being recorded here.

MUSICAL
RECORDINGS
ON CD

DEEP FRIED HARRY
Della Rita Heywood Vocals
1993

In late 1993, E.J. Gold produced *Deep Fried Harry* with Della Rita Heywood (seated far right) on vocals. Heywood did a satirical rendition of Nilsson's songs with a charming Southern twang that made this album very appealing. The cover artwork was a series of original Gold watercolors on a serigraph background.

In 1994, Nilsson spent a week at Gold's during Christmas time. Aside from listening to *Deep Fried Harry* which was very amusing to Nilsson, there was much catching up to do.

Nilsson and Gold took the time to reminisce about shared memories and laugh about old recording stories amidst plans they made for the future. Music videos were at the forefront of Nilsson's attention. He was a strong anti-arms supporter and had written a song called *Lay Down Your Arms* which he hoped to see produced as a music video. Visual effects were discussed, ideas were bounced back and forth in this delightful meeting of the minds. On the walls are photos of Nilsson taken by Gold in the 1960s when they first worked together.

Photos: Michele-Marie Underhill

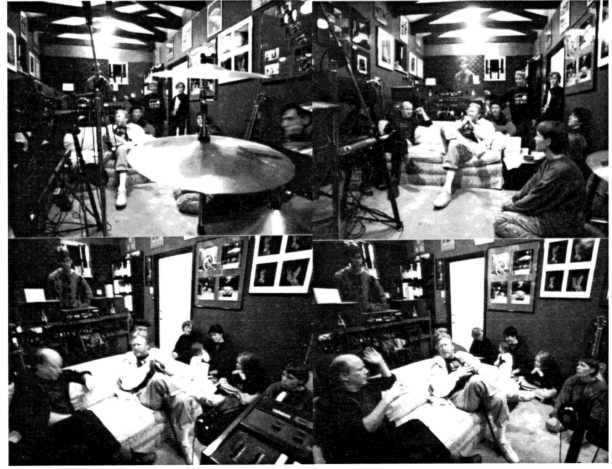

RECORDINGS

The list of recordings produced by E.J. Gold
under various pseudonyms is extremely vast.
Here are some that we have compiled.

A Tribute to Accardi/Gold, Recorded by Various Artists
Accardi/Gold Songbook, Accardi/Gold
Alto Sax Zarathustra, E.J. Gold
Bag Ladies From Hell, Gorebag & The Grunts
Banned In 93 Countries,The Terminators
Bardo Reggae/Bardo Bop, E.J. Gold & Friends
Beatless: Together Again, Various Artists
Best of Elwood Strutter Sutton, Elwood Strutter Sutton & Friends
Blue Smoke, E.J. Gold
Blues From Hell, Zaphod & The New Harmonics
Born to Be Mild, The Satin Experience
Chanting Induction, E.J. Gold
Children of the Night, E.J. Gold
Christmas Album, Insane Investors Club
Cogitate, John C. Lilly, M.D. and E.J. Gold
Creation Story Verbatim, E.J. Gold
Dance of the Hi-Tech Shaman, E.J. Gold
Drone (The), Accardi/Gold
Ducks With Breasts, Ducks With Breasts
E.C.C.O. 2, Dr. John Lilly over Gold
Epitaph For An Ego, E.J. Gold
Evolver, Zaphod & the New Harmonics
Galaxians, Zaphod & the Alien Allstars
God's Greatest Easter Scam, Accardi/Gold
Good Vibes, Accardi/Gold
Gorebag at Midnight, Various Artists
Gorebag in the Morning, Various Artists
Harlem Daze, Accardi/Gold & Friends
Hippie Heaven,The Satin Experience
Hot Night in Hell, Gorebag & the Grunts
How I Raised Myself from the Dead / Resurrection, E.J. Gold
How To Overcome Writer's Block, Robert Sheckley & E.J. Gold
I Can Free You, E.J. Gold
In Your Face, Gorebag & the Grunts
It Pays to be Ignorant, The Morons
Janitors From Outer Space, Menlo Macfarlane & E.J. Gold
Jazz Koto of Eugene Yamamoto (The), Eugene Yamamoto
Jazzmobile, Jeff Spencer Trio
Last Set at the Rembrandt Room (The), Bob Canatsey Quintet
Lazy Man's Guide to Death & Dying, E.J. Gold
Liberation, Accardi/Gold
Live at RCA, E.J. Gold & Friends
Live at the Philharmonic I, E.J. Gold
Live at the Philharmonic II, E.J. Gold
Live at the Philharmonic III, E.J. Gold
Lycanthrope, Accardi/Gold
Miles From the Dead, The Cool Jazz Ensemble
Mostly We'll Rock, Zaphod & The New Harmonics
Music From the Heart of the Galaxy, Zaphod & the New Harmonics

Mystical Journey of the Hi-Tech Shaman, E.J. Gold
Night Blooming Jazzman, E.J. Gold
No Bread Lotsa Jam, Accardi/Gold & Friends
One Single Outbreath, E.J. Gold & Friends
Only Sleeping, E.J. Gold & the Galaxians
Post Pop Festival, Accardi/Gold
Pythagorean Harp & Harmonium Improvisations, E.J. Gold
Rates of Passage, E.J. Gold
Return of Children of the Night, Accardi/Gold
Ride That Carousel, E.J. Gold & Friends
Ritual of the Cave, E.J. Gold
Saturday Night in the Higher Dimensions 1 & 2, E.J. Gold
Sax Pistol, Zaphod & The New Harmonics
Send Money or the Fairie Dies!!!, Insane Investor Quartet
Shaman Ritual Series II: Golden Age, E.J. Gold
Shapeshifter/Timetripper, E.J. Gold & Friends
Shearing (The), E.J. Gold
Songs of the Gold Rush, Gold Rush Boys
Songs We Wrote Tomorrow, Accardi/Gold
Spacing Out, E.J. Gold
Surrender, Overlords of Jazz
Tokyo Tour, Evan Lurie/E.J. Gold
Venus Rising, E.J. Gold
Wall Street, Insane Investors Club
Way Beyond the Veil, E.J. Gold
Wizzards, Accardi/Gold
Wonderland, Gorebag & the Grunts
Workstation, Jimmi Accardi & the P.V.T.s
Yiddish Blues, E.J. Gold
Zaphod & the New Harmonics
Zaphod & the New Harmonics with Elwood Strutter Sutten

sENd mONeY oR tHE FalRiE DiES!!!

Never short of a good story, Gold had this to say as an Intro to sENd mONeY oR tHE FalRiE DiES!!!:

"Honey, there's a fairie in our garden," my wife muttered in my ear as I lay sleeping peacefully, thoughts of work and stress completely out of my jurisdiction for the duration... I woke up sweating. Fairies in my garden. My first thought--they'll wreck my prize dahlias. Without a second thought, I reached for the Remington 870 Police Riot Special I use for home defense and varmints...

"No! No! Don't shoot that fairie!" shrieked my wife, and I clicked the safety on again, momentarily... "This is no time to be sentimental," I replied. "Those are my prize dahlias, and if that little son of a..."

"Now, now," she soothed... "Listen...what if you captured it instead?" "Captured a fairie?" I chortled. "What on earth would we do with a fairie?" "I don't know," she sighed... "what about...selling it on eBay?"

So that's the whole story, and if somebody doesn't buy this little critter, why... I guess we can use it for medical experiments or something...

MUSICAL RECORDINGS
ON CD

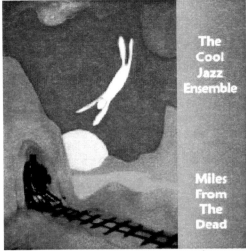

GOREBAG IN THE MORNING

Gorebag in the Morning offers the best of the best with wry commentary by host Gorebag. Humorous, offbeat and always entertaining, Gorebag regales us with warmth, humor and irreverance as he introduces each song in the format of a "not quite so ordinary" radio show.

Gorebag -- of online and otherworldly fame -- delivers the blow-by-blow, detailing this incredible musical catalogue. You are invited to sample over 32 cuts that are excerpted from songs by various artists.

Featured songs include *Mostly for Martians* -- a love song from another plane; *Blue Smoke* -- a hypnotic jazz piece that echoes from a dark and cavernous space; and *The Clear Light* -- most definitely outta site.

A wonderful offering for the musically discerning.

RIDE THAT CAROUSEL

A jazz favorite of E.J. Gold's -- reminiscent of the carousel of life. Awakening is to voluntarily ride the carousel -- to work within the wheel of karma -- the endless rounds of death and rebirth. Liberation is to get off the wheel. Awakening and realizing that one is trying to escape something that doesn't even exist, the wheel of Samsara, presents a theatre of its own.

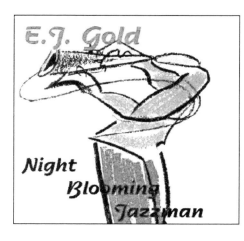

NIGHT BLOOMING JAZZMAN

Riffs rolling round and around broadcasting interstellar signals, beaming faster than light through the blackness of night. Jazz men constructing Sun Ra-like interstices of sound and mood to carry you through the cold darkness of a long, hard night. Tone scientists, men of Jazz bloom brightly telling ancient tales and future sight. Blowing nightly every day the jasmine Jazzmen are here to stay.

IN YOUR FACE

Gorebag & the Grunts punctuate Gorebag's online gaming world of dark dungeons, underground passageways, flickering lights, and explosive weapons with songs that praise the ultimate goal, challenge players, warn of hazards, and bemoan the never ending fate of these short-lived online characters. With intense force and new wave humor, Gorebag & the Grunts produce an album to play while gaming to add another dimension to your fun online.

SQUAWK BOX

The Insane Investors Quartet

LIVE PERFORMANCE

1999

For a long time, Gold and musician friends were regular listeners of the stock market program *Squawk Box* on CNBC hosted by Mark Haines, David Faber, Joe Kernen, Maria Bartiromo and Marci Rossell who mix business news with a fast-paced banter. Their common interest in the stock market sparked a creative frenzy resulting in a collection of songs relating to the good times and bad times of the stock market.

It was only a short leap from a financial website called *The Insane Investor* to *The Insane Investors Quartet.* Their first hit album *Wall Street* tracked the ups and downs of the Nasdaq and the Dow, and was sent to the Squawk Box crew at CNBC as a gesture of thanks for all the fantastic market tips they've broadcast to investors worldwide at the dawn of every stock market day.

When the 4th Anniversary celebrations for *Squawk Box* came around, producer Fran Zarnitzky invited the band to play live. CNBC's satellite uplink truck pulled into Penn Valley at 2 a.m. Friday morning August 6, 1999 for coverage of the Insane Investors Quartet tribute to Squawk Box.

The band assembled at Gold's studio, joining the Pacific Satellite Uplink Crew to beam a mini-concert over to the East Coast. The 4:00 a.m. PST broadcast opened with clips from the music video *Wall Street* which features the stock market hits as well as the band's acappella renditions of Happy Birthday.

The Insane Investors Quartet gave a live performance of its rock/country stockmarket hits *Kahuna and the Brain, Clipping Coupon*s and *Squawk Box* and made history with their musical interlude!

Host Mark Haines interviewed Gold, the "Insane Investor" himself about the band and the club's investing strategies. Gold spoke about the benefits of charitable donations of stock rather than cash and credited Mark and the Squawk Box crew for popularizing this idea. Haines said that the Club's work is outstanding in this area.

In addition to being "the number one song on the Squawk Box Hit Parade," the Insane Investors Quartet's *Kahuna & the Brain* was also the top listing in the "Hot New MP3's" of the Featured Music and Artists category on the MP3 website, which boasts over 100,000 song listings. This song and many others from the group's albums can be downloaded from MP3.

Squawk Box is aired by cable and satellite simultaneously to the United States, Great Britain, the Middle East and South Africa. According to its website, CNBC serves 150 million households in 70 countries worldwide.

MP3 HITS

MP3 is an exciting new website that makes over 100,000 songs available online. It employs a revolutionary new audio technology that enables consumers to easily listen to and download music from the Internet.

Topping the charts in three categories and a respectable third, fourth and sixth in three others, the Insane Investors Club took MP3 by storm.

The Insane Investors Club's hit single *Kahuna and the Brain* was #3 overall in Rock on MP3, and #1 in Guitar Rock and in Country Rock. *Squawk Box*, the band's tribute to the popular CNBC early morning stockmarket program, was #1 in the Country Rock category on the site. Both songs also ranked in the TOP TEN in the Pop & Rock category. Six of the songs from the *Wall Street* album made it into the top thirty.

The Insane Investors Club and members include world-renowned songwriter / artist E.J. Gold, Jimmi Accardi, who played with The Monkees and B.B. King, and the Laughing Dogs. Other members of the band include Bob Bachtold on drums and background vocals, Menlo Macfarlane on slide guitar and background vocals, Robbert Trice on bass and background vocals and David Christie on percussion and background vocals.

Here are more MP3 statistics that will make you dizzy.

No. 1 in Surf Rock out of 130 songs, *Kahuna and the Brain*, Insane Investors Club
No. 1 in Guitar Rock out of over 2300 listings, *Kahuna and the Brain*, Insane Investors Club
No. 1 in Country Rock out of over 400 songs, *Squawk Box*, Insane Investors Club
No. 3 in Rock Overall out of over 14,106 listings, *Kahuna and the Brain*, Insane Investors Club
No. 4 in Pop & Rock, *Squawk Box*, Insane Investors Club
No. 6 in Pop & Rock, *Kahuna and the Brain*, Insane Investors Club
No. 4 in Guitar Rock out of over 2349 songs
No. 7 in Guitar Rock out of over 2349 songs

Top 10: Guitar Rock, Country Rock, Surf Rock, Pop & Rock, overall Rock
Top 10: Entire MP3 Playlist of over 100,000 songs
    # 10: *Squawk Box*
Top 20: 6 songs from *Wall Street* in Country Rock :
    #1: *Squawk Box*
    #7: *Give Me Bonds*
    #10: *Clipping Coupons*
    #12: *Internet Stocks*
    #17: *Everybody's Gotta Have a Stock*
    #20: *Bottom Dweller*
Top 40 entire MP3 playlist:
    #21 *Kahuna and the Brain*, Insane Investors Club
Top 40 Pop and Rock
Top 40 Classic Rock:
    #9: *Lousy Miner*
    #25: *The Car That Takes You Home*
    #35: *Work You Sneakers Work*
    #36: *Deep on the Ocean Floor*
    #37: *You're Under Arrest*
Top 40 Free Jazz:
    Bach Told Me So
Top 30 Classical Crossover:
    #27: *On the Threshhold*
Top 40 Rock'n'Roll:
    All Phenomena Is Illusion

No. 26; of all Artists in downloads out of 100,000 songs listed
2693 downloads on August 6th, 1999

E.J. Gold

Mystical Journey of the Hi-Tech Shaman

E.J. GOLD
PYTHAGOREAN
HARP & HARMONIUM
IMPROVISATIONS

MUSICAL
RECORDINGS
ON CD

Live at the
Philharmonic II

E.J. Gold

E.J. Gold

Live at the Philharmonic I

E.J. GOLD

VENUS RISING

ARTISTIC EVENTS

THE EIGHTIES

ISIS UNLIMITED
BEVERLY HILLS
1988

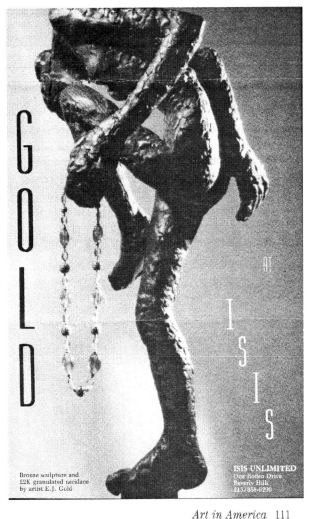

Bronze sculpture and
22K granulated necklace
by artist E.J. Gold

ISIS UNLIMITED
One Rodeo Drive
Beverly Hills
213/858-0290

Art in America 111

In 1983, Gold began a jewelry company called Jewels of Ancient Lands with museum designer Linda Corriveau. The jewels incorporate ancient stones, precious stones and granulated 21K Gold beads in designs inspired by antiquity. They are created as if ancient craftspeople were making them today.

In no time at all, Jewels of Ancient Lands was featured at the splendiferous gallery of Isis Unlimited in Mill Valley and one of the most prized real estate locations in the world--the corner of Rodeo Drive and Wilshire Boulevard in Beverly Hills. Here we see an ad for Isis Unlimited featuring *The Dancer* by Gold holding a 21K Gold Granulation necklace with Amethyst and Citrine. Such designs have helped earn the high reputation that Jewels of Ancient Lands enjoys today.

Jewel McInroy and David Franco attended the elegant opening at Isis Unlimited in the luxurious Beverly Hills gallery on Rodeo Drive.

JEWELS OF
ANCIENT LANDS

Gold works in the most traditional manner, assembling a 22K gold and granulation necklace incorporating ancient glass beads. A lover of antiquities, he has reconstructed many museum quality pieces to be preserved for posterity. His lectures and talks about archaeology convey his enthusiasm for and expertise about the subject. The beauty and quality of his work is legendary.

Gold's jewelry designs are considered very high aesthetic and typically sell in galleries, finer gift shops and museum gift shops. His creations incorporate precious or semi-precious stones, ancient beads and 22K Gold granulation. It was in the early seventies that Gold first began making jewelry and he still designs for JAL when he is not painting, recording, writing or game developing.

Gold's love of ancient materials and artifacts has led him to create necklaces using the most ancient and exotic material of all--meteorites from distant stars and galaxies.

JEWELS OF ANCIENT LANDS

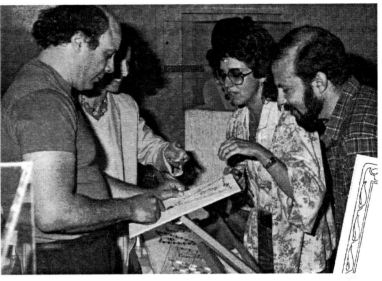

Jim Anthony and Gloria Trujillo from Gallery Arcturus in Toronto during one of their visits to Gold's jewelry studio where they selected a collection of necklaces and earring designs to sell in Canada in exclusive locations. Some of the sets include ancient beads and most are one-of-a-kind creations. These unique designs are inspired by ancient Western Asiatic artifacts and the beading traditions and principles of those civilizations.
Photos courtesy: Aviko

Restoration of an 18th Dynasty vulture pectoral spanned three years.

AN ICE-BREAKER, 1986

After a number of years with art in the background, Gold once again turned his attention to painting in a major way. Here we see him painting the *Pomegranate* in 1986. This was the first of many large scale *Odalisques* he has painted over the years.

THE PAINTING STUDIO
1987

Gold producing ink washes in his studio, 1987.

MANIFESTO
OF
REDUCTIONISM

The Manifesto of Reductionism was signed by twenty-one artists and marked the launch of the Grass Valley Graphics Group at the Frankfurt Fair in 1988. The original signers were: Tom X, Claude Needham, Willem de Groot, Julia Glasse, Tabatha Jones, Zoe Alowan, Della Heywood, David Christie, E.J. Gold, Kelly Rivera, Nancy Christie, Rudy Udarbe, Victor St-James, Brigitte Donvez, R.C. Trice, Stephanie Boyd, Tim Elston, Menlo Macfarlane, Karen Hellmich, Iven Lourie, and Lily Nova. Several more artists have joined the group while a few have moved to distant hills....such as Australia, and Canada.

MUSEUM OF ANCIENT AND MODERN ART
NEVADA CITY
SANITARIUM SERIES
1987

This dramatic series of images was seminal to an ongoing series of haunting solitary figures in a chamber which Gold relentlessly depicts. These paintings were part of a one-man show which took place at the Museum of Ancient and Modern Art in Northern California in 1987 and marked a new entrance into the art world for Gold.
Photos courtesy: Museum of Ancient and Modern Art.

Larry Roberts

GRÄFIN GALLERY
PASADENA
DIMENSIONS IN ART
1987
Planar Contiguities

Linda Corriveau, Gold's curator, and Larry Roberts, Grafin Gallery, Pasadena, California, 1987.

"Dimensions in Art" opening at Gräfin Gallery, Pasadena, 1987. Top: Larry Roberts and E.J. Gold moments before the opening. Lower: Tom X., guests, Larry Roberts, Gräfin director and owner, and E.J. Gold in one of his very rare gallery opening appearances.

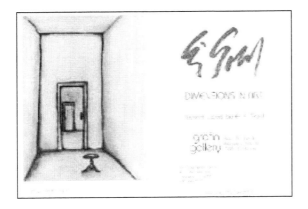

Impromptu School Reunion

Tom "Lucky" Dean at Grafin opening recalls the legendary night E.J. Gold was kicked out of Otis—for artistic reasons. Students were so shocked by this event, explained Dean, that they were still talking about it years later.

Tom "Lucky" Dean recalls his own run-in with Renzo Fenci at Otis a few years after Gold's very noticed departure. Opening of *Dimensions in Art*, Gräfin Gallery, Pasadena, 1987.

Brightside Crossing, Oil on canvas, 1986.

Just Out for a Morning Stroll, Oil on masonite, 1987.

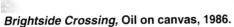

Just Keeping My Shape, Oil on canvas board, 1987.

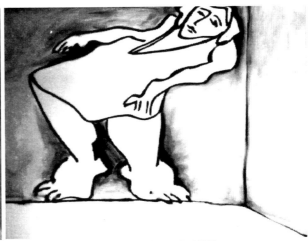

Crossover, Oil on canvas board, 1987.

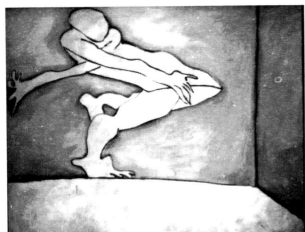

Bebop Man, 1987. Collection of Jim and Gloreen Rowe, Santa Barbara.

On the Line, Oil on canvas, 1987.

GRÄFIN GALLERY
Larry Roberts

Larry Roberts, the director of Gräfin Gallery, is an eclectic collector who has private art parties such as this one in 1991.
Photos courtesy: Larry Roberts

Larry Roberts sits in front of an E.J. Gold canvas in his home replete with exotic artifacts and oriental treasures.
Photos courtesy: Larry Roberts.

Tom Dean and friends share an evening of aesthetic hors d'oeuvres with Gold's art shining on the stage as the main course.
Photos courtesy: Larry Roberts.

December, 1987   71

21 DOWNEY MUSEUM OF ART
10419 So. Rives Ave., Downey 90241 • (213) 861-0419

GRÄFIN GALLERY • The Fair Oaks Group • Contemporary Artists •
18 S. Fair Oaks Ave., Pasadena 91105 • Mon.-Sat., 9am-7pm • (818) 440-9179
Director: Larry M. Roberts
Showing: Through January 1: Eugene Jeffrey Gold, 'Dimensions in Art,' recent works.
Representing: E. J. Gold, Len Berzofsky, Sagi Vas, Dawn Mari, Elizabeth Chandler, Francis Block, Mary Servin.

Larry Roberts has been representing Gold's work as a private art dealer since 1987. His initial show with Gold of his *Planar Contiguities* has been followed by many other shows exhibiting the variety of Gold's work from charcoals to paintings, to sculpture, to ceramics.

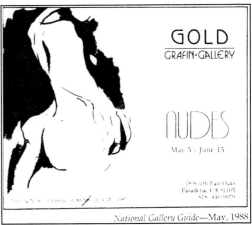

GOLD
GRAFIN·GALLERY

NUDES

May 5 - June 15

18 South Fair Oaks
Pasadena, CA 91105
818-440-9179

National Gallery Guide—May, 1988

141

SHIRO IKEGAWA

During the late sixties, Shiro Ikegawa and E.J. Gold were members of the *California Nine*. They had many shows together over a period of a couple of years and then gradually lost touch with each other. The Grafin show afforded them an opportunity to get together again after many years.

At Shiro Ikegawa's beautiful old Pasadena home, both artists enjoyed an afternoon of eightball and conversation much of which had a nostalgic flavor with reminiscences of past experiences and fun shows they had worked on together.

Photos: Barbara Haynes.

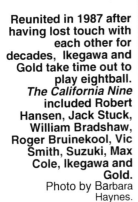

Reunited in 1987 after having lost touch with each other for decades, Ikegawa and Gold take time out to play eightball. *The California Nine* included Robert Hansen, Jack Stuck, William Bradshaw, Roger Bruinekool, Vic Smith, Suzuki, Max Cole, Ikegawa and Gold.
Photo by Barbara Haynes.

COLEMAN - GREENE GALLERY
NEW YORK
RECENT WORKS ON PAPER
1988

New York collectors, Tamara Murray, Barry & Bruscilla Campbell pause with Dr. Janet Greene the director of Coleman-Greene Gallery, New York.

Matthias Schossig flew in from Germany for the event. Schossig is an international writer and private art dealer who travels frequently between the United States and Europe where he represents Gold.

More recent projects have included working for the Disney studios in Germany on the most popular family program in that country with director/producer Peter Clausen who later came to work with Gold on script ideas.

In 1988, the Coleman-Green Gallery held a show of Gold's works on paper focussing in particular on some of his dramatic charcoal portraits.

Above on the left, Brigitte Donvez of Editions Le Chaos, Paris and Montreal, translated one of Gold's books into French. It was published in 1994 with Les Editions du Relie in Paris. Editions Le Chaos represents Gold's art and music as well as his written opus. Here Brigitte Donvez enjoys the company of Dr. Janet Greene, author of *Where You Are*, a New York collector, private art dealer and co-owner of the Coleman-Greene Gallery on 57th Street in New York.

Photo: Coleman-Greene Gallery.

Gold's painting studio as this show took place in New York, in 1988. At this time, it was located in the upper floor of an extension to the artist's home. In the studio we can see a painting from the *Between Heaven and Hell* series, a couple of large acrylic portraits, and some figures with landscapes. Gold rarely attends his openings and rarely travels so he did not make it to this one.

Photo: Barbara Haynes

Connell Foundation for the Fine Arts

EAST HAVEN

MIRO MATISSE GOLD

1988

The Connell Foundation has had numerous shows over the years including *Color and Form, Gold/Giacometti, Portraits, The Dark Hours,* and *Recent Acquisitions.*

New Haven ARTS
The Arts Council of Greater New Haven   October 1988

Cellist Yo-Yo Ma. (Photo: Bill King.)
Violinist Viktoria Mullova. (Photo: Christian Steiner.)
Maestro Murry Sidlin conducts on stage and screen at New Haven Telecom's Beethoven

N-E-W H-A-V-E-N
A-R-T-S
Join the Arts Council, and we'll

Richard D. Altman
Elizabeth Arakelian
Mimi Autmann
Rick Camp
Janet Saleh Dickson
William Ellison
Timothy Foresten
John Gonlero
Elizabeth Haas
Caroline B. Jackson
Paul James
Paul Klein
Ruth Lapides
Faith Middleton
Nitda Morales
Lawrence Russ
C. Newton Schenk, III
Jane Snaider
Barbara Wareck
Raymond E. Washburn

Staff

Beverly Richey
  Director of Communications
Marry Schuck
  Director of BVA
Soozet Chun
  Director of Operations
Barbara Segaloff
  BVA Associate Director
Eleanor Marie Pidsall
  Benefit Plan and Membership Coordinator
Anne Campbell
  Administrative Assistant
Joyda Greenfield,
  Financial Assistant

The Arts Council is supported by its unions, artist, business and corporate members, as well as grants from The Connecticut Commission on the Arts and The New Haven Foundation.

THE DARK HOURS
Recent Serigraphs by E. J. Gold

OCT. 10—DEC. 10

Edge of Thought, Serigraph,
Edition of 75, 1987, Black Ink,
Rives BFK, 22" x 30"

CONNELL FOUNDATION FOR THE FINE ARTS
2 Meadow Place
East Haven, CT 06512
(203) 468-8177

Miró Gold matisse
Connell Foundation
Oct. 25–Nov. 30
East Haven, CT

E.J. Gold
Gold
Alberto Giacometti
Giacometti

C·F
F·A   Connell Foundation
        for the
        Fine Arts

-Presents-

Color and Form:
Matisse, Miro, Gold

THROUGH
January 22, 1988

This unusual collection of original works on paper by Henri Matisse, Joan Miro, and E.J. Gold will surely stimulate that natural response, in each of us, which can appreciate the aesthetic value of fine art works.

-Catalog Available-
For Appointment Information:
(203) 468-8177

E J G O L D

CONNELL FOUNDATION FOR THE FINE ARTS
PO BOX 611
EAST HAVEN, CT
203/ 468-8177

Art in America 107

CONNELL FOUNDATION
FOR THE FINE ARTS
Miro Matisse Gold
1988

The Connell Foundation for the Fine Arts is a private
gallery situated on a grand estate in East Haven,
Connecticut. Connell is a long time collector of
Matisse and Miro works on paper. It was in the late
eighties that he expanded his collection to include
works on paper by E.J. Gold. This was his first show
combining his three favorite artists.
Photos courtesy: Connell Foundation for the Fine Arts.

Collector Pierre Lefevre and Mark
Connell, Director of the Connell
Foundation for the Fine Arts enjoy
a moment at the opening of *Miro
Matisse Gold*.
Photos courtesy: Connell Foundation.

The foyer of the Foundation, 1988.

MUSEUM OF ANCIENT & MODERN ART
NEVADA CITY
EXPRESSIONIST LANDSCAPES

1988

E.J. Gold art exhibit
Expressionistic Landscapes, **1988.**
Photos courtesy: Museum of Ancient and Modern Art.

Gold collector Devoy White watches as E.J. Gold shares some serious laughs with artist Menlo Macfarlane.

Dr. Claude Needham, Museum of Ancient and Modern Art President, Linda Corriveau, curator, Michael Himowitz of Himowitz Gallery in Sacramento, Gold's wife Morgan Fox, Himowitz guest, and E. J. Gold.

Magdelene Wiebe interviewing Tamara Murray, Director, Galerie Matrix, New York, Bruscilla and Barry Campbell, New York collectors who flew in for the occasion.

Morgan Fox, Penelope Rose, the artist E.J. Gold, Joyce Kenyon of Spiral Gallery in Los Angeles, interviewed by Magdelene Wiebe.

Tabatha Jones and Lee Perry president of Samadhi Tank Company share a moment together at the foot of a mountainous landscape by Gold at the opening held at the Museum of Ancient and Modern Art in Northern California in 1988.

Museum of Ancient & Modern Art
EXPRESSIONIST LANDSCAPES

Linda Corriveau chats with collector Ellie Orr.

Conservationist Nancy Christie interviewed by Magdelene Wiebe.

Mrs. Fereshteh Sadeghieh from Vancouver.

Glenn and Lee Perry of Samadhi Tank Co. flew in from Los Angeles.

Glass blower Mark Einert drinking up the beauty of the vistas.

E.J. Gold exhibit, *Expressionistic Landscapes.*
Photo courtesy: Museum of Ancient and Modern Art.

The Himowitz party (Himowitz Gallery, Sacramento) arriving by limousine at the Museum of Ancient and Modern Art.

Lin & Leslie Smith, Nevada City collectors interviewed outside the Museum building as they enter the Opening for *Expressionist Landscapes.*

EMROSE ART CORPORATION
EAC GALLERY
NEW YORK
Pure Gold
1988

You Are Cordially Invited
To The Opening Reception
PURE GOLD
SATURDAY EVENING, 10 DECEMBER, 1988
The Paintings, Sculpture and Original Graphics
of
E.J. GOLD

eac
GALLERY

Works on Display, December 10th - December 31st
R.S.V.P. by December 1
516-248-4163
RECEPTION 7-10 PM

eac
GALLERY
emrose art corporation
838 willis ave., albertson, new york 11507
(516) 248-4163

THE ARTIST, E.J. GOLD

E.J. Gold boasts a rich and diversified background beginning with his first years in New York where he grew up surrounded by the Who's Who in the arts in America of the 40's
and 50's.

A precocious child, he had his first major showing at
the *Museum of Modern Art* in 1948 and in the same year met
Henri Matisse whose impromptu art lesson left an indelible
mark on him.

In the late fifties, he became associated with the *Cedar
Tavern Group* of the New York School and regularly met with
Pollock, Kline, and de Kooning.

After this auspicious debut, Gold moved to Los Angeles
where he studied and taught at the Otis Art Institute, while
at the same time producing and selling art, as well as working with Lebrun and Schwaderer.

During the sixties, he became famous within the *California Nine* and was widely recognized for his invention of soft
and breathing sculptures.

The seventies led him into many directions including
music production and writing in the field of science fiction
and transformational psychology where he soon became a
respected authority.

Since his reemergence in 1986, Gold has entered a
prolific period boldly reasserting himself as an experimental
artist. His diversity and proficiency leave critics and admirers
astonished: ink washes, pastels, gouaches, acrylics, oils, charcoals, linocuts, serigraphs, pen and inks—all clearly
demonstrate his awesome talent and discipline.

LONG ISLAND

PURE *Gold*

Recent Works including Oils,
Pastels, Sculpture, Serigraphs
and Multiples

DEC. 11 through DEC. 31
Gala Reception: Sat., Dec. 10, 7-9 p.m.

He Waits Very Attentively, But for What?,
Serigraph, Arches, 22" x 30", Edition of 75, 1988.

eac
emrose art corporation, 838 willis ave., albertson, ny 11501 (516) 248-4163
Mon. – Fri.: 9 am-5:30 pm; Thurs.: 'til 7 pm; Saturday: 10am-5pm

Pure Gold
THE CURRENT WORKS
OF E.J. GOLD

EAC Gallery very proudly announces the exclusive acquisition of the line
of **Flanagan Graphics, Rosenbaum Fine Art** and **Heidelberg**

Included in these lines are the limited edition works of **Beryl Cook, E.**
McCombs, Oku, Eng Tay, Frank Stella, Russell Nowlin
and available for viewing and purchase.

In addition to these exciting new limited edition fine art graphics, **EAC**
original oil paintings of this region's top upcoming artists. We deliver
customized to your client's specifications.

Our entire inventory is backed by our **Gallery Exchange Program**
work of art at the full value of your original purchase.

Please call **(516) 248-4163** today to arrange an appointment
edition graphics, oil paintings, watercolors from mainland China, custom
our contemporary abstracts, or just forward the enclosed card and
at your location, or from

Thank you,
Emrose Art Corporation

838 willis ave., albertson, new york 11507
(516) 248-4163

**E.J. Gold had a one-man show titled *Pure Gold* at EAC
Gallery, New York, 1988, Larry Rosenbaum, Director. It was
a showing of his current works including original paintings
and prints, lithographs and serigraphs.**
Photos courtesy: EAC Gallery

Marilyn Feinstein at Art Expo proudly displays some large original serigraphs such as *Big Bird* by E.J. Gold. *Big Bird* is part of a very small edition of 20.

Gold's upswing in artistic productivity after 1986 enabled H.E.I. representative in New York, Marilyn Feinstein, to offer more than one-hundred different prints in both lithograph and serigraph form. Here we get a glimpse of the *Chess Player* serigraph left which was published in an edition of 75, and *Lady With Hairdo* below left which exists in an edition of 15. The serigraph on the right is already sold-out.

Several of the smaller editions were immediately sold out. Gold's multiples are almost always produced on Arches paper, Rives BFK, Sennelier and other fine art papers. The editions sizes are typically small, usually 25, 50, or 75. Some editions are as small as 6 while others may go to 200. *The Horn Player* (right) is a pencil signed edition of 75 on 22"x15" Arches paper.

Photos courtesy: Marilyn Feinstein

ARTEXPO '88
Jacob Javits Center
New York

Two Sisters serigraph published in an editon of 75 by Heidelberg Editions International, Gold's official fine art publisher.

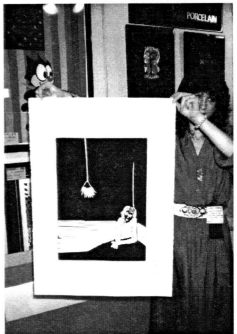

Show posters presented at ArtExpo New York in 1988 amid many large and colorful serigraphs by the artist. Gold's work has been represented many times at such events over the years both in Los Angeles and New York.

149

SALON DES ARTISTES
NEW YORK
DARK HOURS
1988

ART NOW/NEW YORK
Gallery Guide
A SELECTED LISTING OF CURRENT MUSEUM AND GALLERY EXHIBITIONS/JUNE 1988

My life as an art patron is to serve humbly as a guide and herald. Passionately I dream of and am committed to restoring civilization's birthright to enlightenment through creative expression. I believe the art world of late has become perverted, desolate, ugly and submerged in the darkness of negativity, betraying the essence of classical humanism. Sadly, in the closing hours of this century, aesthetic consciousness has suffered an immense loss, finally being brutally severed from its umbilical cord to beauty, wisdom and truth. My promise to humanity is to nurture the regeneration of this primal connection, expelling cynicism, resurrecting idealism in its place. I will bring ideas of great consequence into public attention and pledge myself to you wholeheartedly, striving for the magnanimous elevation of mankind into a great society.

Hvgo Garcia de Pagano
Founder, Salon des Artistes

E.J. **GOLD**

The Dark Hours
Serigraphs by E.J. Gold
June 15-June 30
Catalog Available

"The Woman Who Wasn't There Sitting in the Kitchen With Coffee Cup" - serigraph on Archos, 22" x 30", 1967.

SALON DES ARTISTES
79 Mercer St., NYC 10012
Open Tuesday-Sunday, 12-7 p.m.   212-925-6309

NY-35/Soho

THE NEW YORK ARTS GUILD
and
SALON DES ARTISTES
Request the honor of your presence
At an opening reception honoring artist

EJ GOLD
Curated by Tamara Murray

Premiering
Friday, the 17th Day of June 1988
8:00 P.M. to 10:00 P.M. at

SALON DES ARTISTES
No. 79 Mercer Street/SoHo
(between Spring and Broome)

R.S.V.P. (212) 925-6309

This exhibition will continue through July 2nd, 1988.

A show of Gold's serigraphs from the *Dark Hours* series as well as some of his *Odalisques* marked the New York beginning of a tour that carried these multiples throughout the country stopping at several galleries.

The Dark Hours
EJ Gold

Salon des Artistes

Checkered Table at Cafe
Edition of 75, 1987. Black ink, Rives BFK, 22" x 30"

Here is a cafe scene that resonates with the 19th century tradition of Cézanne and Manet, the Montmartre imagery transposed to Greenwich Village. The woman's posture is eerily familiar from all those Parisian cafe portraits, while the manner of portrayal calls up the figures of Schiele and Kirschner, caricatures of night life in Vienna and Weimar Germany. The setting also has an uncanny accuracy, from the reflected bottles and wineglasses to the typical tablecloth. The figure pathos in this image is heightened by her black face blending with dress and background rather than the body.

The Woman Who Wasn't There in the Kitchen with Coffee Cup
Edition of 75, 1987. Black ink, Rives BFK, 22" x 30"

Where is the woman who wasn't there? Is she off in a dream, in a fog, in a wistful memory, in an idle daydream? Her kitchen is boldly present, with the sure strokes that define pans, cooking utensils, stove top, ruffled curtains. In strictly visual terms, the black wall contrasts strongly with the objects in the room and heightens their interest. The nude woman with her morning coffee is a mysterious and ambivalent figure, contorted and flowing with the environment but also in repose. This linocut shows the artist's ability to take simple elements and derive a compelling mood or symbolism from them, as Beckmann and Munch did so well in their works on paper.

very expressionist in feeling. The emotion is ambiguous but definitive. Rainy weather seems to have insinuated itself not only in the raincoat, but also in the grain of floors, walls and skin. It rains throughout the image, and rain unites the figure with its ground.

Are we seeing the same odalisques we have seen in the European tradition of painting and elsewhere in the world? Is it only because we have seen Redon's and Monet's dream flowers, Matisse's and Gauguin's and Utamaro's women, Vermeer's and Van Gogh's interiors that these images have not only a visual correspondence but an emotional connotation for us?

E.J. Gold invites us by way of the eye into his world of archetypal images. His odalisques present as an attractive variation of an ancient artistic tradition, the study of the female. He certainly has synthesized the elements most typical of the modernist painting style, the objects and forms that seem by necessity to dwell in these visions and form their

Odalisque III
Edition of 75, 1987. Five Colors, Rives BFK, 22" x 15"

non-sectarian symbology. Beneath the attractiveness and accomplishment of the paintings and prints, there lies a further aesthetic possibility for the viewer.

Perhaps the meaning of this iconography of the modern is that no matter where you go there you are. These rooms and their resident odalisques are archetypes that we continually encounter, whether in this life or another. The uncanny familiarity of the images may be not from déjà vu, the memory of another such chamber or another similar life, but rather a recall of life as one whole cloth, one single life that simply transforms its outward shimmer as a convenience to its own numerous eyes.

Odalisque IV
Edition of 75, 1987. Five Colors, Rives BFK, 22" x 15"

12

THE ARTIST TURNS AUCTIONEER AND FUNDRAISER

The Prospector
The Union's weekly entertainment magazine
Events for Aug. 21-28

Art museum

Ancient and modern combine at NC gallery
—See pages 10 & 11

Local theater groups nominated for awards
—See page 4

Rain comes to GV and Breeze in NC
—See page 8

Davis and Davidson team up in Tahoe
— See page 9

For several years, Gold volunteered for the Museum of Ancient and Modern Art as their most exciting auctioneer at the fundraising Benefit Auctions which combined education and entertainment.

His humor broke tradition and attracted media attention — KCRA TV, Sacramento and

E.J. Gold hits the pinata that was brought in at a 1988 Benefit Auction where he volunteered as an art auctioneer for one of his favorite community services: a local art museum of very high aesthetic standards.
Photos: Museum of Ancient and Modern Art

Channel 10 covered several events. The auctions were marathons that lasted as long as seven hours with Gold going non-stop with digressions of every kind about the historical significance of an artist, the differences in techniques, the importance of conservation, the artistic merit of a piece, all of this topnotch information peppered with stories, anecdotes and jokes. Most people would stay until the very end many of them having driven for three or four hours.
Photo courtesy: Museum of Ancient and Modern Art.

PETER HEINEMAN FINE ARTS
DENVER
DIMENSIONAL TWEAK
1988

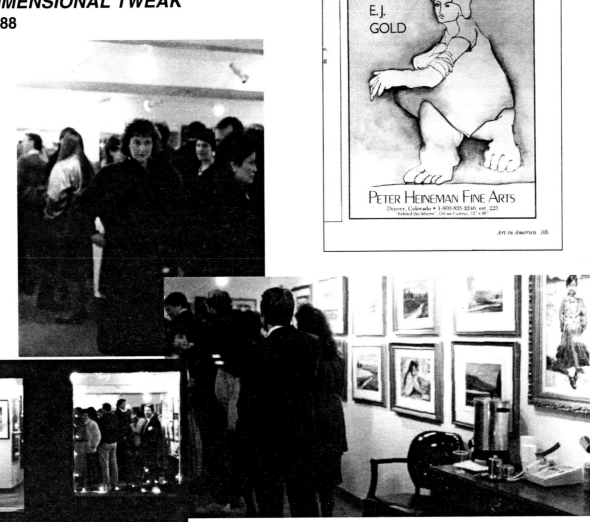

A Wee Slip of a Girl,
72"x96" Oil on canvas by E.J. Gold.

E.J. GOLD

PETER HEINEMAN FINE ARTS
Denver, Colorado • 1-800-835-2246, ext. 223
"Behind the Mirror", Oil on Canvas, 72" x 96"

Art in America 105

Photos courtesy: Peter Heineman Fine Arts.

One of several openings Peter Heineman Fine Arts has had over the past decade or so showing originals and multiples, 1990.
Photos courtesy: Peter Heineman Fine Arts.

PETER HEINEMAN
FINE ARTS
DIMENSIONAL TWEAK
1991

Photos courtesy: Peter
Heineman Fine Arts.

SPIRAL GALLERY
LOS ANGELES
Inside Outside
1988

Joyce Kenyon is a private art dealer, Hollywood script writer and Reiki instructor who combines aesthetics with her quest for harmony and well-being.

After falling in love with Gold's art in 1987, she included him in her stable of artists and has been very successful selling his work to her own extensive private client list which includes movie directors and producers, actors, and entrepreneurs both American and Oriental.

and Baj.

SPIRAL GALLERY • Twen-
sters and Con-
1440 Veteran
90024 • By Ap-
(213)479-7503
Joyce Kenyon
y: E.J. Gold: Ear-
tings, drawings,
s.
bid, Johnson and
also available by:
e, Picasso,
hagall, Calder,
s.

Vol. 7, No. 5   January, 1988

ARTSCENE
The Monthly Guide to Art in Southern California

E.J. Gold, 'Seated Woman #1,' a/c, 48x36", 1987, is featured at Spiral Gallery during January.

Spiral Gallery, Los Angeles, 1989 opening. From left to right: collectors Peter Jordt, Marilyn Charles, David Shore, Pierre Lefevre and Joyce Kenyon, gallery director.

Kreditkassen
Oslo
ODALISQUES
1989

Brigitte Donvez European art representative for Heidelberg Editions International at one of several exhibits in Oslo curated by Per Heiberg. Donvez introduced the *Manifesto of Reductionism* to the European market at the Frankfurt Book Fair in 1988.

E.J. Gold installation of *Odalisques* curated by magistrate and collector Per Heiberg at Kreditkassen, Oslo, Norway, 1990.
Photos by Per Heiberg, 1990

HOHO GALLERY
MOUNT HOLYOKE
ARTISTS IN RESONANCE
NONA HATAY & E.J. GOLD
1989

Photos courtesy: Amherst Art Associates

NONA HATAY

Curators, Sydney and Steve Kunin are pleased with the attendance on opening night.

Nona Hatay is an experimental photographer whose work has been published in several books, including her most well-known, *The Jimmi Hendrix Portfolio*.

As a photo artist she experiments with color, superimpositions, transparency, texture, and surrealism. Nona Hatay is the daughter of print dealer Pamela Hatay-Stratton and is renowned as a rock star photographer.

HOHO GALLERY   AMHERST ART ASSOCIATES

Photos courtesy: Hoho
Gallery, Holyoke.

Amherst Art Associates curators Sydnie and Steve Kunin enjoy the results of their labors for this show which brought together experimental photographer Nona Hatay and multi-faceted artist E.J. Gold of whom she did many photographic studies prior to the show.

(c)1997hei

PAGE 24   DAILY HAMPSHIRE GAZETTE

Editor,
Maretta Prichard

Arts & Entertainment

'Artists in Resonance'

Film foundation k with Oscar-winnin

'Walking piano' part of new Mandrell act

Photographer Nona Hatay used artist E.J. Gold for the subject of her photographic studies and experiments with his art in the background or superimposed in combination with paintings, sculptures and serigraphs by Gold.

The exhibit took place in the HoHo Gallery located in an old factory which has been renovated and given a new life serving the arts.
Photos courtesy: Amherst Art Associates

Amherst Art Associates
ARTISTS IN RESONANCE
1989

380 Dwight Street

ARTISTS IN RESONANCE

April 27-May 21

"E.J. Gold"   Nona Hatay   "A Boy and His Dog"   E.J. Gold

Advertisements for two shows from 1988 at Amherst Art Associates: *Pure Gesture* and *Odalisques.* Director Steven Kunin was the president of Kunin Felt Company and became an avid collector of Gold's while at the same time representing him in the Northeastern states.

True to tradition, *Artists in Resonance,* a collaboration between Nona Hatay and E.J. Gold, also offered an afternoon poetry reading by well-known poet Iven Lourie from his 1988 collaboration book with drawings by Gold inspired from Miro's starving artist period, titled *Miro's Dream.*

THUNDERBEAR GALLERY
SANTA FE
E.J. GOLD WORKS ON PAPER
1989

Thunderbear Gallery in Santa Fe, New Mexico caters to the Southwest crowd of art collectors who favor Gold's *Odalisques*. The colors of his palette break through conventional barriers.
Photos courtesy: Thunderbear Gallery.

Barbara Haynes Heidelberg Editions International consultant at Thunderbear Gallery opening in Santa Fe, 1989. Heidelberg Editions International is Gold's art publisher.
Photos courtesy:
Thunderbear Gallery.

Collector Jean-Pierre Sauve at Gold opening at Thunderbear Gallery, 1989.
Photos courtesy: Thunderbear Gallery.

The Thunderbear Gallery
presents

E.J. GOLD

WORKS ON PAPER

The Old Oak Tree

E.J. Gold

Friday, September 1, 1989
through
Saturday, September 30, 1989

Opening Reception
Friday, Sept 1, 5-7 pm

The A.D.A.M. Inc. Thunderbear Gallery
113 Washington Street Suite 109
Santa Fe, New Mexico

Hologramm

Nr. 54 Mai 1988 DM 5,– C 20356 F

Das ganzheitliche Magazin · erscheint vierteljährlich

HOLOGRAMM
Interview
1988

KUNSTBLATT
Interview
1989

Rein

Der High-Tech-Schamane E.J. Gold

Ein Porträt

Brigitte Donvez & Linda Corriveau

E.J. Gold, 1987

Mandalas
Bilder au

E.J. Gold hilft in der Küche seines
Lieblingsrestaurants

62. BERLINER Kunstblatt

Die Kunst

DER KÜNSTLER, E.J. GOLD

Inside Outside,
E.J. Gold 1987
Kohlezeichnung

39

The German art market was receptive to the work of E.J.
Gold as these art magazine interviews demonstrate.
Gold has been represented in Germany by art dealer
Matthias Schossig for many years. *The Dark Hours*,
because of their expressionist style and dark mood,
were a natural match for the German public taste and its
particular angst.

Artistic Associations: Barry Moser
ALICE IN WONDERLAND OPENING
Museum of Ancient & Modern Art
1989

Making an exception, Gold went to the opening of the Barry Moser exhibit at the Museum of Ancient and Modern Art to pay homage to a fine artist. Moser is a student of Leonard Baskin whom Gold reveres so it was an event he could not pass up. The two artists enjoyed sharing their artistic similarities and found mutual friends too. From left: E.J. Gold, museum supporters actor Devoy White, Barry Moser, and artist Faye White.

Gold has a genuine appreciation of Barry Moser's elaborate woodcuts and Moser was graciously accommodating and autographed a copy of his *Alice in Wonderland* book for fan, E.J. Gold.
Photos courtesy: Museum of Ancient and Modern Art.

THE CALIFORNIA
ART REVIEW

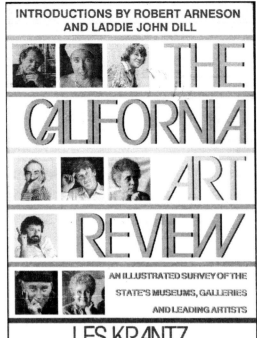

THE CALIFORNIA ART REVIEW

This richly illustrated volume is an in-depth survey of California's art world. Reviews of hundreds of California's museums and galleries are included, as are individual profiles of more than 2,000 contemporary artists. Accompanying the text are over 1,600 reproductions, making this volume an indispensible reference for collectors, curators, critics, dealers, and all those following the contemporary art scene.

The Museums: Descriptions of their collections, new acquisitions and programs, highlighted by photographs from recent and upcoming exhibitions.

The Galleries: Reviews of over 200 of the state's most influential galleries, citing specialties and gallery artists.

The Artists: Profiles of more than 2,000 artists, many accompanied by color and black and white reproductions of their works.

Artist Resources: A listing of influential museum personnel is included, categorized by department heads and listing their titles. Also included are art associations, with listings of programs, exhibitions, services and other activities.

Cross-Referencing: Galleries cross-referenced according to specialty.

Index: Alphabetical listing of museums, galleries, and over 5,000 artists from both individual profiles and gallery stables.

The California Art Review is yet another trade publication in which E.J. Gold's biography has been included. The number of publications of this nature in which references to Gold can be found has considerably grown over the years. Now, with the Internet, there are more services and directories than ever.

Anecdotally, on this page in the *Review* readers will see Gold listed on the same page as one of his most beloved art teachers from Otis Art Institute, Bob Glover.

GLOVER, ROBERT LEON (Ceramist, Sculptor)
6015 Santa Monica Blvd., Los Angeles, CA 90036

Born: 1936 *Awards:* Ford Foundation Grant *Collections:* First Federal Savings, South Pasadena; Southern California Container Corporation *Exhibitions:* San Francisco Museum of Fine Arts; Space Gallery, Los Angeles *Education:* Chouinard Art Institute; Los Angeles County Art Institute *Dealer:* Space Gallery, Los Angeles

His ceramic sculpture is formal and abstract, dealing with the natural attributes of clay as both medium and metaphor. Early upright forms were rounded, closed and engraved with designs suggestive of bricks or stonework. These made references to standing stones and conceptually linked the manmade object with the natural. Recent work is modular and composed of units that are placed in natural settings or arranged within an interior space to create a "site." The curving stoneware slabs of his piece *Dial O* are arranged in a circle ten feet in diameter. Connotations of prehistoric earthworks, archaeological sites and techniques, and the natural landscape are activated by these pieces.

GLOWIENKE, CARL (Sculptor)
2316 Bancroft St., San Diego, CA 92104

Born: 1955 *Collections:* Greenpeace Permanent Collection *Exhibitions:* American Cetacean Society Biennial Symposium; Scrimshaw Gallery, San Francisco *Education:* Cal. State-Northridge

He wrote briefly for *ARTWEEK* after taking a degree in music. His subsequent abstract wood torsos were heavily influenced by Moore and Nakian. In 1985, he went to the Sea World Research Center and began studying marine mammals. His work of the period was influenced by Randy Puckett and Jerry Glover. He is presently continuing to study marine mammal anatomy under Larry Foster and is apprenticing in bronze work under Guillermo Castano of Mexico City.

Palm Springs Desert Museum *Exhibitions:* Milwaukee Museum; National Contemporary Museum, Seoul *Education:* U. of Texas *Dealer:* Natoli Ross, Santa Monica

Her art experience includes painting, drawing, silkscreening, tapestry design, photography and jewelry-making, but she is best known for her outdoor monumental sculptures. Worked in welded steel, her artistic concerns are expressed in both an abstract figurative style and a non-objective, geometric style. Sculptures are either left unfinished or are painted with Rustoleum paints in red, black and yellow. Currently she is working on her painting, using acrylic paint on handmade paper. These geometric works are puzzle-like variations on rectangles.

GOLD, E. J. (Painter)
P.O. Box 1656, Grass Valley, CA 95945

Born: 1941 *Collections:* Museum of Ancient and Modern Art; Connell Foundation for the Fine Arts *Exhibitions:* Museum of Modern Art, New York; Houston Museum of Fine Arts *Education:* Otis Art Institute *Dealer:* Coleman Greene Gallery, NYC; Spiral Gallery, Los Angeles

He has always worked as an experimental artist. The techniques of forced perspective, planar contiguities, color field reductionism and iso-magnification have been important in the development of his work with breathing and soft sculptures. His work has ranged broadly from the figurative to the abstract; in all styles, he has concentrated on gestural refinement. Recent work includes a series of large paintings with figures floating in and out of walls and corridors. Relying on perspective distortions and exposed canvas, they reflect the influence of sumi-e through their use of irreversible lines. A disturbing sense of otherworldliness contrasts with a mood of deep serenity and peace. Also working in small lithographs on his own press, he is collaborating with John Cage on a livre d'artiste to be published in Germany.

THE PRINTWORLD DIRECTORY

THE
PRINTWORLD
DIRECTORY

CONTEMPORARY PRINTS & PRICES
SIXTH EDITION 1994

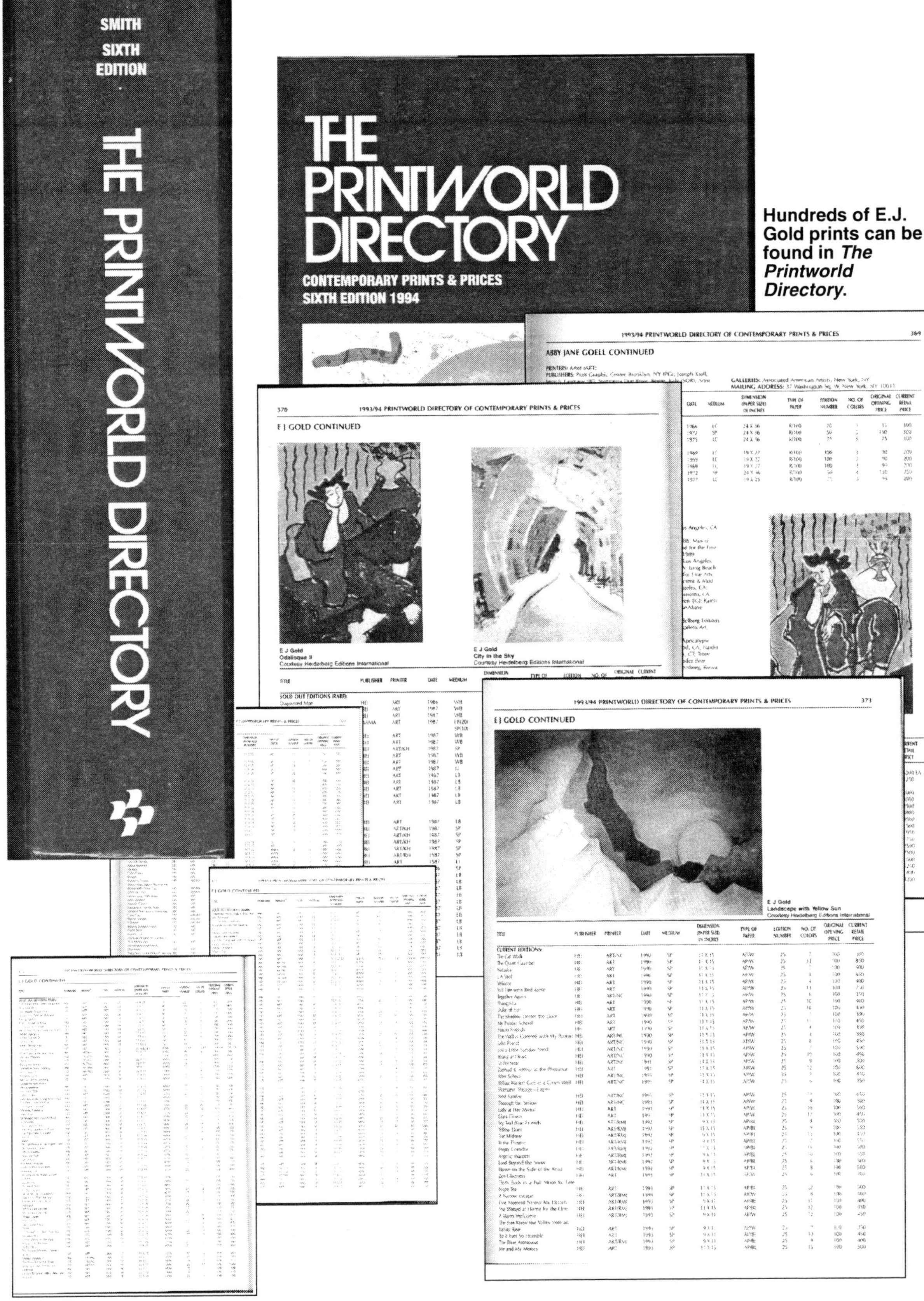

Hundreds of E.J. Gold prints can be found in *The Printworld Directory*.

Bob Bachtold is a head hunter turned collector who is rather eclectic. He enjoys contemporary art as well as Old Masters such as Rembrandt, and modern masters from the School of Paris.

His collection is therefore well diversified. Gold's art shines in this elegant company by its colorfulness and sheer size since Bachtold tended to collect smaller works until he started amassing a sampling of Gold's paintings which measure as large as 48"x60" thus dwarfing the masters around it.

Bachtold's new love is large landscapes with a somewhat abstract flavor as well as bronze sculptures which also have an abstract quality to them such as the *Cubist Torso* by Gold seen in the forefront.

Photos courtesy: Bachtold & Associates

PRINTEMPS GALLERY
DENVER
WORKS ON PAPER
1989

Curated by Peter Heineman Fine Arts

Views of the exhibition and dining area with its impressive staircase and elegant and dramatic decor populated by small black and white hand-pulled Gold lithographs.
Photos courtesy: Peter Heineman Fine Arts.

Gold's art has appeared on the covers of books, magazines, journals, catalogs, newspapers...

Collectors' Profile:
Dr. James & Gloreen Rowe

The late Dr. Jim Rowe was a state lobbyist who when not busy working in Sacramento lived in Santa Barbara with his wife Gloreen. Both were avid art collectors who enjoyed introducing their friends to the work of many artists that inspire them.
Photos by Glenn Perry.

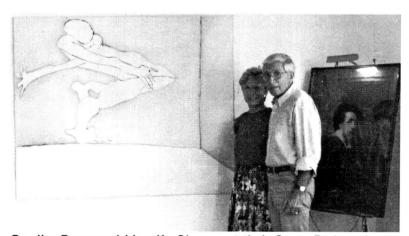

Dr. Jim Rowe and his wife Gloreen at their Santa Barbara home installing *Bebop Man* by E.J. Gold. The Rowes are avid collectors of the Grass Valley Graphics Group and have original works by every one of them.
Photos by Nancy Burns.

Painting the *FUSION* series
1989

A section of one of the vaults where paintings are stored in Gold's "barn".

Painting the *Fusion* series, 1989.
Photos by Mariette Fournier.

Collectors' Profile:

BRUCE & CARYN RENFREW

Caryn & Bruce Renfrew pondering on their final choice of a painting in the studio of E.J. Gold, 1990.

ARTISTIC EVENTS

THE GOODWIN SHOW
SACRAMENTO
1990

Ron and Debra Goodwin, Sacramento art collectors and patrons, hosted a large group show focussing on current works on paper, paintings, and sculptures by all of the members of the Grass Valley Graphics Group.

Art patron Debra Goodwin who hosted the show in Sacramento chats with curator Linda Corriveau standing by a *Planar & City in the Sky Fusion* painting while photographer and sculptor Bill de Groot of the Grass Valley Graphics Group is visible in the background on the left.

Rudy Udarbe is a floral artist who, in collaboration with mobile artist David Christie, incorporated metal forms and sculpted flowers with silk flowers and leaves. *Metallo-Florica* is the name given to one of these creatures.

The program book above left, mobile artist David Christie chats with artist Kelly Rivera whose works were in this group show.

Debra Goodwin with guests.
Photos by Willem de Groot.

Rod Goodwin (right) with guest.

USA - USSR
THE RUSSIAN TOUR
1990-1992

Claude Needham, Vladimir Petrov and Linda Corriveau make a preliminary selection of art for *USA-USSR*.

Dr. Claude Needham with Vladimir Petrov, the Russian Cultural Representative of the Sergei Diaghilev Art Center and coordinator of *USA-USSR*. Works by the Grass Valley Graphics Group were selected to represent the United States in this exhibit which went on tour throughout the Soviet Union and its satellite countries for about three years.
Photos by Willem de Groot.

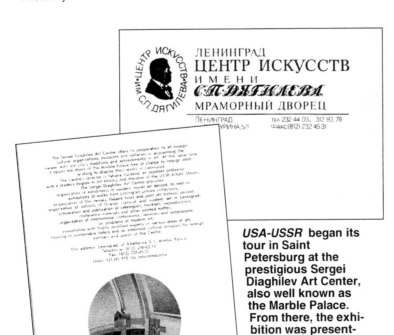

ЛЕНИНГРАД
ЦЕНТР ИСКУССТВ
ИМЕНИ
С.П.ДЯГИЛЕВА
МРАМОРНЫЙ ДВОРЕЦ

USA-USSR began its tour in Saint Petersburg at the prestigious Sergei Diaghilev Art Center, also well known as the Marble Palace. From there, the exhibition was presented at the Anichkov Palace near Anichkov Bridge.

The Manifesto of Reductionism was translated in its entirety into Russian and published in this journal for the tour throughout the Soviet Union and its former satellite countries. The cover art was by Tom X, a member of the Grass Valley Graphics Group. Below we see Dr. Claude Needham with Vladimir Petrov in an early meeting about this project.

РУССКИЙ ВЕСТНИК

Специальный выпуск "Русского Вестника". No 7. Латвия. Валка.

"Слепой".

ОЛЕГ ЯХНИН
ВАЛЕРИЙ МИШИН
МИХАИЛ КАРАСЬ
ВЛАДИМИР ВИДЕ!
АНАТОЛИЙ ВАСИЛ
ЮРИЙ ЛЮКШИН
ИВАН ТАРАСЮК
ВЯЧЕСЛАВ МИХАЙЛ
ЮРИЙ ЮДИН
И. Д. ГОЛД
ТОМ ДЖОНСОН
МЕНЛО МАКФАРЛАН
КЕЛЛИ РИВЕРА
КЛОД НИДХЕМ
СТЕФАНИ БОЙД
ЛИЛИ НОВА
КАРЕН ХЭЛМИК
БИЛЛ ДЕГРУТ
ДЕЛЛА ХЕЙВУД
ДЭВИД КРИСТИ
ТИМ ИЛСТОН
ЗОЯ АЛОВЭН
РОБЕРТ ТРАЙС
ДИК ХАРТ

The Grass Valley Graphics Group and the School of Reductionism found an interested audience in the Soviet Bloc countries who published the *Manifesto of Reductionism* in several different languages including Russian, Lithuanian and Estonian.

The *Manifesto* is an artistic statement produced by the Grass Valley Graphics Group in 1986 and originally launched at the Frankfurt International Book Fair, the largest book fair in the world.

ЦЕНТР ИСКУССТВ
имени
С. П. ДЯГИЛЕВА

★★★★★★★★★★★
ВЫСТАВКА
СОВЕТСКО-
АМЕРИКАНСКОЙ
ГРАФИКИ
★★★★★★★★★★★

ЛЕНИНГРАД —
СЕВЕРНАЯ КАЛИФОРНИЯ

Ленинград
ул. Халтурина,5/1
Мраморный дворец

ОТКРЫТИЕ 11 МАРТА 1991 г.   Выставка открыта ежедневно с 10.30 до 18.30. кроме среды

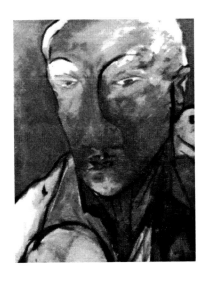

During the Gulf War in 1990, Gold produced hundreds of pastel portraits on 10"x13" Sennelier paper.

These magnificent pieces are memorable for their vivid and often mildly eerie colors. About a dozen paintings were also produced at the time, some of which are in the Meryl and Lenny Beck collection, the Harry Nilsson collection and the Foundation for the Study of Objective Art in Toronto.

On the right, we see a photo of the studio during the production of this series while it was still located in the upper floor of the extension of the artist's home.
Photos by Barbara Haynes.

THE FACES OF WAR
1990

HIDDEN IMAGES STUDIO
BOULDER
Bardo Visions
1991

Hidden Images Studio, Boulder, CO, 1991.

HIDDEN IMAGESTUDIO

PREMIERE OPENING

HIDDEN IMAGES STUDIO is pleased to host AIME FINE ARTS and PETER HEINEMAN FINE ARTS in presenting the MACRODIMENSIONAL TRANSFORMATIONAL works of Internationally reknown west coast author/artist E.J. GOLD.

Also featured are the multi-media prints and pastels of MENLO MACFARLANE and the sensuous blown glass objects of MARK EINERT, members of the GRASS VALLEY GRAPHICS ARTISTS group in California.

Peter Heineman supervising gallery installation, Boulder, 1991.
Photos courtesy of Peter Heineman Fine Arts.

Hidden Images Studio, Boulder, 1991.
Photos courtesy: Hidden Images Studio.

HIDDEN
IMAGESTUDIO
GALLERY OPENING

WOMAN IN SHOWER

E.J. GOLD

FEATURING WORKS OF

E.J. GOLD- *Internationally renown artist/author*

RECEPTIONS:

FRIDAY NOV. 15th, 6-10pm SATURDAY NOV. 16th, 6-10pm

SHOW HOURS: NOV.18th-20th, 3-7pm

4575 N. 11th

Nov. 14-17, 1991

WEEKEND

Art when Free is a
four-letter word
—See Weekend Entertainment section, page 35

Six pages of letters
—See Opinion section, page 30

p.29

The Weather

Weekend

Colorado Daily

Serving the university community since 1892

VOL. 99 NO. 66 (122-38)

Four CU profs claim age bias

Say after 55, the raises stop coming

By KEVIN BLOCKER

Volume 15, Number 11 • DENVER'S NEWS & ARTS WEEKLY • November 13-19, 1991 Free

p.47

Westword

RUNNING ON EMPTY

drivers went to
lost control
heir company.

BY ALAN
PENDERGAST
Page 10

HIDDEN
IMAGESTUDIO

THE BARE BULB   E.J.GOLD

HIDDEN IMAGES STUDIO
Bardo Visions
1991

Completed installation.
Photos courtesy of Peter
Heineman Fine Arts.

HIDDEN IMAGESSTUDIO

HIDDEN IMAGES STUDIO is pleased to host *PETER HEINEMAN FINE ARTS* and *AIME FINE ARTS* in presenting **BARDO VISIONS** - the evocative serigraphs of **E.J. GOLD**, internationally recognized artist.

" E.J. Gold makes every effort a finished work. He boldly and candidly asserts his indefatigable humor coupled with classicism of line and gestural mastery."

Also featured will be the equisite blown glass works of **MARK EINERT**.

OPENING RECEPTIONS
Fri. 6-10 pm Nov. 15th
Sat. 6-10 pm Nov. 16th
Show runs through Nov. 18-20th, 3-7 pm

HIDDEN IMAGES STUDIO
Ph. (303) 440-6234

4575 N, 11TH ST., U
(1 blk West of Br

THE ARTS ALT

ICON

Cau
ICON

NOVEMBER 9

New
Western

Live Reviews with Live music

Photos courtesy:
Hidden Images Studio.

175

PENINSULA GALLERY
PALOS VERDES
Contemporary Creations, Group Show
1990

Contemporary Creations was a group show in which some of Gold's *Faces of War* series were included. They were abstracted portraits of faceless individuals with a very eerie quality to them. Here is an excerpt from a review published in the *Palos Verdes Peninsula News* and written by Diane Kaminski:

... "Three works of E.J. Gold, an experimental artist, make a statement about artistic reductionism, in which the impressions of the viewer's mind draw upon the individual's stored perceptual patterns, to assist in the development of a new image about the simplistic art form.

An abstractist, Gold relies upon "the viewer experiential expectation" process to evoke impressions of his work. The three small drawings exhibited were reminiscent of Picasso's geometrically designed subjects, and included a starkly drawn facial study of a woman, an odd assemblage of hands and feet entwined behind a circular object, and a champagne flute, each conveying a distinct subject in an abstract presentation..."

Barrett DeBusk's "I Want My MTV," a wire wall relief sculpture inspired by images of the artist's past.

Art Nouveau Decos Local Gallery

By DIANE KAMINSKI
News Entertainment Writer

A faint clinking of glass, the wafting scent of hors d'oeuvres, and the restrained buzz of quiet conversation discussing beaux objets d'art appointing the walls and floor of the Peninsula Gallery, filled the air at the well-attended opening last weekend.

Contemporary creations by more than 20 artists were represented in classic sculpture, wire sculpture, paintings, drawings and three-dimensional media inventions. The collection of 70 or so works displayed was diverse, ranging from the tribally serene chalk drawing by Ben Macala, a South African artist, to the innovative, high profile relief wire sculpture with neon, "I Want My MTV" by Barrett DeBusk. Street scenes and trendy city life themes livened the character of the modernist collection amassed from domestic and international art figures.

I like a collection with a little fun," said Dori Hansen, gallery director, about the work of DeBusk, 34, a Texan sculptor, constructs three-dimensional wall reliefs of cold hand-bent blackened steel, welded and framed 3 inches away from the wall surface, so that his images recreate themselves as shadows on the wall behind.

The subjects cast by DeBusk are minimalist, geometric figures, frozen at a commonplace moment in day-to-day life. The sociability of the relief's setting, warmly offsets the cold presence of the twisted steel, provoking a curiously entertaining and ambient mood.

Also on the lighter side, this replete with parked vehicles, ethnic folk attending to their daily business, and puffy clouded electric blue skies with rising hot air balloons, all scream for attention.

Fazzino's three-dimensional works of "primitive" art are acrylic on rag paper, portraying the unfettered, happily conducted urban activities. Likened to Haitian art for its bright coloring and busy appearance, Fazzino's street scenes are depicted colorfully and three-dimensionally, by raised cut-out squares applied to the surface of the painting. The 34-year-old artist's controlled lines and attractively bold imagery succeeds in conveying a very polished, but spontaneous appearance of ordered confusion.

The more interesting and unusual genre of works displayed were Marko's paintings on woven reed or rattan. These multimedia works, each emphasizing a road, highway or thoroughfare as its main theme, against a city or countryside background, employ decoupage to highlight bordering palm trees, storefronts, or baby-booming passersby drifting through the foreground. Additional texture accomplished through the use of burlaps and other roughly manufactured textiles, complements the muted, though strongly toned coloring applied generously to the woven face.

Three works by E. J. Gold, an experimental artist, make a statement about artistic reductionism, in which the impressions of the viewer's mind draw upon the individual's stored perceptual patterns, to assist in the development of a new image about the simplistic art form. An abstractist, Gold relies upon the "viewer experiential expectation" process to evoke impressions of his work. The three small drawings exhibited were reminiscent of Picasso's geometrically designed subjects, and included a starkly drawn facial study of a woman, an odd assemblage of hands and feet entwined behind a circular object, and a champagne flute, each conveying a distinct subject in an abstract presentation.

Sculpture artists Stefan LeTete and Ed Radow distinguished the collection with the elegance of LaTete's bust of woman's upper body in ivory white on a marble pedestal, and Radow's western bronze rodeo figures. The American historical retrospective of a cowboy on a saddle bronc, a cowboy atop a rearing stallion, a gunslinging cowboy, and a lone standing cowpoke completed the collection of four sculptures, each standing about 30" high.

Moderately priced selections from the low hundreds to the two thousand range were the norm for this gallery of fine art, also providing framing and matting service.

KIMBER WOODS TENNIS CLUB
FREMONT
E.J. Gold
1990

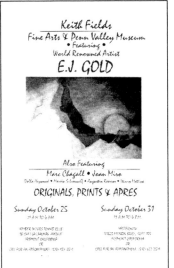

Silicon Valley private art dealer Keith Fields organized a one-man show of E. J. Gold original paintings and prints at the exclusive Kimber Woods Tennis Club. From there, the show went on to the Yesternow Gallery in Fremont. Fields caters to the nouveau-riche computer program developers, inventors, and hardware and software giants of all computer persuasions.

LIVRES D'ARTISTES

A Short Waltz Through the Bardos
A Pleasant Conversation
Abstract Impressions
Asylum
La Corrida
Cosmo Street
Dark Hours
Faces of War
In Old Greenwich Village
Juan Tepozton
The Planar Contiguities
Mes Voyages
The Nude
Rhythm & Movement
Spirit Photography
Views from an Open Casket

Views from an Open Casket
1992

Over the years, Gold has created a few dozen *Livres d'Artistes* highly decorated with original art. He has printed most of these himself. This limited edition book had a very haunting quality to it as its name can easily suggest and Gold accommodatingly posed for the camera when the subject of this book was brought up to him...

THE HERMIT
Serigraph

E.J.GOLD

> "Art should reveal another world, a different dimension, a different way of seeing. It should strip the ordinary senses away and show the world which is unperceivable with ordinary sight and feeling."
>
> E.J. GOLD from PURE GESTURES; Gateways Publishing

"BARDO VISIONS"
A Showing of Limited Edition
Serigraphs and Lithographs

Featuring the works of **E.J. GOLD**, international
artist/author

Presented by
AIME FINE ARTS & PETER HEINEMAN FINE ARTS

OPENING RECEPTION
Friday **January 24th, 1992** 6PM-8PM

SHOW DATES
January 24th, 1992 through **February 28th, 1992**

Hosted by
THE NAROPA INSTITUTE
2130 Arapahoe Avenue
Boulder, CO
(303) 444-0202

Chess Player, left, and *Shrimp Boat Boy*, below, original serigraphs, edition of 75 on Arches paper.

> "Art should reveal another world, a different dimension, a different way of seeing. It should strip the ordinary senses away and show the world which is unperceivable with ordinary sight and feeling."
>
> E.J. GOLD from PURE GESTURES; Gateways Publishing

"BARDO VISIONS"
A Showing of Limited
Serigraphs and L

Featuring the works of E.
artist/auth

Presented
AIME FINE ARTS & PETER

OPENING RE
Friday **January 24th,**

SHOW D
January 24th, 1992 throu

Hosted
THE NAROPA I
2130 Arapaho
Boulder,
(303) 444-

THE INSIDE TRACK ■ MOVIES ■ MUSIC ■ THEATER ■ ART ■ NEW VIDEOS ■ CALENDAR

NEW RADIO HIGHLIGHTS COLUMN PAGE 31

FRIDAY MAGAZINE

EVOCATIVE IMAGES: Tonight marks the opening of "Bardo Visions," a show of limited edition serigraphs and lithographs by critically acclaimed painter E.J. Gold at Naropa Institute, 2130 Arapahoe Ave., Boulder. The opening reception goes from 6 to 8 p.m. and the show continues through Feb. 28. Call 444-0202.

BEST OF THE WEEK

THREE FILM CLASSICS
See three of the greatest films ever made this week at the University of Colorado. Orson Welles' epic **"Citizen Kane"** shows tonight at Muenzinger Auditorium. The Marx Brothers brilliantly funny **"Duck Soup"** is screened tonight, Saturday and Sunday in The Forum Room in the UMC; Alfred Hitchcock's terror classic **"The Birds"** shows there Wednesday and Thursday.

THREE HOT CONCERTS
Boulder's mysterious Grammy-nominated flatpicking guitarist **Charles "Slade" Sawtelle** returns to the concert stage with his band **The Bluegrass Pals** — including former Hot Rize bandmate Tim O'Brien — at 8 tonight at Denver's Swallow Hill Music Hall. Saturday at 8 p.m. outstanding New England singer/songwriter **Cheryl Wheeler** joins **Carla Sciaky** at Swallow Hill while sometime Jerry Garcia sidekick, organist **Merle Saunders**, performs with his **Rainforest Band** at The Mercury Cafe in Denver.

SUPER SUNDAY FUN
Get out of the house Sunday before you hunker down for the evening Super Bowl rituals. The **Denver Zoo** offers free admission with proof of Colorado residency. Boulder's **Thordis Simonsen** — author of "Dancing Girl" — will read from her book and show slides taken during her two year residency in Greece at 2 p.m. at Boulder's Meadows Branch Library.

177

BLUE CREEK WEST GALLERY

<small>BOULDER</small>
WORKS ON PAPER
1991

This colorful exhibit was curated by Peter Heineman Fine Arts as a traveling show. It included a variety of works on paper both originals and multiples.

Gold has created over two-hundred lithographs most of which are on Arches paper, and over one-hundred serigraphs on Arches paper. Many of these editions are completely sold out.

In the late nineties, he reluctantly began producing the ubiquitous *giclee* print.

Photos courtesy: Peter Heineman Fine Arts

National Centre for Atmospheric Research
BOULDER
WORLDS IN FUSION
1991

Peter Heineman is an architect, artist, art collector and art dealer.
He has curated numerous exhibits of Gold's art and has been collecting it since the mid 80s.

Gold's art has appeared in many unusual places, including the National Center for Atmospheric Research in Boulder, Colorado in 1991...probably because they improved the atmosphere considerably! *Worlds in Fusion* was curated by Peter Heineman Fine Arts who organized many art exhibits throughout Colorado.
Photos courtesy: NCAR

FREE

Shared VISION

VANCOUVER'S CREATIVE ARTS & LIFE RESOURCE MAGAZINE

ISSUE 38 • OCTOBER 1991

WOMEN IN DISCOVERY

pictures off the wall & remember who I am."

PLACE ON EARTH
by Velva Strong

on the card. Whatever it was, it (and maybe my question) changed him. He no longer seemed threatening. He turned then and faced me directly for the first time since he'd entered the shop. With both hands on the counter he leaned toward me.

"My name's William — what's yours?"

"Velva," I answered.

We spoke of many things then — rocks, crystals, books, our philosophies of life. He was very knowledgeable — that surprised me at first and disturbed some of my judgements about bikers. I have no idea how long we talked nor all we talked about — what I remember clearly is the energy in the room — it was intense.

Eventually another customer entered the shop and broke the spell. William said it was time he was leaving. Suddenly this tough, coarse-looking man was terribly concerned about the finger marks he'd made all over the glass countertop. He offered to clean it before he left. I told him it gave me something to do. He pulled out a rough piece of rose quartz from his jacket pocket and handed it to me.

"Say your name again," he said. I repeated it.

As he opened the door he turned and looked back at me.

"Velva," he said softly, "It's engraved on my soul." And the door closed behind him.

I've never seen him again. I never expect to. But I will never forget him, either. I have the piece of rose quartz and the "Course in Miracles" card he chose that I picked up after he left. I have a feeling we played out some ancient karma that wild November afternoon.

The card says :

"The Holiest Place On Earth Is Where An Ancient Hatred Has Become A Present Love."

Earth's crammed with Heaven.

— Elizabeth Barrett Browning

E.J.Gold

Equus: Alliance

I ride you
And breathe the world
Through your nostrils.
Pre-historic
Pre-dawn
You inhale
And I live.

Afraid of how you kill me
Throwback
Impassive
I climb your inclement mountain
And see an effortless universe
Through your cloudless eyes.

Other beasts stand
Servant/slave/quiet
Little quiver dry throat
I cry out
At the cold lump of steel
Stilling their tongues;
Your pounding echoes
And burns down this corridor.

I dream of you relentlessly
Your lathered flanks
Are crimson satin
My bedroom mirrors steam and crack
Your big legs tear my sheets in half.

I would mate with you
All my heart for Chiron;
Our children would be centaurs
With the faces of gods
And hoofs
Hard as rock

— *Reisa Stone*

Dear John . . .

I have seen you as my property, a carcass already rotting beneath my claws. I don't really want you. I want to drag around a spineless, castrated, mesmerized, only-looking-at-me, devoted-like-a-dog, has-only-eyes-for-its-Master, hunk of flesh.

A trophy. My claws are still in you or perhaps is that a fake-diamond-studded collar around your neck and aren't you panting, looking up at me mesmerized for life?

I walk on the world pleased now. I'm wearing black tight clothes, a silk black diamond-studded cowboy-style shirt, dragging you along, some of your blood flows from the corner of my mouth. I smack my lips deliciously. What a kill!

SCENE TWO

I have my claws into you. Long curved nails 2" into your flesh, bones, tendons, gristle.

My eyes tear up. How can I do this to you? I care for you.

My claws sink a little bit deeper. "You are mine." my voice cackles. I cry. I try to pull my witch away and chuckle inside. She's part of me. I can't get rid of her. I talk to her. She releases her claws and the ten wounds in your flesh automatically heal over.

The witch comes towards me very interested in me, becomes lighter and has no interest for you any longer. There is only instant healing and light around you.

Her interest is now with me. She has turned to me.

I cry. Has it really taken me 40 years to discover my witch, my power, my balance?

She is right beside me now on my right looking in the same direction...

— *Blanche Brusovski*

My chant is the beating of my heart.

- *Peggy Lagodny*

"I must undr

Dancebody

A mysterious pool lies behind the patterns of our everyday lives. Through movement we can bathe in these waters to rejuvenate our souls, heal our wounds and integrate our transitions.

Dance coaxes us out of our numbness and contraction fostered by cultural conditioning, family patterning, early trauma, daily stress and world events.

Many of us stifle our emotions or spill them carelessly over our worlds. Both ways have limited effectiveness. Dance can evoke archetypal tides of emotion and teach us how to simply embody our humanity with nobility and effective power.

Dance is a catalytic key that opens many doors of our humanity. Locked in our cells are memories including those of our deep wounds, emotions associated with those events and much, much more. There is innate wisdom, healing powers, ecstasy and the capacity for deep intimacy with our fellow humans and all life.

Dance is a healer. It is preventive medicine, psychotherapeutic as well as nurturing to the soul or journey. It takes us out of our isolated pathologies in mandalic patterns of relationship and resolution. In fertile ground new ways of being together as a World can grow.

— *Lizanne Fisher.*

figure why. I guess you're right — I am searching." He paused. "You know, I think I came in here to steal some of your energy."

"Energy is our gift — it's a renewable resource — take all you like!" I told him. "And perhaps — if you're searching for the answer to a specific problem, you might like to pick a "Course in Miracles" card from the box there. It's where I often find the answer I need."

He chose a card and a look of shock, awe? crossed his face. I didn't ask what was

E.J.Gold

A woman knows that nothing can be born without darkness and nothing can come to fruition without light.

— *Diane Mariechild*

Life shrinks or expands according to one's courage.

— Anais Nin

E.J. Gold has created a large body of women portraits, odalisques and nudes, and it was not surprising to find that *Shared Vision, Vancouver's Creative Arts and Life Resource Magazine* used Gold's art as illustrations for an in-depth article about women in the process of self-discovery.

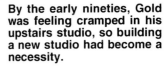

MONUMENTALS
1992.

By the early nineties, Gold was feeling cramped in his upstairs studio, so building a new studio had become a necessity.

In 1992, he moved into his new expanded studio and proceeded to paint many large canvases and murals up to thirty feet in length, including the *Monumentals* which he invented there and then.

The Monumentals are free-standing paintings that are-assembled in triangular triptychs which obviate the necessity to hang. *The Monumentals* can of course be made extremely large, thus rendering them suitable for outdoor architectural installations.

From the outside, the studio looks like a barn and that is what it has been called. The barn with its elevated cathedral ceiling, incorporates a recording studio as well as a painting studio, sculpture studio, library, writing office and smaller painting studio where he works on miniatures, pastel work-ups and jewelry.

Photos by Willem de Groot.

Photos by Willem de Groot.

Painting the *Monumentals*

Photos by Barbara Haynes

MAD RIVER POST
Anima Terra
1992

MAD RIVER POST is one of a select group of corporations using their working environment on an ongoing basis, to showcase exciting, contemporary art.

Far from the mundane "corporate art" that fills most offices, MAD RIVER POST displays a new exhibition three times a year of emerging and established artists that are all a part of the fast moving contemporary California art scene.

Anima Terra was curated by plein-air artist Nancy Sadler. This show included all of the members of the Grass Valley Graphics Group, some of whom were able to attend the opening in Los Angeles.

A partial view of the location with some of the art of the Grass Valley Graphics Group hanging in the background.

The opening at Mad River Post attracted a smorgasboard of visitors from hi-tech people to the Hollywood crowd with a sprinkling of artists and collectors.
Photos courtesy: Scott Norris.

MAD RIVER POST
Anima Terra
1992

Nancy Sadler, curator, *Anima Terra*, and Michael Elliott, co-owner Mad River Post, Los Angeles, 1992.
Photo courtesy: Till Bartels, Berlin.

M A D R I V E R
P O S T

`Anima · Terra

E. J. Gold	Judith Reifman
Basmat Porath	Linda Ortiz
Jari Havlena	Lori Wolf
Bret Purpus	Jennet Inglis
Laurie Bender	Morgan Green
N. C. Sadler	John Hyatt
Menlo MacFarlane	Judith Schonebaum

Artists Reception - Thursday

Curated by Sadler

M A D R I V E R
P O S T

Frank O. Gehry • Edgemar Building
2415 Main Street
Santa Monica, California 90405

MAD RIVER POST is one of a select group of corporations using their working environment on an ongoing basis, to showcase exciting, contemporary art. Far from the mundane "corporate art" that fills most offices, MAD RIVER POST displays a new exhibition three times a year of emerging and established artists that are all a part of the fast moving contemporary California art scene. Please be our guests at a wine and cheese reception and view MAD RIVER POST's current collection.

Grass Valley Graphics Group artist Menlo Macfarlane at the Mad River Post opening.
Photos courtesy: Till Bartels, Berlin

SHOPPING, DINING, ENTERTAINMENT, ATTRACTIONS, EVENTS · MARCH 1992

WHERE
·LOS ANGELES·

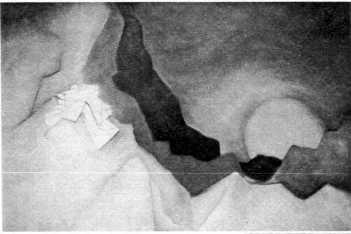

your negotiating skills by offering less than the asking price — a little haggling is encouraged, and you can sometimes get things for half of whatever the original price was. Bring cash, because you're dealing with private parties, and not all of them are equipped to take credit cards. Any of these shows will make for a good weekend browse.

Shopping

In addition to its wonderful museums, L.A. has its share of wonderful museum gift shops, too. For instance, there are beautiful displays in the shops in the **Southwest Museum** between ... and downtown L.A. (213/221-2164), ... **port Harbor Art Museum** in New... (714/759-1122), and in the massive ... **ty Museum of Art** on Wilshire ... 57-6111.

... there are also some museum gift ... in locations other than just at the ... selves. The **Laguna Art Muse-** ... ese, a lovely cliff-top museum ... e Orange County coast that has ... filled with art and artifacts in-

More

For more information on the city's magnificent museums, check the *This Month in L.A.* article and the listings in our *Shows, Events and Attractions* section; details on some of the city's most prominent art galleries are in the following listings.

ACCENT ON ART — 8533 Melrose Ave., West Hollywood (310/855-1944). Featuring original works and graphics by contemporary Chinese artists Jianghua Su and Huangli Yang. Also available by other contemporary artists are posters, rare graphics and originals.

AFRICAL GALLERY — 2430 Main St., Santa Monica (310/289-0425). A gallery committed to the preservation of African culture and antiquities. A percentage of all sales goes to Africa-related charities. Open daily 11 a.m.-6 p.m.

ANGELS GATE CULTURAL CENTER — 3601 So. Gaffey St., San Pedro (310/519-0936). New exhibition: "Solo Series of Three," works by Joanne Hayakawa, Elizabeth ... and Victor Hugo, opens 3/8.

E.J. Gold's Between Heaven and Hell *(detail shown at the top of the page) is in the group show at the Beverly Plaza Hotel; David Ligare's* Landscape with an Archer *(detail shown above) is at the Koplin Gallery.*

Open Mon.-Thur. 10 a.m.-5 p.m., Fri.-Sat. 11

BEVERLY PLAZA HOTEL

MONUMENTAL LANDSCAPES

1992

Beverly Korenwasser, Heidelberg Editions International representative in Los Angeles, co-ordinated *Anima Terra* **at Mad River Productions, Los Angeles in 1992 as well as a special show of** *Monumental Landscapes* **at the Beverly Plaza Hotel during the same year.**
Photo courtesy: Till Bartels, Berlin.

Monumental Landscapes, **Beverly Plaza Hotel, 1992.**
Photos courtesy: Scott Norris.

ASHLEY + CRAIG GALLERY
Monumentals
1992

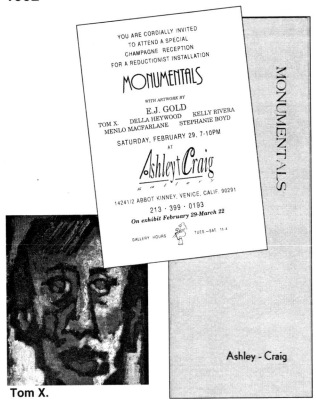

Tom X.

Photos courtesy: Scott Norris

Rudy Udarbe of the Grass Valley Graphics Group ponders among the giants.

The photo above shows works by Gold left and center, and Kelly Rivera to the right. The other photos show paintings by Gold some of which were eight feet tall.
Photos courtesy: Till Bartels, Berlin.

ASHLEY + CRAIG GALLERY
Monumentals
1992

At the opening reception, gallery owners Ashley Collins and Craig Connors chat with artist Menlo Macfarlane, center, of the Grass Valley Graphics Group whose work was part of the group show.
Photo courtesy: Till Bartels, Berlin.

Painting by Menlo Macfarlane on display at Ashley+Craig Gallery.
Photos courtesy: Scott Norris

Three paintings of Della Heywood, two portraits by Tom X. and an eight foot *Monumental* by Gold.
Photo courtesy: Scott Norris

A Gold *Monumental* in the forefront with two Kelly Rivera paintings on the right.
Photo courtesy: Scott Norris

The well-known German photographer Till Bartels visited the studios of several members of the Grass Valley Graphics Group and did photo essays on them during the preparations for this series of shows.
Photo by Scott Norris

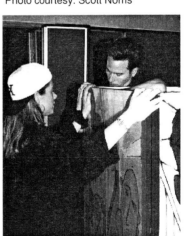

Photos courtesy: Scott Norris

GALLERI TONNE, OSLO
MONUMENTER
1992

Monumenter, Galleri Tonne, Oslo, Norway, 1992. Galleri Tonne is a contemporary gallery usually bustling with activity and situated in the heart of downtown Oslo. This prestigious gallery is internationally reputed for its restoration work which is sought after by many museums throughout Europe. Galleri Tonne is owned and directed by Terje and Ulrike Tonne who permanently represent Gold's art in Oslo.
Photos courtesy: Galleri Tonne.

The one-man show *Monumenter,* Galleri Tonne, Oslo, Norway, 1992.
Uppermost photo: a view of the spacious mezzanine; upper left: a view of one exhibit hall; upper right: the gallery entrance looking out to the street; lower left: another view inside the gallery; lower right: the program book, gallery brochure and show invitation. Tonne, which also represents Odd Nerdrum, is an important pace-setters in Scandinavia.
Photos courtesy: Galleri Tonne.

E.J. GOLD

Malerier

Vi har den glede
å invitere til åpningen

Torsdag 14. mai kl. 18.00

Utstillingen varer
til 2. juni, 1992

Galleri Tonne A/S
Fr. Nansen plass 7, Oslo

E.J. Gold: Figure with Landscape

Monumenter, **Galleri Tonne, Oslo, Norway, 1992.**
Photos courtesy: Galleri Tonne.

NARDIN FINE ARTS LTD
E.J. Gold Odalisques
1992

Mrs. Nardin in her office.
Photos courtesy: Nardin Fine Arts.

Show sponsors
Edwin & Elizabeth
Schneider.

E.J. GOLD

October 20 - November 15, 1992

NARDIN FINE ARTS LTD.
Yellow Monkey Village • Cross River, NY 10518
(914) 763-8451

Gallery Hours · Tuesday thru Sunday 10-5

New York entrepreneur and collector Jim King, Elizabeth Schneider, and curator Lisa Martini who all helped prepare this colorful show.
Photos courtesy: Nardin Fine Arts

Last minute preparations for the opening keep everyone on their toes for this beautiful show.

"Sitting", E.J. GOLD, Oil on Canvas, 36" x 48", ©1990

NARDIN FINE ARTS LTD
Cross River, NY
E.J. Gold Odalisques
1992

This one-man show at Nardin Fine Arts in Cross River, New York took place in the fall of 1992. It included brightly colored *Odalisques* paintings from the Edwin Schneider Collection as well as some smaller works on paper with related themes--notably serigraphs from the *Dark Hours* series.

Photos courtesy: Edwin Schneider.

Right: Gallery owner Mrs Nardin and her daughter and gallery assistant.

THE OLD CEDAR BAR

E.J. Gold paintings at the Cedar Bar used a black background technique where the figures were created in the negative space field.

THE OLD CEDAR BAR

New York
1992

Following the early influence of the Woodstock Impressionists and the Art Students' League in Woodstock which he attended, the next artistic center of gravity for Gold was the New York School of Abstract Expressionism which congregated at the Cedar Bar.

The Cedar Bar was an artistic and literary haven which made a profound impact on Gold who, as a Village artist, frequented it in the late fifties and rubbed shoulders with painters and poets the likes of Franz Kline, Willem de Kooning, Jackson Pollock, Museum of Modern Art curator Frank O'Hara, poet Margaret Randall, and dozens more who contributed to making the Cedar a vibrant hangout.

Abstract Expressionism left its imprint and made Gold receptive to artists like Rico Lebrun whom he was soon to meet in Los Angeles, as well as Fritz Schwaderer, a student of Schmidt-Rottluff and Hans Burckhardt.

Under that banner, Gold turned to Figurative Expressionism as a preferred vehicle.

In 1992, Gold honored fellow habitues of the Cedar with the unveiling of a collaborative book with Margaret Randall, *The Old Cedar Bar,* and an exhibit of the same name which was installed at the current Cedar Tavern. The book and exhibit contain a literary memoir written by Randall and images created by Gold in the late fifties.

The following images are part of this series. Several of these miniature pastels were translated to larger canvases for the exhibit. The photographs show the opening reception in 1992 and some of the Cedar Bar celebrities who attended the event.

Upper right: World-famous exhibited *Portrait of Frank O'Hara* **painted in 1992 by Gold that was part of the Cedar Bar exhibit.**
Photo by Priya.

Lower right: Jerry Tallmer's NEW YORK POST review of the opening of *The Old Cedar Bar* **with texts by Margaret Randall and art by E.J. Gold.**
Reprinted with permission: New York Post

Drinking up the '50s

EYE ON ART

JERRY TALLMER

WE ALWAYS exaggerate the glamour of the places of our youth, but the Cedar Bar in those days really was something. Those days? Here's a tiny story. Not long ago I had occasion to sit side-by-side in a small screening room with Shirley Clarke during a projection of "The Connection," a movie she'd made in 1962 from the Living Theater's 1959 production of the Jack Gelber play.

From time to time I'd ask her things like: "Shirley, how'd you ever get the cockroaches to run up the wall right then?," and she'd laugh and say: "They were in the guy's hand, and he just opened his hand." When the movie was over, Shirley turned to me, her eyes dancing, as we waited for the elevator. "Jerry," she said, "weren't the '50s *wonderful*?"

Those days. The off-Broadway movement was starting, the Village Voice was starting, and the Abstract Expressionist movement was more than starting — it was in full flower at the galleries on 10th Street plus a few uptown, and, every evening, at the Cedar Bar, the original Cedar Bar on University Place just north of Eighth Street.

I wasn't all that young either, not as young as Margaret Randall, a New Yorker and aspiring writer who'd come back from Albuquerque in her early 20s and started going to the Cedar with her best friends, the painters Elaine de Kooning and Pat Passlof; not as young as 18- or 19-year-old E.J.

Gold, a budding artist whose girlfriend was Renee Rosenberg, niece of critic Harold Rosenberg, one of the three great gurus of the New York School of painting, the others being critic Clement Greenberg and critic/poet/Museum of Modern Art associate curator Frank O'Hara.

Gold, who lived in nearby Stuyvesant Town, started going to the Cedar in 1959, seven years before O'Hara was tragically, absurdly killed at age 40 by a dune buggy while sleeping on the beach at Fire Island. "He was someone I looked on with awe," says musician/author/artist Gold, whose painting of O'Hara is to my mind the strongest, surest, most striking of the 36 expressionistic canvases by the one-time awestruck kid in a show called "The Old Cedar Bar," upstairs over the "new" Cedar Bar, three blocks north of the old one.

Margaret Randall also remembers Frank O'Hara — "a real tender guy and a wonderful poet."

Ms. Randall has gone on to write more than 50 books of poetry, oral history, essays, feminism, translations, novels; won headlines by coming home from Nicaragua in

1984 only to find herself ordered deported under the "ideological exclusion" clause of the McCarran-Walter Act; won headlines again by winning her four-year case against the government.

The exhibit is half words, half pictures, words by Randall, pictures by Gold. Also available (for $125) is an elegant hand-tooled limited edition of the same words, same pictures. Here are some of the words. They get all my juices stirring again:

"The Cedar was what happened when the sun went down ... We'd walk over to The Cedar, eat what may have been the first full meal of the day for many, drink to whatever degree each of us did that, and meet our friends ...

"The time at the bar was an interlude, with a life of its own ...

"I don't think most of my generation at The Cedar were heavy drinkers. We smoked dope instead, calling it grass back then. Our older mentors, like Franz Kline and Bill de Kooning, drank a great deal. Perhaps their battles with alcohol were a warning to the younger among us to go easy on the stuff ...

"A few monumental moments surface now. One focuses on the photographer Robert Frank ... a maker of independent films back then, and his wife of those years, the sculptor Mary Frank. They screamed at one another down the length of the bar. She was doing most of the screaming: righteous anger, and also a rebellion it would take others of us years to cultivate. Robert's eyes seemed to speak confusion, sadness ...

"We shared work, we met old or new friends. Sometimes we went home with one of them ... John Cage made his music, and Martha Graham, Merce Cunningham, and Erik Hawkins danced ... The most important thing I can say about The Cedar was that it was a home to me for a while. Home in a way that few places become."

Yes, Shirley, Yes, Margaret, it was a wonderful time.

Terrace Gallery, Cedar Tavern, 82 University Place at 11th Street, (212) 929-9089, to July 31. Limited edition ($125) available at the exhibition or c/o curators Oz and Yanesh Fritz, Troov Gallery, 118 Greenpoint Ave., Brooklyn 11222, (718) 389-2011, where E.J. Gold and poet Harry Nilsson share a "Moonbeam" show through Tuesday, (212) 929-9089.

Cedar Bar, c. 1958-59. Pencil drawing by E.J. Gold, 1969.

THE OLD CEDAR BAR

After much intense labor, the Old Cedar Bar paintings were displayed on the studio walls just prior to being shipped to New York.
Photos by Willem de Groot.

196

Warm moments at the opening were shared by Margaret Randall, Valerie Peterson, Oz Fritz, Troov Gallery director and curator of this exhibit, and Rhoda Waller.
Photo by Priya.

From left to right: Collectors Edmund and Marjorie Luycks, Una Dora Copley, and Guy Kaldis display their E. J. Gold original canvases.
Photo by Priya.

The current face of the Old Cedar Bar.
Photo by Priya.

Top: Jaswant Bains, a Vancouver private art dealer, who has organized Gold's *Moonbeam* show at the Richmond Art Center in Vancouver; Oz Fritz, Troov Gallery Director and *Cedar Bar* show curator, Fielding Dawson, writer emeritus, and Ken Ahrns, Michigan art dealer.
Photo by Priya.

Arnold Weinstein signing the guest book as curator Yanesh watches at the Old Cedar Bar.
Photo by Ken Ahrns.

The Cedar Bar show presented a slice of history, bringing together Randall's literary recollections, and Gold's mood-capturing canvases where new and old fans mingled in a mildly nostalgic atmosphere. Through word and gesture, the poet and artist paid homage to the masters of expressionism.

Randall and Gold recognize the influence of the Cedar Bar, its philosophy and its denizens. Randall owes much of her literary discipline to discoveries made during this period which fueled her thirst for penetration of ideas. Much of Gold's art is gestural and spontaneous thus speaking for the dynamic energy of expressionism at the core of his artistic endeavors.

THE OLD CEDAR BAR
1992

Top left: Lisa Martini, Curator with Nardin Fine Art in Cross River planning a show of Gold's art, chats with Elizabeth Ann & Edwin Schneider, private representatives of Gold in Armonk, Westchester County, NY.
Photo by Priya.

Marjorie Luycks and Margaret Randall have a warm greeting for each other.
Photo by Priya.

Arnold Weinstein pauses by the Frank O'Hara painting at the Old Cedar Bar opening.
Photo by Ken Ahrns

The Troov Gallery
is pleased to invite you
to attend the opening of

The Old Cedar Bar
a collaboration of literary and visual art

Margaret   &   E.J.
Randall   Gold

Saturday, June 6, 1992
7:00 pm to 10:00 pm
at the Cedar Tavern
82 University Place, New York City

R.S.V.P. -- (718) 389-2011
On exhibit through July 31, 1992

Margaret Randall shone brightly at the opening. E. J. Gold, right, was unable to attend but was there in spirit.

Guests look at the Old Cedar Bar book and assorted posters for recent exhibits and upcoming shows including the one Gold will be doing later in 1992 with John Cage. On the wall are current pieces Gold produced around the Cedar Bar theme. These are primarily spatial studies.
Photo by Priya.

Top: Oz Fritz, Troov Gallery, who curated the exhibit lends an ear to artist, Frances Avery.
Photo by Priya.
Bottom: Jean Davidson, Oz Fritz, Frances Avery, Guy Kaldis and Jean Cohen.
Photo by Priya.

Margaret Randall addresses the gathering with thoughtful comments expressing what many are feeling.
Photo by Priya.

NEW YORK—Pat McKenty, left, of Heidelberg Editions International art publishers, with writer Margaret Randall at the opening of "The Old Cedar Bar" exhibit at the 'new' Cedar Bar. The multimedia show featured prose-poetry by Randall and artwork by E.J. Gold, who frequented the old tavern during its heyday in the '50s as a hangout for painters, writers, and musicians. "Frank O'Hara at the Cedar Bar" by Gold is shown.

SUMMIT, N.J.—St. Lifer Art Ex Lifer joins artist Arie Galles dur pastels for his "Heartland" and

TROOV GALLERY
MOONBEAM
FEATURING THE POETRY OF HARRY NILSSON
AND ART BY E.J. GOLD
1992

Robert Soares, who popularized Lambada music from Brazil a few years ago, with Yanesh, gallery director.

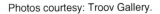

Photos courtesy: Troov Gallery.

Music producer Bill Laswell (with hat).
Photos courtesy: Troov Gallery.

Jazz great, Ornette Coleman and gallery director Oz Fritz at sneak preview of *Moonbeam*, Troov Gallery, 1992.
Photo courtesy: Troov Gallery.

Oz Fritz with Buddy Miles, former Jimi Hendrix drummer.

Jonas Helborg, bassist/composer/ producer of John McLaughlin fame visits the show.

Solo artist, Bootsy Collins, Parliment/ Funkedelic bass player, formerly with James Brown.

Matt Stein, producer/ engineer chats with Yanesh Troov Gallery director.

Top: Oz Fritz and Ramelzee.
Middle: Clive Smith and wife with Oz Fritz.
Photos courtesy: Troov Gallery.

Photographer Priya in conversation with artist Robert Soares.

TROOV GALLERY
MOONBEAM
FEATURING THE POETRY OF
HARRY NILSSON
AND ART BY
E.J. GOLD
1992

Ed Kelleher

Composer Evan Lurie, gallery director and award-winning sound engineer Oz Fritz, with composer/musician John Zorn at the opening of *Moonbeam.* Because of the musical connection, the *Moonbeam* show attracted many rock musicians and performers.

Guitarist Andy Hawkins from *Blind Idiot God Band* with Oz Fritz at *Moonbeam* opening.

Oz Fritz with Jay Crawford, guitarist and Warner Bros. recording artist with "Bomb."

Photos courtesy: Troov Gallery.

**Yanesh, Clive Smith
and his wife.**

**Charles Jones of the Charles Jones
Art Gallery in Cincinnati.**
Photos courtesy: Troov Gallery.

**Oz Fritz, John Zorn, Jim King and
Evan Lurie.**

Amy Singer, Oz Fritz.

**Upper: Ray Reyes, art patron Jim King, Oz Fritz.
Lower: Guests including Lisa Dominick in white hat.**

H. HEATHER EDELMAN GALLERY
SOHO - New York
MASTERWORKS
Lecture on Nothing from *Silence*
1992

Writings by
John Cage
Paintings by
E.J.Gold

Installation at the Heather Edelman Gallery.
Photos courtesy: H. Heather Edelman Gallery.

H. HEATHER EDELMAN GALLERY
MASTERWORKS
Lecture on Nothing
1992

H. Heather Edelman

***Masterworks, Lecture on Nothing* show at Edelman Gallery, 1992.**
Photos courtesy: H. Heather Edelman Gallery.

Lecture on Nothing* from *Silence had long been a favorite book of Gold's and for many years he toyed with the idea of doing art-work for it.

An early version of the project was to be published in Germany with Propylean Verlag but the necessity to travel to Germany made it impossible to realize.

When the time came for this project to material-ize it began as a series of original illustrations for a *livre d'artiste* but quickly grew into a series of large paintings in the Monumental for-mat.

Cage was very pleased with the art but unfortu-nately passed away days before the opening and so was never able to see the completed project in all its aspects.
Photos courtesy: H. Heather Edelman Gallery.

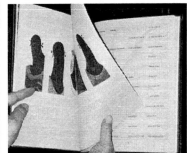

November 3, 1992•Vol. XXXVII No. 44• The Weekly Newspaper of N

BASQUIAT: THE BLUE-CHIPPING OF A BLACK ARTIST (

THE MONSTER IN THE BOX: DONALD FREED ON BUS

THIS MUD'S FOR YOU: LESLIE SAVAN ON PRESIDENTIA

the village **VOICE**

H. Heather Edelman Gallery
is proud to exhibit

★ John Cage ★ ★ ★
★ ★ ★ E.J. Gold

Masterworks from an art collaboration of two stars

E.J. Gold's illustrations on canvas of
John Cage's writing, "Lecture on Nothing"
from his book, Silence

Special Champagne Reception
on
October 28, 1992
6 pm to 9 pm

The exhibition will continue from
October 22 through November 12, 1992.

386 West Broadway, 3rd floor
New York City, New York 10012-4302
Telephone: (212) 226-2943

H.Heather Edelman visiting
the artist's studio in
California prior to the show
in New York.

H. Heather Edelman and to her left,
Menlo Macfarlane who did a reading
from *Lecture on Nothing* at the opening of the show, seen here engrossed
in a discussion with visitors.
Photos courtesy: H. Heather Edelman Gallery.

H. HEATHER EDELMAN GALLERY
ARTEXPO '92
Jacob Javits Center
1992

Left: Heather Edelman in her spacious booth at the Jacob Javits Center, 1992. In the photo below, we see Walter Edelman (center) who works with her and spends a lot of time on the road servicing about 300 galleries throughout the country.
Photos courtesy: H. Heather Edelman.

Above and left: Larry Rivers -- an artist and a saxophonist -- was the subject of one of the portraits Gold created for the *Cedar Bar* show which had taken place earlier in 1992 in New York.

As it turns out, Rivers was scheduled to perform in a band at the 1992 Art Expo where H. Heather Edelman had a very large presence.

As part of the festivities, Edelman presented Rivers with the *Monumental* portrait Gold did of Rivers on sax. Here we see them on stage for this presentation after his performance.
Photos courtesy: H. Heather Edelman Gallery.

A Sculptural Fugue

E.J. Gold sculpting a clay nude between painting large canvases in 1992. The sculpture was later cast in bronze in a limited signed and numbered edition of 22.
Photos by Michele Marie Underhill.

IN-BETWEEN GALLERY
HOLLYWOOD
Life Is a Carnival
CURATED BY SCOTT NORRIS FINE ARTS
1992

Paul Westfall, editor and publisher of *"In"* Magazine, Los Angeles, poses in front of Gold's paintings at the In-Between Gallery.

Brook Lizotte, owner of the In-Between Gallery and Councilman Michael Woo at the inauguration of Theatre Row.

Brook and Teresa Lizotte, owners, In-Between Gallery, Theatre Row Hollywood, stand in front of some E.J. Gold paintings at the opening of *Life Is a Carnival.*

Councilman Michael Woo, Renee Taylor, James Carey, Pres. Theatre Row Hollywood, Jerry Schneiderman, Bruce Bal, Cultural Affairs.

Michael Woo, Renee Taylor and James Carey, Pres. Theatre Row Hollywood, and artistic director, Attic Theatre.

Jerry Schneiderman, art patron, and Michael Woo enjoy the reception at the In-Between Gallery on Theatre Row in Hollywood.

Liz Reilli, Artistic Director, Hudson Theatre poses in front of a serigraph by E.J. Gold.
Photos by Scott Norris

AIME FINE ARTS
DENVER
Open House
CURATED BY
KATHLEEN DREIER
1993

GENRE GALLERY   *present*   AIME FINE ARTS

"HEY!THIS AIN'T
SOUTH WESTERN!"
or
"WHY DON'T HE
...O NORMAL
...NTINS?"

...ening with artist
...as Boyd Jr.
...AY APRIL 30th
...:00-11:00pm

...ord art"   photo

...EP INTROSPECTION."
...DENVER WEEKLY NEWS

...OW WHAT TO SAY"
...OW ARTIST AND FRIEND

...DON'T TAKE IT PERSONAL"

...sic you
...erience by
...REALITY

GENRE GALLERY 2301 CHAMPA (303)298.7417
(corner of Park Avenue & Champa)

for more information about Lucas Boyd's
Graphic Design or Fine Art
call his agent Kathleen Dreier at
(303)722.4573

refreshments will be served

**Left center & lower: Kathleen Dreier
gives a presentation of Gold's works
on paper, jewelry and essential oils at
one of her many events at Aime Fine
Arts in Denver. She has organized
numerous *Open Houses* in her
gallery.**
Photos courtesy: Kathleen Dreier.

AIME FINE ARTS
Picasso Was a Kid Too
Group Show
1993

Aime Fine Arts in Denver organized several shows with the art
of E.J. Gold, one-man shows
and highly successful group
shows that included live entertainment and lots of visitors.
Kathleen Dreier, the director of
Aime Fine Arts, has always
favored combining art shows
and traditional arts such as perfume and jewelry.
In some of these photos, we see
small colorful serigraphs by E.J.
Gold.

AMITYVILLE A NEW GENERATION
Fourth thriller in the famous series
Hollywood Movie Set 1993

In 1993, when the horror/suspense sequel to the hit horror movie *The Amityville Horror, Amityville A New Generation* was shot, the production company requested the use of some of Gold's *Monumental* paintings for a scene that was to be filmed in a coffee shop.

A large selection of the paintings were hung throughout the movie set for the coffee shop scenes and have since become part of film history.

Photos courtesy: Scott Norris Fine Arts

At about the same time as this filming was taking place, Tim Elston, formerly of Filmation, Disney Studios, and Will Vinton Studios, was creating this virtual reality experiment in computer animation based on E.J. Gold's art.

Amityville A New Generation

Fourth thriller in the famous series
1993

Top photo: Leading star Ross Partridge on the set of *Amityville A New Generation* with Gold's art prominent in background. The movie was director John Murlowski's second.

The full cast included Ross Partridge, Lala Sloatman, David Naughton, Richard Roundtree, Terry O'Quinn and Julia Nickson.

The synopsis of the movie reads as follows:
A beautiful but strangely dark antique mirror opens a doorway to gleaming, modern horror as a young artist discovers the secrets of his past, and the terrifying future that awaits him.
Photos courtesy: Scott Norris Fine Arts.

HELEN JONES GALLERY
SACRAMENTO
STROKES OF GENIUS
Group Show
1993

Pam Harley, far right, curated *Strokes of Genius* at the Helen Jones Gallery in Sacramento in March, 1993.
Photos by Della Heywood.

Strokes of Genius was a group show representing the work of members of the Grass Valley Graphics Group: E.J. Gold, Tom X, Kelly Rivera, Menlo Macfarlane, Della Heywood, David Christie, Robbert Trice. Art patron Don Harley helped organize this show and we see him standing with an unidentified guest in front of an *Odalisque* and a *Faces of War* painting by E. J. Gold.

Brightly colored ceramics from Gold's studio were also offered at the Helen Jones Gallery in Sacramento.

Musicians playing in front of three mid-size *Haunted Corridor* paintings by Gold.

HELEN JONES GALLERY
STROKES OF GENIUS
Group Show
1993

Kelly Rivera original drawings on these panels.

Collectors David & Trish Akiyoshi with Menlo Macfarlane at the opening reception of *Strokes of Genius*. The Akiyoshis have been collecting works by the Grass Valley Graphics Group for over a decade. They came from the Bay area to attend this group show. In the photo above, we see *Odalisque* serigraphs of Gold's.
Photos courtesy: Helen Jones Gallery

The buffet table at the opening brought visitors in close contact with one of Gold's larger paintings from the *Haunted Corridors* series.

H.HEATHER EDELMAN GALLERY
NEW YORK
ART EXPO '93
1993

H. Heather and Walter Edelman fell in love with Gold's art when they first discovered it in 1992. The Edelman's have been Gold's art representatives in New York ever since.
Walter Edelman supplies over 300 galleries throughout the country and now offers them Gold's art in his stable.
Photos courtesy of the artist

E.J. Gold Miniature Marvels and Houses of Imagination

Miniature Museum Space
E.J. Gold
Mixed Media

Odalisque #2
E.J. Gold
Gouache

Miniature Night Gallery
E.J. Gold
Mixed Media

Miniature fine art
for fine art collec
and dealers. Orig
from one inch to

An outstanding collection of drawings, graphics, acrylic and oil on gouache, pastels,limited-edition sculpture (bronze, sterling silv 18K and 22K gold) by E.J. Gold.

H. Heather Edelman Gallery
386 West Broadway, 3rd Fl, New York, NY 10012-4302
(212) 226-2943   Fax: (212) 226-4422

A poster for the 1993 Art Expo in New York where H. Heather Edelman presented a large selection of miniatures and ceramics created by E.J. Gold.

Above right: Photography session of the miniatures prior to their being sent to New York. All of Gold's art is catalogued and numbered before it leaves the studio so it can be included in the ongoing *Catalogue Raisonne* of his work. Thus far, well over 30,000 works have been catalogued by Gold's archivist Barbara Haynes each with its own reference number, description, history, and photograph in color and in black and white. The Catalogue Raisonne is currently being digitized.
Photos by Barbara Haynes.

Houses of Imagination

Miniature fine art
for
fine art collectors and dealers.
Originals from one inch to life size.
by
E.J. GOLD

216

H. HEATHER EDELMAN GALLERY

ART EXPO '93
Houses of Imagination
Miniature Marvels
1993

H. Heather Edelman Gallery at *Art Expo '93*. On the left Walter Edelman in the gallery during preparations. On the far left and above H. Heather Edelman. Staff wore t-shirts and leather skirts with original graphics.
Photos courtesy: H. Heather Edelman Gallery

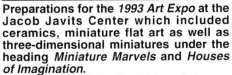

Preparations for the *1993 Art Expo* at the Jacob Javits Center which included ceramics, miniature flat art as well as three-dimensional miniatures under the heading *Miniature Marvels* and *Houses of Imagination*.
Photos courtesy: H. Heather Edelman Gallery.

THE WHITE HOUSE PROJECT
1992

Scalamandre
FABRIC SAMPLES
FOR THE WHITE HOUSE

Among the galleries and decorators in Walter Edelman's roster was Kaki Hockersmith who happened to be the decorator for the Governor of Arkansas at the time. When the governor became the President, the decorator found that she had a new house to oversee, namely the White House.

From there it was only a step to inviting Gold to submit some paintings for possible use in the presidential abode. Thus was born, the *White House* series. In order to produce the *White House* series, E.J. Gold was provided with fabric samples to guide him in his choice of colors.

Dimensions were provided to the artist who began in earnest to paint some *Odalisques.* After producing over a dozen of these, it was discovered that the wrong dimensions had been given and new ones were provided. Taking it all in stride, the artist began afresh and went on to create a memorable series.

Here we see him clowning with the Scalamandre fabric and paint samples provided by White House decorator Kaki Hockersmith. The colors were part of his preferred palette and the fabrics extremely tasteful.

The net result was that Gold created over seventy paintings in this series. In the end, a Matisse was chosen for the designated area and that settled that!

However, during the process, several *Odalisques* serigraphs made it into the White House collection as well as some of Gold's beautiful hand-crafted ceramics which lived in the White House Solarium for several years. Not to mention some delicious truffles delivered from The Truffle Shop in Nevada City which were greatly appreciated by the First Family!
Photos by A.V. Hopcroft.

CATHERINE OXENBERG
The Model

A visit by actress and friend Catherine Oxenberg coincided with the *White House Project* and Ms. Oxenberg agreed to pose for some of the paintings.
On another such visit, the artist photographer took the opportunity to photograph the actress between work sessions.
Photos by E.J. Gold.

A sampling of one of The White House Collection of *Odalisque* serigraphs.

Aside from posing for some of the *White House* paintings, Oxenberg and Gold have developed a working relationship in which movie scripts get hammered out and finalized with long, intense improv sessions and numerous rewrites.

They have worked on manuscript drafts, recording of stories for the *Galaxy Audio Project,* and story ideas for continuing collaborations over the course of many visits.
Photos by E.J. Gold.

CATHERINE OXENBERG MODELS

Model Catherine Oxenberg and artist E.J. Gold take a break from the serious work of painting and posing. As the posing sessions wore on, the atmosphere actually grew more buoyant. These *Queen's Chamber* pieces, with teddy bear, music box, carousel, toy fox, harlequin doll and dollhouse were the happy result.

THE ROSE ROOM MODEL
prepared by E.J. Gold

A miniature scale model of the Rose Room in the White House "reference maquette." The Rose Room is the specific room in which the painting was to be placed. Many variations of paintings were first produced in the form of watercolor sketches before the larger canvases were begun.

The model includes silk carpets from the Kashishian Collection, d. Ann Ruff curtains, Bespaq clavichord, and Derek Perkins fireplace mantle.

Presidential Notecards
for *Bill Clinton*

for *Hillary Clinton*

E.J. Gold in the quiet of his private studio works on miniature watercolor notecards for his closest friends. The cards are never sold and are only given as gifts.

for *Chelsea Clinton*

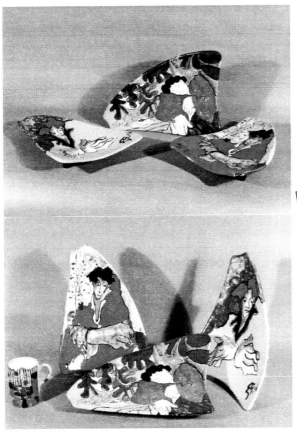

WHITE HOUSE CERAMICS
Odalisques
1992

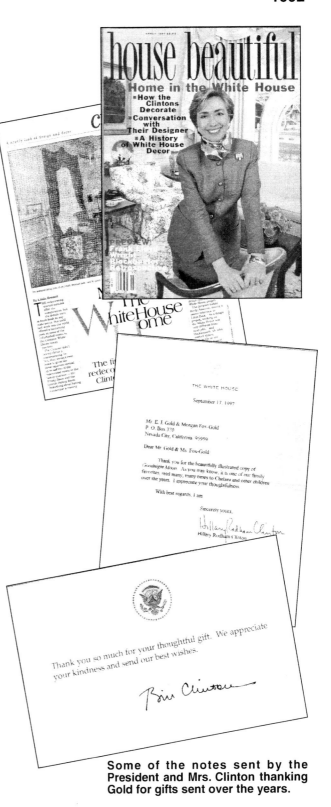

To top off the White House adventure, Gold decided to send some rare Charles Houston ceramic platters which he hand-painted and kiln-fired in his ceramic studio. The platters were garnished with truffles prepared by world-famous friend, photographer and chocolatier, Willem de Groot.

The platters and truffles were then hand-delivered to the First Family by White House decorator Kaki Hockersmith.

Kaki Hockersmith has remained a friend and continues to keep in touch with Gold and his always new and exciting projects.

The Clintons acknowledged their appreciation by sending champagne flutes from Camp David as Christmas gifts as well as their thank you notes pictured here.

Chocolatier Willem de Groot was equally thanked for his wonderful truffles in this note from Hillary Clinton's Special Assistant, Capricia Penavic Marshall.

Some of the notes sent by the President and Mrs. Clinton thanking Gold for gifts sent over the years.

Collectors Lenny Beck and Meryl Hershey Beck pause for a moment with Gold's wife Morgan Fox in front of a painting from the *White House* series during one of their visits to Gold's studio where they acquired several magnificent paintings.

Meryl Hershey Beck and dreaming woman Heather Valencia, a very close friend of hers with her niece Sonia LaVenture, radiate excitement and enthusiasm as they sit and enjoy a private art presentation in Gold's studio.

Private presentations often occur in Gold's studio where assistants love to play *Show and Tell.* The presentation of canvases can take several hours and guests usually consider it the experience of a lifetime.
Photos by Aviko

Gold plays hide 'n seek with Lenny Beck after dinner when everyone gets to sit back and relax.

Lenny Beck takes a quiet moment to catch his breath after viewing a large number of paintings recently produced by the prolific Gold. The sheer quantity of works to see is often overwhelming to even the most seasoned collector.

From left: Sonia LaVenture, Heather Valencia, Meryl Beck, Lenny Beck, Rose Gander, and Barbara Haynes placing the canvas.

Collectors' Profile

Denbridge Corporation

Gold poses one last time with this well-loved canvas before it goes to its new home across the border in Toronto, Canada. Denbridge Capital Corporation in Toronto acquired this four by five foot painting, *Mountain Pass Arcturus*, from the *Between Heaven and Hell* series for its corporate offices.

Billy Barty

Recently deceased legendary actor Billy Barty stands beaming in front of his Gold landscape in 1993.

Peggy Carlson

The late Peggy Carlson was a good friend and collector of Gold's art. She also followed his advice about the stock market and came out a winner. Here collector and artist pose with a recent trophy: *Monique*.

Evan Lurie

Composer Evan Lurie and entrepreneur Jim King acquired this painting by E.J. Gold and have since added several others to their New York penthouse collection. Lurie did the musical score for *Oswald the Octopus* as well as *Johnny Stecchino* directed by Oscar-winner Roberto Begnini.

Doreen and Everett Ping

Everett and Doreen Ping are the manufacturers of the famous and oh so fine *Ping Ware* which is among the best cookware you can ever hope to have in your kitchen. They fell in love with Gold's art when they weren't all eyes for each other and have been living happily ever after together... with Gold's art.

RICHMOND ART GALLERY
RICHMOND, B.C.
MOONBEAM
1993

RICHMOND ART GALLERY
MOONBEAM
1933

The beautiful Richmond Art Gallery located outside of Vancouver, British Columbia hosted the *Moonbeam* show on one of its many stops throughout the country. This show was curated by Jaswant Bains of Bains Fine Art.

The show included tall free-standing paintings in the Monumental format as well as colorful ceramics hand-produced in Gold's ceramic studio.

Evening lighting gave the exhibit a magical look as seen in all the pictures.

"The Most Magical Christmas since the First"
Harry Nilsson
1994

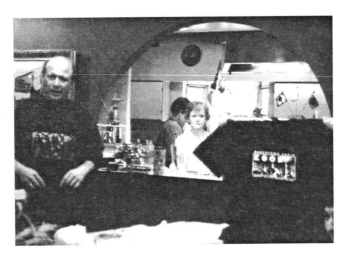

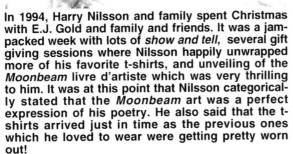

In 1994, Harry Nilsson and family spent Christmas with E.J. Gold and family and friends. It was a jam-packed week with lots of *show and tell*, several gift giving sessions where Nilsson happily unwrapped more of his favorite t-shirts, and unveiling of the *Moonbeam* livre d'artiste which was very thrilling to him. It was at this point that Nilsson categorically stated that the *Moonbeam* art was a perfect expression of his poetry. He also said that the t-shirts arrived just in time as the previous ones which he loved to wear were getting pretty worn out!

The Many Faces of Harry Nilsson

A happy Harry smiles his warm, loving and playful smile as he sits back and watches the incredibly festive activity around him, meeting new friends and old admirers who take the opportunity to let him know how much they appreciate his music. Harry Nilsson, a true gentle man, watches his family enjoying their Christmas vacation. Lower left: Nilsson holds his own ashtray made especially for him in Gold's ceramic studio. Lower right: Gold's Odalisque in the background keeps an eye on Nilsson.

Photos by Michele-Marie Underhill

REMEMBER (Christmas)

Una and Harry Nilsson give a warm smile by the Christmas tree.

Harry Nilsson in a familiar gesture chats around a candlelight dinner that stretches on for hours.

Nilsson's greatest wish had been to be published in *Galaxy* magazine which he grew up avidly reading as a science fiction lover. Gold granted him his wish and published in the March 1994 issue of *Galaxy* a story authored by Nilsson of which he was very fond, *"The Boy Who Always Said No."*

Days went by with the reunited friends eating, talking, reminiscing, planning, laughing, joking, enjoying the company of artists, recording engineers, studio assistants, children, music, *X-Minus One.* They listened to music and even recorded together.

And then the inevitable departure where Gold and Nilsson exchanged warm hugs. Nilsson passed away about two weeks later.

WORKSPACE GALLERY
NEW PALTZ, NY

The Art of Reductionism:
Paintings, Serigraphs, Ceramics by E.J. Gold, Tom X and Menlo Macfarlane
1994

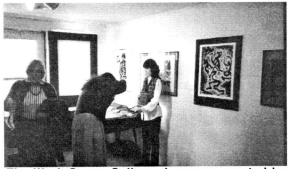

The Work Space Gallery show was curated by Grant Abrams and his wife, artist Judy Gonzalez.

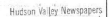

Hudson Valley Newspapers

Work Space Gallery Opens With Exhibit On Reductionism

Grant Abrams and his wife Judy Gonzalez, above, with works of ceramic art in their Work Space Gallery at 62 Henry W. DuBois Drive.

NEW PALTZ(HVN): Work Space Gallery, a small gallery and frame shop at 62 Henry W. DuBois Drive, opened its doors to the public with a reception on Sunday, February 27. Owners Grant Abrams and Judy Gonzalez have organized an exhibit on the Art of Reductionism, featuring three California-based artists: Tom X, E.J. Gold and Menlo MacFarlane, all well known on the West Coast but not as familiar to New Yorkers.

The three artists are known for their unconventional shows and for "reductionism," a style of art that "explores new forms of perception which force the viewer to confront new modes of perception."

On display will be ceramics, serigraphs, paintings and other surprising mixed media until March 26.

Hudson Valley Newspapers

A PAID CIRCULATION NEWSPAPER   50¢ A COPY

The NEW PALTZ NEWS

Combined With Wallkill Valley World   EDI

Vol 106, No. 9   New Paltz, N.Y. Wednesday, March 2

WOODSTOCK TIMES

ARTS

California dreaming

Another gallery offering Gold's ceramics is the charming Crafts People in Woodstock, New York pictured below.

OPEN SPACE
A CELEBRATION OF THE OPENING OF
WORK • SPACE GALLERY
PAINTINGS, SERIGRAPHS, CERAMICS BY ARTISTS OF THE CALIFO
BASED
SCHOOL OF REDUCTIONISM
E.J. GOLD   MENLO MACFARLANE   TO
SUNDAY, FEBRUARY 27, 1994
914-255-2898 FOR DIRECTIONS & INFORMATION

ARTWORKS GALLERY
Vancouver
MOONBEAM
1994

ArtWorks is an experimental studio/gallery in Vancouver, British Columbia run by artists.

MoonBeam

Harry Nilsson & E. J. Gold
A Collaboration of Poetry and Art
Opening Tuesday, April 5, 7:00pm
Showing Through April 16, 1994
— ARTWORKS —
237 East 4th Avenue, Vancouver, B.C. V5T 1C6   (604) 874-7607

"Who Searches for the Moonbeam" Original Serigraph. ©1994 E. J. Gold

---

Bains Fine Arts Unlimited & Desert Moon

present

MOON BEAM

HARRY NILSSON & E. J. GOLD
A collaboration of poetry and art

Opening Tuesday, April 5th, 7:00 p.m.

Artworks
237 East 4th Avenue,
Vancouver, B.C. V5T 1C6
(604) 874-7607

On exhibit, April 5-16, 1994.

*"Who Searches for the Moonbeam"
E. J. Gold, 72" x 30". Acrylic on Canvas. 1991*
Photo by Kanwal

Hamming it up for the camera after the CBC television crew completed a news segment are from left to right, Jaswant Bains with gallery directors Lesley Moseley and Kevin Hutt.

The Vancouver Sun

THE LORD MUST BE . . . As for stars, U.S. artist **E.J. Gold**'s series of reductionist paintings dedicated to the late singer-songwriter **Harry Nillson** has quietly cropped up again. This time, Gold's exhibition will hang until April 16 at the Artworks studio-living space complex, 237 East Fourth.

Khalsa Credit Union manager **Jaswant Bains** and friends **Nadiya Szram, Lesley Moseley** and **Kelvin Hutt** also showed the acrylic-on-canvas *Moonbeam* series in Richmond late last year.

Nillson won a Grammy for the *Midnight Cowboy* theme *Everybody's Talkin'*, which might happen were **Ringo Starr** and others to attend Gold's show here as they do in Los Angeles.

ARTWORKS GALLERY
Vancouver
MOONBEAM
1994

FREE Volume 22, No. 57

July 16, 1994

22nd Year Of Publication

Twice A Week
Community Newspaper

THE LINK HOUSE
#202, 336 E. 17th Avenue,
Vancouver, B.C. V5V 1A8

THE LINK Weekend Edition   July 16, 1994   79

MARKETPLACE

TINU MATHUR   R. PAUL DHILLON

GALLERY OF FUNCTIONAL ART
PRESENTS

J. GOLD
MOONBEAM SHOW

Ex-Dynasty star Catherine Oxenberg and daughter with Jaswant Bains

Ceramic Earthen Works by E.J. Gold

The Art Lover

Jaswant Bains is a manager at The Khalsa Credit Union by day and an art aficionado by night. He says his love for the arts got him started in art collection and dealership about three years ago. He became interested in a company called Bains Fine Arts Unlimited, which distributes a fictional literary magazine called Galaxy, edited by E.J. Gold, a musician, writer and artist. "We had a show of works by E.J. Gold done in the poster of Harry Nilsson, who passed away recently, at the Richmond Art Gallery and Artworks. Then we took all the pieces to Los Angeles and had a show there", he said.

Brooklyn born, Los Angeles bred singer-songwriter and two time Grammy Award winner, Harry Nilsson, created poetry called Moonbeam, which was used as inspiration by Gold to create the artworks. Bains, who owns works by Gold, helped organize the shows in Vancouver.

The luminaries in attendance included ex-Dynasty star, Catherine Oxenberg. Also present at the opening were Galaxy writers and recent Nebula Award nominees for fictional writing, Jean Marie Stine and Brad Linaweaver.

Saturday, March 26, 1994

ROUND & ABOUT
KEEPING IN TOUCH WITH THE LOWER MAINLAND

Singer Nilsson's work 'on display'

AT THE PRESS CONFERENCE CALLED BY THE BEATLES TO ANNOUNCE THE FORMATION OF THEIR NEW COMPANY, APPLE RECORDS, A REPORTER ASKED JOHN LENNON WHO HIS FAVOURITE AMERICAN SINGER SONGWRITER WAS. HE REPLIED, "NILSSON! MOMENTS LATER, PAUL McCARTNEY WAS ASKED WHO HIS FAVOURITE AMERICAN GROUP WAS. UNHESITATINGLY, HE SAID "NILSSON!"

Moonbeam is the title of an exciting collaboration combining the art of E.J. Gold and poetry by singer/songwriter Harry Nilsson. These two renowned artists were friends and colleagues in the '60's and '70's, when their collaboration led to exciting album cover design and an intimate photographic essay by Gold about Nilsson, which captures his many moods and delightful sense of humor.

Nilsson is author of the classic lyrics and music of "Me and My Arrow," "Lifeline," and many other hit songs; and he won a Montreux Festival Award for his work on the movie The Point. This animated feature also yielded a gold record, one of 19 for Nilsson. E.J. Gold is like Nilsson, a native New Yorker who became known in Los Angeles during the 1970s for his work as a sculptor/painter/author/comedian/movie studio consultant and at one time, co-worker of Nilsson at Capitol and RCA records, helping produce and design several albums.

When Jaswant Bains learned of the collaboration between E.J. Gold and Harry Nilsson, he felt that this show would be ideal for a Vancouver gallery. The interplay of Nilsson's lyrics as poetry with E.J. Gold's brightly coloured series of Reductionist canvases produce dynamic and startling art exhibit. There are also fine art posters created especially for this show.

Fittingly this current exhibition was first shown in New York and was on display in November 1993 at the Richmond Art Gallery. This is a series of commemorative shows with the next one scheduled for 15 May 1994 in Los Angeles. Harry Nilsson passed away in January earlier this year.

A collaboration of Art and Poetry by E.J. Gold and Harry Nilsson Featuring Original Canvases and Ceramics.

Opening 7 p.m. Tuesday April 5th, 1994, ARTWORKS, 237 East 4th Avenue, Vancouver, 874-7607 Curator Jaswant Bains 327-3071

The *Moonbeam* show curated by Jaswant Bains of Bains Fine Arts Unlimited and Nadja Szram of Desert Moon got extensive press and television coverage during its month-long run. Bains had the pleasure of meeting movie star Catherine Oxenberg at an opening.

GALLERY OF FUNCTIONAL ART

Los Angeles
THE MOONBEAM SHOW
1994

Una Nilsson and gallery director Lois Lambert at the Moonbeam Show opening.

E. J. GOLD
THE MOONBEAM SHOW

A tribute to Harry Nilsson

On Exhibit May 14 - July 10, 1994

The Gallery of Functional Art
At Edgemar

2429 Main St., Santa Monica, CA 90405, (310) 450-2827

The artist was represented at this *Moonbeam* show by Patricia Elizabeth and Morgan Fox pictured here with gallery director Lois Lambert. Guests included many intimates of Nilsson.

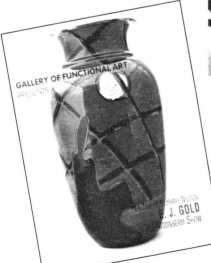

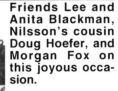

Friends Lee and Anita Blackman, Nilsson's cousin Doug Hoefer, and Morgan Fox on this joyous occasion.

234

GALLERY OF FUNCTIONAL ART
THE MOONBEAM SHOW
1994

Left from top to bottom: Una Nilsson and Stuart Lerner. Moonbeam Ceramics at the show during the set-up. Morgan Fox, Patricia Elizabeth and Stuart Lerner. The entrance to the gallery. Right from top to bottom: Anita Blackman, Morgan Fox, and Lee Blackman. The show sign. The invitation to the show. Una Nilsson, Anita Blackman and Patricia Elizabeth.

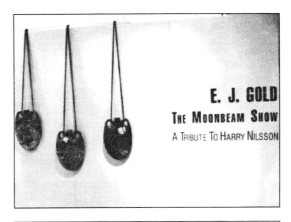

E. J. GOLD
THE MOONBEAM SHOW
A TRIBUTE TO HARRY NILSSON

When John Lennon was asked who his favorite singer was he replied, 'Nilsson'. When Paul McCartney was asked who his favorite group was he replied, 'Nilsson'. Gold's tribute to Nilsson represents an act of love and reverence. Gold will donate his proceeds to The Audio Galaxy Magazine For The Blind

POETRY

MUSIC

CERAMICS

MONUMENTALS

SERIGRAPHS

JEWELRY

A TRIBUTE TO HARRY NILSSON
E. J. GOLD
THE MOONBEAM SHOW

A COLLABORATION OF TWO ARTISTS

YOU ARE CORDIALLY INVITED TO A RECEPTION HONORING THE ARTIST, SATURDAY, MAY 14 1994, 6PM - 9PM.

EXHIBITION WILL CONTINUE THROUGH JULY 10 1994 GALLERY HOURS TUESDAY-FRIDAY 11AM- 7PM SATURDAY & SUNDAY 11AM - 6PM

GALLERY OF FUNCTIONAL ART, 2429 MAIN STREET, SANTA MONICA, CA 90405 PHONE 310-450-2827 FAX 310-450-4831

235

GUMP'S
SAN FRANCISCO
ODALISQUES CERAMICS
1994

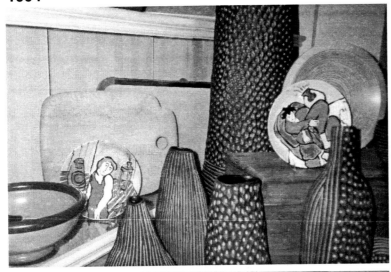

Since 1861, buyers from the prestigious Gump's in San Francisco have traveled all over the world, seeking out rare, unique and imaginative treasures of the past and present.

Gump's specializes in higher end gift items and caters to the upwardly mobile crowd. They offer distinctive home furnishings, home décor accents, corporate gifts, and executive gifts.

In 1994, Gump's began carrying E.J. Gold's ceramic Odalisques. Here we see some of them on view at the In-Store Housewares Display.

Photos courtesy: Gump's San Francisco

BILL GRAHAM
AND DOTTIE GRAHAM
STUDIO VISIT
NOVEMBER 1995

Gold and longtime friend Bill Graham, of record giant BMG Productions are reunited after many years.

Gold points to album cover photos of their friend Harry Nilsson. Graham gifted Gold with a plaque and Gold Record given to him by RCA for producing the million hit song of Nilsson's *Without You.*

Graham and his wife Dottie thoroughly enjoyed the reunion and shared a few good laughs too.

Reminiscing about the past during the studio tour which Gold conducted through the mementos gathered over years of working with a plethora of musical groups.

Show and Tell is always an exciting discovery. Here Bill and Dottie look at an earlier hard-cover first edition of Gold's photobiography.

Special visits like this one are always too short and will be remembered very fondly by everyone involved. On the occasion of Gold's birthday roast later that same year, Bill Graham sent a video clip of himself paying tribute to Gold. He told of a dream he had about him and how Gold had been given so many gifts with which to live this life. It aptly described his deep feelings about Gold whom he profoundly admires and cherishes as a friend.

FOUNDATION FOR THE STUDY OF OBJECTIVE ART
TORONTO
MASTER IN BLACK
1995

THE FOUNDATION FOR THE STUDY OF OBJECTIVE ART
533-A Parliament St, Toronto, Ont. M4X 1P3.
Tues-Fri 2:30-5:30, alternate Saturdays 10-4
(Dec 9 & 23, Jan 6 & 20)
(416-972-0401. Fax 416-964-0199)
Extended to January 31:
E. J. Gold, 'Master in Black,' 32 original
charcoals. Just a few lines establish the Zen
like mastery of E. J. Gold, a former student of
the Japanese Gutai School and founder of the
contemporary American School of
Reductionism. In this extraordinary exhibition
of reductionist method, stark simplicity
expresses subtleties of mood transcending
the limits of the medium.
Works are not for sale. Admission is free.

Master in Black
32 original charcoals by E.J. Gold
October 4 - December 15, 1995
Just a few lines establish the Zen like mastery of E.J. Gold, a former student of the
Japanese Gutai School and founder of the contemporary American School of
Reductionism. In this extraordinary exhibition of reductionist method, stark simplicity
expresses subtleties of mood transcending the limits of the medium.

The Foundation for the Study of Objective Art
533-A Parliament St , Toronto, Canada M4X 1E7
Tel. (416) 972-0401 Fax (416) 964-0199
Tues.- Fri. 2:30 - 5:30 pm & alternate Sat. 10 am - 4 pm
Works are not for sale. Admission is free.

Curator and gallery manager Gloria Trujillo helped select and prepare this stunning display of charcoals by E.J. Gold.

E.J. Gold's first show at the Foundation for the Study of Objective Art in Toronto included thirty-two original charcoal drawings.

The Foundation has gone on to acquire an extensive permanent collection of works by E.J. Gold and has hosted a dozen one-man shows since then, as well as several group shows with artists of the Grass Valley Graphics Group.

The Foundation is a center for the scholarly study of Objective Art in its numerous forms and has a research library at its disposal as well as its own collection which students and scholars can freely research. It hosts a number of programs in addition to the regular art exhibits that it offers. The Director of the Foundation for the Study of Objective Art is James Anthony, a prominent businessman and art collector.

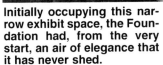

Initially occupying this narrow exhibit space, the Foundation had, from the very start, an air of elegance that it has never shed.

HOLLYWOOD ARTS COUNCIL
HOLLYWOOD
FEAST FOR THE SENSES
Grass Valley Graphics Group
1995

The entrance to Gallery 6161 on Santa Monica Blvd in Hollywood where *Feast for the Senses* was held.

Feast for the Senses drew large crowds to its opening as wave after wave of appreciative viewers streamed in.

Grass Valley Graphics Group artist, the late Tom X, chats with visitors at the opening reception of *Feast for the Senses.*

This glowing smile would seem to indicate a very happy customer with a Zoe Alowan original graphic.

Visitors stop in front of this huge mural by E.J. Gold from his series of *Visions from the God World.*

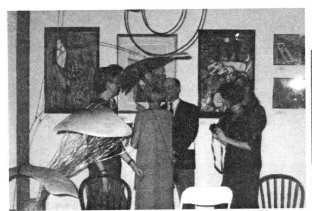

Dr. Jerome Berman, director of the California Museum of Ancient Art, enjoys the show with other guests.

A view of this Grass Valley Graphics Group show organized by the Hollywood Arts Council in collaboration with Lofty Productions.

HOLLYWOOD ARTS COUNCIL
Feast For the Senses
Grass Valley Graphics Group
1995

Tom X with longtime Grass Valley Graphics Group collectors Jim and Gloreen Rowe from Santa Barbara who couldn't miss the opportunity to see more works by their favorites.

Sculptures by Willem de Groot on display in the center of the large exhibit space.

Beverly Korenwasser who curated the show for Heidelberg Editions International and who represented the Grass Valley Graphics Group at the opening of *Feast for the Senses* enjoys the success with art patron Jerry Schneiderman.

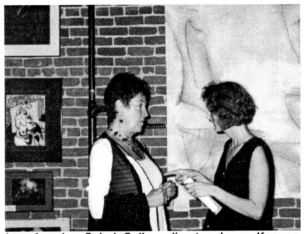

Los Angeles Spiral Gallery director Joyce Kenyon and Nancy Burns Trice, representative for Heidelberg Editions International, mix business and pleasure.

Feast for the Senses included large paintings as well as smaller graphic works seen right. In front, a large David Christie mobile hovers dramatically near Willem de Groot's *Soldier*.

New Friends Old Friends
CURTIS ARMSTRONG:
HARRY FEST
1995

The *Moonbeam* show which took place at the Gallery of Functional Art in Los Angeles attracted lots of attention from Nilsson and Gold fans alike.

One fan who missed the show and only heard about it after it had closed, decided he couldn't let the opportunity pass him by so he came to visit E.J. Gold in person. This turned out to be a wonderful beginning to a great friendship between Curtis Armstrong and E.J. Gold. Armstrong has since made many visits to Gold's home and studio where he is always welcomed as an old friend.

Of course, the initial visit was particularly exciting as an ice breaker when the *Revenge of the Nerds* star was immediately recognized by his fans as the infamous *Booger,* a memorable offbeat character Armstrong will never live down...

So Armstrong hit it off with the children as well as the adults. What better friend than one who is loved by all age groups!!

These photos show a few scenes from some of these visits and discussions that occurred as Curtis Armstrong began the preparations for a *Harry Fest* that he organized in Los Angeles and that has since become an annual event.

Armstrong is captivated by some audio bytes of Nilsson that Gold pulled out of his bag of tricks.

No level of seriousness will defer some clowning around which is *de rigueur* on this set.

Ever the gentleman, Armstrong takes a moment to sign a few autographs for his younger fans who beam with pleasure at having a real hero in their midst.

Armstrong enjoyed taking a peak at an unpublished manuscript of Gold's in the middle of a whirlwind of activity.

New Friends Old Friends
CURTIS ARMSTRONG:
HARRY FEST
1995

Armstrong is quite focussed on the artwork Gold is presenting him as they prepare for the first *Harry Fest.*

A video viewing and discussion was part of the activities Armstrong got to enjoy with the group that had gathered during his visit.

Curtis Armstrong came looking for artwork and material he could offer fans at his *Harry Fest*. He was particularly pleased with the ceramics he came away with.

Looking a little hagard after his senses have been bombarded in every direction, Armstrong sits in awe at the sheer diversity...

The group discusses strategy for the upcoming *Harry Fest.*

After all this business, a warm hug says it all.

Artisans on Ward

NELSON, BRITISH COLUMBIA
ART AND SOUL
May 2-31, 1996

"Flower and Heart"   E.J. Gold

Fairy tales often begin with a dream. Living in the bucolic setting of Nelson, British Columbia, Jim and Mary Donald had a dream of sharing art which they loved with others, even in such an isolated area. And their dream came true.

Paradise, in the form pictured above, usually comes without art. Some would say, that's its only drawback...

With the help of a few friends, they organized *Art and Soul* featuring the Grass Valley Graphics Group, and took the show on tour.

Jim Donald sits amidst his treasures savoring the diversity, energy and exuberance of these paintings soon to be displayed locally.

Art lovers came out of the woodwork and enjoyed the show tremendously.

The *Art and Soul* show reflected the philosophy of curator Donald, a devoted family man, who provided music for this event as well as a wholesome setting for all age groups.

The Kooteneys
ART AND SOUL
July-August, 1996

Jim and Mary Donald's enthusiasm for art spilled over into yet another show in remote British Columbia. Like the preceding exhibit at Artisan's on Ward, this show also offered a multi-media event for visitors to enjoy. Donald is an accomplished musician and music was an important part of this art celebration.

When word got out that Donald was cooking up another extravaganza, helpers came forth to assist in making it a huge success.

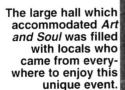

The large hall which accommodated *Art and Soul* was filled with locals who came from everywhere to enjoy this unique event.

TESORO'S
BEVERLY HILLS

soulful bowls

There's nothing cookie-cutter about the stuff at Tesoro, a tabletop and home-accessory shop recently relocated to Canon Drive from its original Robertson Boulevard home. Nearly every item—anthropomorphic etched-steel bar stools, wineglasses fashioned from coconut shells, hand-painted rolling pins—is made by an artist and, according to owner Marlene Riceberg, "has a soul." Riceberg encourages customers who don't find precisely what they're looking for on the shelves to collaborate with her talent. She also offers the services of on-staff design consultants, who make house calls to show customers just how coconut-shell wineglasses might fit into the greater scheme of things.

—Andrea Feldm

401 N. Canon Dr., Beverly Hills; (310) 275-9990

Co-owner Tara Riceberg

African-motif ceramics by E.J. Gold, $382–$387; coconut accessories, $23–$96; African sisal figures, $27 each; saks vessel by Jun Kaneko, $315.

January 1998 article in Buzz Magazine article about Tesoro's Gift Shop prominently displayed E.J. Gold's Blackware ceramics in the form of platters, serving trays, salt and pepper shakers, vases and serving bowls.

The prestigious and elegant Tesoro's has been representing E.J. Gold's *EarthenWorks* since 1996.

Located in Beverly Hills on Canon Drive, Tesoro's caters to a star-studded clientele with movie industry buyers as well as tourists always looking for the latest and hottest trends to bring home and show off.

Owner Marilyn Riceberg runs the elegant shop with her daughter Tara Riceberg who is the manager. Riceberg senior is known for her impeccable taste, and has helped maintain standards of excellence that contribute to the reputation of this upscale location.

LOS ANGELES COUNTY MUSEUM OF ART
Gift Shop
BLACKWARE
1996

E.J. Gold's *Blackware* ceramics have been extremely popular wherever they have been offered. The LACMA Gift Shop was one of the select locations in Los Angeles where they could be found. Details of this unique line of ceramics can be seen on this page. Platters, pitchers, vases, creamers and coffee pots are sprinkled throughout the shelves.

E.J. Gold's ceramics are handmade in very small editions that make them all the more cherished and desirable.

Overall view of the elegant Los Angeles County Museum of Art Gift Shop where Gold's ceramics have been very popular for years.

BLUE LADDER GALLERY

CHICAGO

The Grass Valley Graphics Group
1996

The Blue Ladder Gallery is directed by Fred Schill. The gallery offers a very eclectic collection of art: paintings, prints, ceramics, sculpture, jewelry, books. Above the door is a Grace Kelly Rivera painting.

The large mural by E.J. Gold titled *Blue Angel* was an appropriate selection for the Blue Ladder Gallery and dominated the space with grace and elegance.

Visitors have access to the second level gallery through the French doors.

Visitors have a history of swarming to the Blue Ladder openings which always offer new artists to discover, fine art that's off the beaten path, alternative works that are refreshing to a jaded crowd.

A nighttime view of the Blue Ladder offers a bit of magic that attracts passersby and invites them in...

BLUE LADDER GALLERY
The Grass Valley Graphics Group

The Blue Ladder Gallery is on the gallery circuit and joins in the festivities of special art tours that occur throughout the city of Chicago at certain times of the year.

Behind the counter, Mark Einert, a glass blower from the Grass Valley

Graphics Group lends gallery director Fred Schill a helping hand in this busy season and provides the special touch of the presence of the artist that turns any gallery into a very sought after place.

FOUNDATION FOR THE STUDY OF OBJECTIVE ART

TORONTO
HIDDEN DOMINIONS
Feb. 3 - April 27, 1996

Castle Near The Central Sun

Hidden Dominions was the second show held at the Foundation for the Study of Objective Art. At first located in a very small but elegant space, the Foundation quickly felt its facility was too cramped for its big plans, and by the third E.J. Gold show, it had opened a new spacious gallery in a beautiful, renovated building where it has been ever since.

THE FOUNDATION FOR THE STUDY OF OBJECTIVE ART
533-A Parliament St, Toronto, Ont. M4X 1P3.
Tues-Fri 2:30-5:30, alternate Saturdays 10-4
(Feb 3 & 17, Mar 2, 16 & 30).
(416-972-0401, Fax 416-964-0199)
To April 27:
E. J. Gold, 'Hidden Dominions,'
works on canvas and paper. Normally,
landscapes capture the mood of a particular
place. E. J. Gold works in reverse.
Exploring certain moods and sensations,
he finds a corresponding place within
and hidden landscapes shimmer into view.

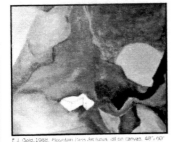

E.J. GOLD
HIDDEN DOMINIONS
Works on canvas and paper

FEBRUARY 3 - APRIL 27, 1996

Normally, landscapes capture the mood of a particular place.
E.J. Gold works in reverse. Exploring certain moods and
sensations, he finds a corresponding place within and
hidden landscapes shimmer into view.

THE FOUNDATION FOR THE STUDY OF OBJECTIVE ART
533-A Parliament Street, Toronto, 1-8, 972-0401, Fax. 964-0199.

Tuesday-Friday 2:50 p.m. - 5:30 p.m
Alternate Saturdays 10 a.m. - 4 p.m

E.J. Gold, 1988, Mountain Pass Arcturus, oil on canvas, 48" x 60".

This show included recent Gold acquisitions by the Foundation: some *Odalisques*, a few landscapes, some figures, a *City in the Sky* acrylic, some Kelly Riveras, as well as *Twilight Figures* by Della Heywood. Foundation Director James Anthony is seen above on left with guests.

GALLERY ARCTURUS
TORONTO
LARGE AS LIFE
July 30 - August 30, 1997

This one-man show presented for the first time, the *Monumentals* of E.J. Gold to a Toronto audience.

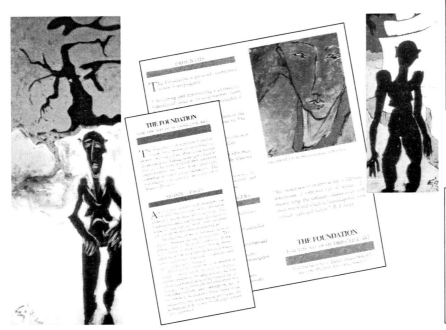

Some of the *Monumentals* on the wall of the artist's studio before being shipped to the show in Toronto. The *Monumentals* have been extensively presented throughout North America and Europe.

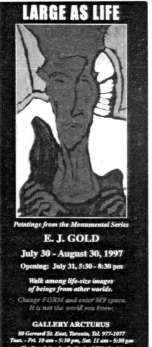

LARGE AS LIFE

Paintings from the Monumental Series

E. J. GOLD

July 30 - August 30, 1997
Opening: July 31, 5:30 - 8:30 pm

*Walk among life-size images
of beings from other worlds.*

*Change FORM and enter MY space.
It is not the world you know.*

GALLERY ARCTURUS
80 Gerrard St. East, Toronto, Tel. 977-1077
Tues. - Fri. 10 am - 5:30 pm, Sat. 11 am - 5:30 pm
The Foundation for the Study of Objective Art

FREE Gallery Arcturus: Paintings by E.J. Gold. This relatively new gallery offers innovation—a study centre for research, opportunities for students and artists to teach and learn, and publications on the Internet. Gold's work is big, bold and aggressive; it hovers between emotionally charged expressionism and coolly controlled abstraction. Here, he addresses a major concern of painters—how to introduce three-dimensional space into two-dimensional surfaces—by painting his images at human scale and mounting them on triangular bases that create a sculptural environment. July 30 to Aug. 30. 80 Gerrard St. E. (977-1077).

AMERICAN McGEE
Quake II
1997

In 1997, Gold was invited to create sound effects for the extremely popular 3D game *Quake*. American McGee, famous for his weapons, sounds, and most loved levels in *Quake I* and *II* flew out to Gold's recording studio with his computer and there directed the production of sound effects for *Quake II*.

In the world of online gaming, American McGee is a hero of the younger generation which he has inspired to follow in his footsteps as creative computer programmers and intrepid gamers. Here he sits with a young fan enraptured by the presence of this mythical giant known for his online speed and the fact that he cannot be beaten.

Prior to this visit, Gold had been developing his own 3D games and playing online games long before *Wolfenstein* hit the streets and became the most popular early 3D game of the computer gaming industry and won the Game of the Year award in 2001.

During his visit, McGee got to meet game developer Claude Needham, far right, and computer animator, Tim Elston, top, as well as hosts Morgan Fox and E.J. Gold. After working for a few years at id Software, the producers of *Quake I, II* and *III,* as well as *Doom* and *Wolfenstein,* McGee later went on to develop *Alice,* a 3D action shooter based on the Lewis Carroll classic.

Tim Elston, Bob Bachtold, Samantha Weingart, American McGee, Morgan Fox, Claude Needham, and E.J. Gold pause at the end of a whirlwind visit for a quick group shot.

MAGICAL BLEND MAGAZINE
1998

The interview with Michael Langevin editor of *Magical Blend Magazine* was a glorious event with E.J. Gold in full form. Langevin recorded the interview for several hours and walked away with his head spinning. In the end he had gathered enough material to separate it out into several different issues. Langevin got the royal treatment: Gold painted for him, showed him some ceramics, a few *livres d'artistes* and even gave him a tour of the recording studio where they listened to Gold's most recent CD.

Langevin stated in his editorial that he has interviewed an array of inspiring people, but not even the likes of Robert Anton Wilson, Timothy Leary or Merilyn Tunishende had prepared him for this charming and mesmerizing encounter. He was simply dazzled by Gold's genius.

GALLERY ARCTURUS
TORONTO
MY OTHER SELF
GROUP SHOW
April 23 - May 30, 1998

**Collaboration of Tom X
and E.J. Gold**

The Biggest Star in the Sky

It was very exciting for the Grass Valley Graphics Group to explore the theme *"My Other Self."* The divergent results spoke for the unique style of each artist which shines through even when they are united by a common inspiration.

The high quality art was matched by the elegant decor that enhanced the presentation of these dramatic works several of which were mural size.

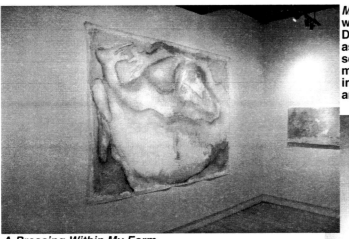

A Pressing Within My Form

My Other Self was a group show featuring the works of E.J. Gold, Della Heywood, Tom X, Denise Wey and Doug Truth. Here we see an assortment of works by Gold that enhanced this selection. The show included some very large murals as well as smaller works on canvas all including renditions of figures in one form or another.

The facade of the elegant brownstone in which Gallery Arcturus is located in Toronto.

Wizard

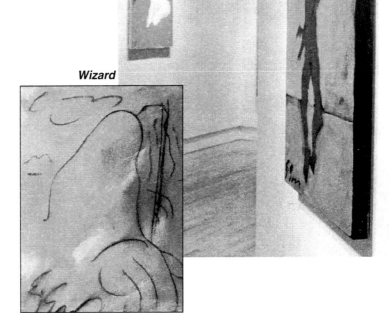

The Formless One

A self-portrait by Tom X is visible on the immediate left. Beside it, a painting by Della Heywood of her *Twilight Figures.* Far left, a haunting faceless portrait by Gold. This show represented works from the School of Reductionism.

Los Angeles County Museum of Art
RHAPSODIES IN BLACK,
ART OF THE HARLEM RENAISSANCE
July 26 - October 19, 1998

In addition to carrying E.J. Gold's *Blackware* in the Museum Gift Shop, LACMA set up a special gift shop for the *Harlem Renaissance* exhibit where not only the ceramics were a hit, but also Gold's numerous *Jazz Musicians* prints which he has been creating for years.

LOS ANGELES COUNTY MUSEUM OF ART
RHAPSODIES IN BLACK,
ART OF THE HARLEM RENAISSANCE
July 26 - October 19, 1998

Duke Ellington is always a best-seller among Gold's Jazz Musician prints.

GALLERY ARCTURUS

Toronto
BARDO TOURS
THE OLD CEDAR BAR
40 YEARS LATER
September 10 - October 17,1998

Gallery assistant Annavie.

Unidentified art guest with gallery manager Cathy Stilo at opening reception for *Bardo Tours, The Old Cedar Bar 40 Years Later.*

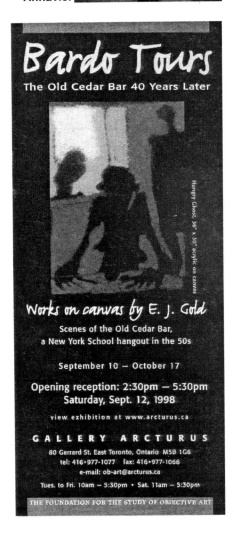

Bardo Tours

The Old Cedar Bar 40 Years Later

Hungry Ghost, 36" x 30" acrylic on canvas

Works on canvas by E. J. Gold

Scenes of the Old Cedar Bar,
a New York School hangout in the 50s

September 10 — October 17

Opening reception: 2:30pm — 5:30pm
Saturday, Sept. 12, 1998

view exhibition at www.arcturus.ca

GALLERY ARCTURUS

80 Gerrard St. East Toronto, Ontario M5B 1G6
tel: 416•977-1077 fax: 416•977-1066
e-mail: ob-art@arcturus.ca

Tues. to Fri. 10am — 5:30pm • Sat. 11am — 5:30pm

THE FOUNDATION FOR THE STUDY OF OBJECTIVE ART

Guests enjoyed the spacious location and haunting images that took them on an unusual tour through the past and through another world.

A continuous stream of visitors attended the opening reception.

The show *Bardo Tours* included about thirty paintings by E.J. Gold. Many were produced from small pastel drawings created by Gold...about 40 years ago, and recently translated to paintings of all sizes including some larger ones like the one pictured above in center of photo.

The entrance to the gallery and its staircase to the upper levels have some intriguing art...

Gallery Arcturus has been opened for just a few years now and it is shows of this calibre that have helped it gain a solid reputation among collectors and art critics.

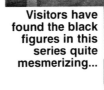

Visitors have found the black figures in this series quite mesmerizing...

MAD RIVER POST
Recent Paintings and Sculptures
Grass Valley Graphics Group Show
SAN FRANCISCO
Nov. 20 - March 1, 1997-98
LOS ANGELES
March 12 - July 12, 1998

Bowing to the Giant

The Bay

At the Foot of the Giant

Troubled Waters

The Grass Valley Graphics Group has had several shows with Mad River Post over the years and these two are the most recent ones. Like the name implies, Mad River Post is a post production company with a strong advocacy for the arts, and art exhibits are one way that they show their support.

The shows have been curated by Nancy Sadler and are typically well attended by industry people and the public at large.

Because of the spaciousness of the exhibit spaces, the artists were able to present several works each. E.J. Gold introduced his series of *South Seas* landscapes which he had just created at this time.

The Other Side of the Mountain

GALLERY ARCTURUS

TORONTO

SLIGHTLY OFF THE WALL

RECENT WORKS BY THE SCHOOL OF REDUCTIONISM

September 3 - 27, 1997

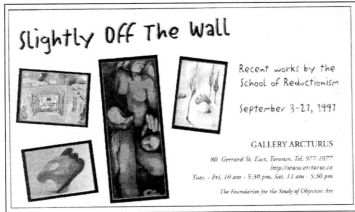

Gallery Arcturus

TORONTO

A Voyager's Guide to:
LIFE IN THE LABYRINTH

November 4- December 24, 1999

Gallery Arcturus has been a champion of the School of Reductionism and has had numerous one-man shows and group shows for Gold and the Grass Valley Graphics Group.

The Gift Shop and its ceramics, *livres d'artiste*, posters, notecards and prints from the Grass Valley Graphics Group.

Paramount Studios
SISTER, SISTER
1998

Entertainment Weekly proclaimed *Sister, Sister* "...a situation comedy featuring charming real-life twin sisters Tia and Tamera Mowry... The twins are glowingly likable..."

In 1998, *Sister, Sister* was the first Warner Brother series to hit a landmark 100 episodes. It also launched its off-net syndication that year. Cast and crew included the Emmy award-winning executive producer, Suzanne de Passe, the series stars identical twins Tamera and Tia Mowry, Emmy award-winning actress Jackee Harry and veteran comedy actor and producer Tim Reid.

Sister, Sister's debut season on The Warner Brothers Television Network in 1993 quickly established the sitcom as the #1 comedy program on the network bringing unprecedented double-digit shares among teens and kids for the first time ever.

Sister, Sister won its time period among kids and ranked #2 among teens in both its Wednesday time slots during the 1997/98 season. Further, *Sister, Sister* established itself as one of the few prime time series which promoted and encouraged family values. The series continued to chronicle such realistic and mature issues as the college sorority and fraternity rush, relationships, etc.

Rick Hawkins (*The Wayan's Brothers, Mama's Family*), who serves as *Sister, Sister's* executive producer along with Suzanne de Passe and Suzanne Coston, explained in 1998, "This season will continue to focus on the growth of each individual character and how their progress has changed the dynamic of the family."

Sister, Sister captured the hearts of audiences in the pilot episode when identical twins Tamera (Tamera Mowry) and Tia (Tia Mowry) explained how they came to live together as one family. Viewers have continued to watch the sisters grow into mature young women and very close friends, and in 1998 the twins went away to college.

The changes in the script and the addition of the college called for new props. Set designers decided that the newly invented college hang-out and Student's store could use the boost of some compatible artwork and voilà they turned to Gold's *Blackware* Ceramics and *Jazz Musicians* to dress up the set.

Ceramics from the *Blackware* series were tucked away in the bookshelves in the Student's Store, and prints from Gold's series of *Jazz Musicians* including Duke Ellington, Cab Calloway, Annette Washington, Thelonious Monk among others, produced in conjunction with the *Harlem Renaissance* show at the Los Angeles County Museum of Art were hung on the walls of the hang-out where students retreated for a much needed break.

Sister, Sister had a 1999 off-network launch in 32 of the top 35 markets representing 70% of the country.

Sister, Sister is a de Passe Entertainment Production in association with Paramount Network Television and is taped before a live studio audience at the Paramount Studios in Hollywood. The Paramount Television Group is part of the entertainment operations of Viacom Inc..

TRIBUTE TO MILT HINTON
1999

Actress, teacher and jazz singer Cynthia Baldessare a.k.a. Cynthia Henderson acted as Gold's emissary to gift a collection of jazz musician prints to legend-ary bassist, Milt Hinton.

Baldessare and her son Justin spent the day with Milt Hinton and his wife, Mona, talking about art and listening to music while going through the portfolio of jazz musicians which included Hinton. He was fascinated by the variety of musicians portrayed and appreciated the private art show too.

Cynthia Henderson

Without Him

Baldessare recently recorded a jazz album titled *Without Him*. The CD was released on the Cloister Recordings label in 2000. It was produced by E.J. Gold, engineered by Oz Fritz & Jimmi Accardi, and recorded at Union Label Studios.
Photo by Douglass-Truth

Bassist Milt Hinton was among the dozens of jazz musicians Gold has paid tribute to over the years with his numerous pastel portaits which have been translated into prints.

Milt Hinton print on Arches paper by E.J. Gold.

Baldessare found a home for the Duke Ellington Jazz print at the Duke Ellington School in Manhattan where it now hangs beside the official school plaque.

GALLERY ARCTURUS
TORONTO
GESTURE IN BLACK
April 23- May 30, 2001

Arcturus Gallery director James Anthony visits with Gold.

...everything seems connected

events occur at the same

moment we happen to think

of them; external extensions

of our moods and thoughts,

we are so attuned to events

that we seem to be creating

them in the moment.

E.J. Gold
Life in the Labyrinth

Another dazzling show at Gallery Arcturus where E.J. Gold's charcoals are regularly shown to the delight of visitors who recognize his talent for this medium. Gold credits his teacher, master Rico Lebrun, for his powerful and bold use of shading.

GESTURE IN BLACK

E.J. Gold
charcoals on paper

February 10 – April 14, 2001
view exhibition at www.arcturus.ca

Gallery Arcturus
80 Gerrard St. E., Toronto, ON M5B 1G6
Tel. (416) 977-3207 Fax. (416) 977-2966
E-mail: cjh-ed@arcturus.ca

Tues.–Fri 12 noon – 5:30 pm, Sat 11 am – 5:30 pm

THE FOUNDATION FOR THE STUDY OF OBJECTIVE ART

March 18, 2001   **Art**   Tandem / Corriere Canadese   Page 15

Arcturus gestural treasures

Art Gallery offers up new classical experimental works

by Donna Lypchuk

Tucked away in a Heritage Home between renovated warehouse buildings at Church and Gerrard you will find Gallery Arcturus — a non-profit exhibition space dedicated to contemporary art. Funded by The Foundation for the Study of Objective Art this pleasant, well-lit space is an off-beat and charming surprise considering that it is located so far away from the galleries clustered along Queen Street and Yorkville.

Currently on display are two very interesting shows, which fall into the category of what I would call "classic experimental" art. Both exhibitions were put together by Arcturus curator Cathy Stilo, with an eye to educating both students and the general public about the often misunderstood genre of gestural art. You can see gestural drawings and paintings anywhere in any gallery in Toronto, but rarely do you see it done well.

One space is devoted to a series of charcoal drawings by American artist E.J. Gold. A member of the infamous California Nine, a guerilla artist group of the sixties, Gold's main claim to fame were his "soft and breathing" sculptures. This solo exhibit called *Gesture In Black* features a series of line drawings — all portraits done in charcoal of women's heads.

This tight, glossy show of 14 works clearly demonstrates the Reductivist approach to drawing: stark and spontaneously drawn lines are used to express the subtleties of mood and character. Anyone who is interested in gestural drawing will definitely benefit from taking a look at this show. The first seven works have a flair about them that reminds me of Matisse.

These works are very minimalist and rely on the blackness of the paper to express depth and definition. In a drawing such as "Metaduc," for instance, the artist uses very few strokes of charcoal to express the sly character of a man hiding

From E.J. Gold's *Gesture in Black* exhibit.

behind a cape.

The second seven works in the show are more violent in style. Several of the works raucously rape the style of Picasso complete with asymmetrical eyes, bullish noses and trapezoid-shaped faces. This is one of the best appropriations of Picasso's truncated cartoonish perspectives that I have ever encountered in a gallery, and is not surprising coming from such a creative chameleon such as Gold who has created thousands of paintings, drawings and sculpture since the sixties.

He is also one of the few artists who can pull this off with authenticity, as he was part of the retro-cubist movement that was all the rage back then and is becoming all the rage again.

In the second gallery, art teacher and Arcturus artist-in-residence Deborah Harris presents 10 large gestural portraits

called *Angels in Procession*. Created largely from oil and collage, curator Cathy Stilo notes that "each Christmas for the past 10 years Deborah has, in her own words, been delivered an angel."

These figures emerge in the form of a collage each with its own unique gesture and character. The works in this show range from the figurative, such as her bloody and brownish portrait of a red angel squatting with her back to the viewer to the completely abstract, such as her portrait of a greenish angel, who emerges merely as a pair of eyes in a lime green colour field.

One astounding collage features the angel completely splintered and fragmented into landscape filled with body parts, and yet another features an icon-like angel, kneeling and coloured with the classic golds and browns you would find in a traditional religious painting.

This exhibition represents a very earnest attempt to detail the elusive nature of other-worldly spirits. Unlike Gold's show, it is not very cohesive or united by a singular purposeful style. However, that is what is unique about it. Harris shows how the content of a painting can dictate its style, as opposed to being dictated by the eccentricities or limitations of the talent behind it.

Both of these exhibitions offer the viewer a lot of food for thought about how gesture can be used to create portraits. Ultimately, both artists fragment and reduce their subjects to find an essence; one using a few broad strokes and the other using collage. Both are extremely well-versed when it comes to expressing spontaneity and authenticity in their visual language.

This is refreshing in a gallery scene full of unmapped mimics who can't grasp the importance of gesture. ◆

Gesture in Black and Angels in Procession are being shown at Arcturus Gallery, 80 Gerrard St. E., 416-977-1077 Until April 14

ALPHA GALLERY
GRASS VALLEY
ANNUAL STUDIO TOUR:
Recent Works
2001

In the month of October, the Nevada County Arts Council has a tradition of setting up studio tours to the numerous artists' studios in a county which has become famous as an art haven. Gold's paintings were selected to be hung in the Alpha Gallery along with a few other artists, including Douglass Truth and Tom X of the Grass Valley Graphics Group.

The front page of the local newspaper carried a large color picture of the gallery installation featuring a few of Gold's offerings.

WYNTON MARSALIS CONCERT
JAZZ ART
November, 2001

Wynton Marsalis, Ted Nash and Wycliffe Gordon are towered by Gold's huge Monumentals of jazz musicians.

"The Jazz Art exhibit created by the collaborative artists of the Grass Valley Graphics Group was the perfect visual compliment to the music of Wynton Marsalis -- a dynamic and stunning feature in the event's presentation of jazz as a purely American art form."

Michael C. McGahan
Editor
Art Matters

WYNTON MARSALIS CONCERT
GRASS VALLEY
JAZZ ART
November, 2001

"...It's like a dream I have of really integrated arts."
Wynton Marsalis

The Marsalis event was a huge success. Newspaper articles abounded. Robbert Trice of the Grass Valley Graphics Group was one of the few individuals who had the opportunity to interview Marsalis between his performances. The interview was published in *Art Matters* which was replete with Gold's art in the background.

The *Monumental* paintings by E.J. Gold are clearly visible on the stage where Marsalis performed to a sold out audience for all three performances.

"This gig is extremely hip. I've never been in a place like this before-- where the music is with things like the art...This was beautiful. It made the space a whole lot more alive! Jazz, jazz themes, different styles of everybody's art...a feeling of community where everybody is coming together in a meaningful way. This is something that surely should happen more."
Wynton Marsalis

Portrait of Wynton Marsalis as a huge 10'x6' *Monumental* that was one of five such paintings to grace the stage.

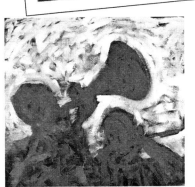

ALPHA GALLERY
GRASS VALLEY
JAZZ ART
December, 2001

The Nevada County Arts Council had the innovative idea of combining art and music in this unprecedented event and turned to the Grass Valley Graphics Group to paint a show in record time. After the concerts, it was a natural to move the art into the huge Alpha Gallery which coincidentally was available at the time. The show received rave reviews from jazz and art lovers alike and will now go on tour throughout the country. The next stops appear to be the Jazz School in Berkeley and, the California Museum of African American Art in Los Angeles with several other museums in queue.

ALPHA GALLERY
JAZZ ART
December, 2001

The installation of the *Jazz Art* exhibit required a huge space and the Alpha Gallery was just perfect for it. The expanse gave lots of breathing room for the large canvases, many of which were free-standing in typical *Monumental* style. The exhibit took place during local holiday festivities with throngs of visitors streaming through. Many commented that they had been to the concert and were delighted to have another chance to view the art.

WESTERN PLEIN-AIR WORKSHOP
Master Art Class
2002

Douglass Truth has been an enthusiastic attendee from the beginning of these classes.

Grass Valley Graphics Group artist Lin Larsen has enjoyed and benefitted from the class immensely.

The *Western Plein-Air Workshop* started as a Sunday art class for professional artists and members of the Grass Valley Graphics Group, several of whom have had very little formal art training. Held at first in the artist's home, the space quickly became too cramped for the ever-growing number of eager attendees and was moved to his larger studio.

The word soon got out and attracted more and more friends to the acclaimed class. In fact, FCAT, the local cable TV network has made its appearance at the class and hopes to videotape it for a wider local audience with a view toward national syndication.

Photos by Aviko

WESTERN PLEIN-AIR WORKSHOP
Master Art Class
2002

Photos by Aviko

The Western Plein-Air Workshop began in the artist's home, then moved to his studio and finally was forced to move to a larger public space which could accommodate the ever-growing number of enthusiastic students.

University of Niagara Film Department
FLOATING WORLD
February 2002

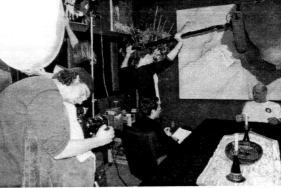

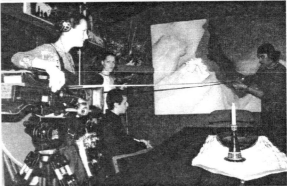

Photos courtesy: University of Niagara Film Dept.

In February 2002, a production team from Niagara University flew out to California in order to interview Gold and Samadhi Tank owners, Glenn and Lee Perry, for a documentary film about Gold's late friend, Dr. John Lilly. Gold and Lilly co-authored the popular *Tanks for the Memories*, a book about the floatation tank.

The crew included director Greg Virc, Producer / boom, Kathryn Kennedy, DOP, Ryan Shaw, Cameraman, Matt Van Allen, Sound engineer, Jenn Godin and Professor Andrew Stevenson.

The film titled *Floating World* is currently in production and slated for release later in 2002.

SIERRA HEALTH FOUNDATION
SACRAMENTO
THE HEALING POWER OF ART
May-July 2002

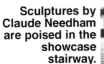

This show offered a selection of works from a few members of the Grass Valley Graphics Group which has maintained, since its inception, that art is not an ordinary activity but one that connects to a larger whole that benefits both the artist creating the work and the viewer observing the artwork.

Sculptures by Claude Needham are poised in the showcase stairway.

The connection to healing esthetics is a doorway to subtle energies that nourish our higher etheric bodies and thus impart to our physical bodies their beneficial effects. Art is therefore a profoundly healing activity for both the generative and receptive participants. Zoe Alowan stands radiantly by her painting at the show.

It is a credit to modern holistic medicine that this once visionary viewpoint is now accepted as part of everyday medical practice, just as now we know that laughter is, indeed, the best medicine and the harmonization of one's environment — as portrayed in the traditional art of Feng-Shui — magnetizes the forces of healing.

The sprawling exhibit space where the art is hung for thousands of visitors to see.

H. HEATHER EDELMAN GALLERY

New York
STREETS OF NEW YORK
June-July 2002

Views of the H. Heather Edelman Gallery from the street.

The H. Heather Edelman Gallery moved to the Chelsea area where many galleries have taken up residence following the shifting tides of location, location, location.

In June 2002, Gold had a show at the H. Heather Edelman Gallery featuring his most recent paintings depicting the streets of New York. This theme is a double favorite for Gold: he has created many street scenes in general and, being a native New Yorker, he has, over the years, returned pictorially to many favorite spots he has frequented. Like many artists, he paints mostly from memory and often refers to *Carlson's Guide to Landscape Painting* and his chapter aptly titled *Painting from Memory.*

Chronology

EUGENE JEFFREY GOLD
1941-

ONE MAN SHOWS / GROUP SHOWS

2002	H. Heather Edelman, New York, *Jazz Art*, October
2002	Vorous Space, Sacramento, *Odalisques and Other Recent Works*, October
2002	California Museum of African Art, Santa Monica, *Jazz Art*, Fall
2002	H. Heather Edelman, New York, *Streets of New York*, June 5 - July 31
2002	Sierra Festival of the Arts, Nevada County Arts Council, Grass Valley, May
2002	Sierra Health Foundation, Sacramento, *Art as Healing, Landscapes from The Grass Valley Graphics Group,* Group Show, April-July
2001	Alpha Gallery, Grass Valley, *Jazz Art,* art from the Wynton Marsalis Concert, Nov. 30 - Dec. 23
2001	Veteran's Hall, Grass Valley, *Wynton Marsalis Concert*, Stage Design with Monumental paintings, Nov. 23-24
2001	Alpha Gallery, Grass Valley, *Open House with Studio Tours,* October
2001	Gallery Arcturus, *Gesture in Black,* February 10 - April 14
1999-2000	Los Angeles Country Museum of Art, Los Angeles, *Harlem Renaissance*, Jazz Musician prints, traveling show
1999	Gallery Arcturus, *Life in the Labyrinth,* November 4 - December 24
1998	Gallery Arcturus, *Bardo Tours*, Sept. 10 - Oct. 17
1998	Gallery Arcturus, *My Other Self*, April 23 - May 30, Group Show with the Grass Valley Graphics Group
1998	Mad River Post, Los Angeles, *Recent Paintings and Sculptures,* Grass Valley Graphics Group, March 12 - July 12
1997-98	Mad River Post, San Francisco, *Recent Paintings and Sculptures*, Grass Valley Graphics Group, Nov. 20 - March 1
1997	Gallery Arcturus, Toronto, *Slightly Off the Wall*, Group Show, Sept. 3-27
1997	Gallery Arcturus, Toronto, *Large as Life*, July 30 - August 30
1997	Gallery Arcturus, Toronto, *Out of Time*, April 16 - May 17
1997	Blue Ladder Gallery, Chicago, *Dreaming Women on a Journey*, November 1 - November 30
1997	Soho Gallery, Vancouver, *Works on Canvas & Paper, from the Art School of Reductionism*, June 15 - August 15
1997	Taf's Gallery, *Art & Soul*, Vancouver, March 2 - March 30
1996	Blue Ladder Gallery, Chicago, *Post-Pop Visions of the Veil*, October - December
1996	Blue Ladder Gallery, Chicago, *Post-Pop Visions of the Veil*, Sept. 5-Oct. 31
1996	The Unicorn Gallery, Chicago, *Art & Soul*, June 10-July 7
1996	Ann Nathan Gallery, Chicago, *Art & Soul*, June 8 -9
1996	Artisans on Ward, Nelson, B.C., *Art & Soul*, May 2 - May 31
1996	Essential Art Gallery, New York, *Art & Soul*, April 15 - April 31
1996	Unison Arts Center, New Paltz, *Art & Soul*, An Explosion of Post-Pop Paintings, March 3 - March 31
1996	Gallery Arcturus, Toronto, *Inner Spaces,* Oct. 15 - December 14
1996	Gallery Arcturus, Toronto, *Hidden Dominions*, Works on canvas and paper, Feb. 3 - April 27
1995	Gallery 6161, Lofty Productions/Hollywood Arts Council, *Feast for the Senses,* with the Grass Valley Graphics Group, October
1995	The Museum Store, Los Angeles, *Post-Pop & the Grass Valley Graphics Group,* October 20 - December 31

1995	Foundation for the Study of Objective Art, Toronto, *Master in Black*, Nov. 15 - Jan. 31
1995	Images Gallery, Nevada City, *E.J. Gold's Post-Pop*, Nov. 3 - Feb. 25
1995	Cappuccino Gallery, Penn Valley, *Between Boundaries*, July 8 - October 15
1994	Gump's, San Francisco, *Ceramics*
1994	Carr & Associates, San Francisco, *Ceramics*
1994	Tesoro's, Los Angeles, *Ceramics*
1994	Gallery of Functional Art, Los Angeles, *Moonbeam*, May 14 - June 30
1994	Artworks Gallery, Vancouver, *Moonbeam*, April 5-15
1994	Workspace Gallery, New Paltz, *School of Reductionism*, Feb. - March
1994	Richmond Gallery, Vancouver, *Moonbeam,* a collaboration of poetry & art, Nov. 18-29
1993	Webster's, New York, *Monumental Figures*
1993	Helen Jones Gallery, Sacramento, *Strokes of Genius*, with the Grass Valley Graphics Group
1993	Art Expo '93, Jacob Javits Center, New York, *Houses of Imagination*, H. Heather Edelman Gallery
1992-93	H. Heather Edelman Gallery, New York, *Lecture on Nothing* with the writings of John Cage and paintings by E.J. Gold
1992	Apocalypse Gallery, Vancouver, *School of Reductionism*, Group Show with the Grass Valley Graphics Group, Nov.
1992	Labyrinth Gallery, Sacramento, *Group Show*
1992	In-Between Gallery, Hollywood, *Life Is a Carnival*
1992	Nardin Fine Arts, Cross River, CT, *E.J.Gold*
1992	River's Edge Gallery, Amherst, MA, *More Gold,* curated by Amherst Fine Art Associates
1992	State Street Gallery, New Haven, CT, *Group Show*
1992	Jacob Javits Center, *Art Expo '92*, New York
1992	Troov Gallery, Brooklyn, *Moonbeam,* a collaboration with Harry Nilsson
1992	Cedar Tavern, New York, *The Old Cedar Bar,* a collaboration with Margaret Randall curated by Troov Gallery
1992	Ashley-Craig Gallery, Venice, *Monumentals,* Group show with members of the Grass Valley Graphics Group
1992	Beverly Plaza Hotel, Los Angeles, *Monumental Landscapes,* Group show with members of the Grass Valley Graphics Group
1992	Mad River Productions, Los Angeles, *Anima Terra,* Group Show curated by Nancy Sadler
1992	Galleri Tonne, Oslo, Norway, *Monumenter*
1992	Naropa Institute Visual Arts Gallery, Boulder, *Bardo Visions*
1992	The National Center for Atmospheric Research (NCAR), Boulder, *Worlds in Fusion*
1992	University of Colorado, Boulder, *Crazy Wisdom Conference*
1992	Keith Fields Fine Art, Fremont, *E.J. Gold*
1992	Charles Jones, Cincinnati, *E.J. Gold,* Permanent Display
1991	Wilshire-San Vicente Plaza, Beverly Hills, *Works on Paper and Multiples,* Reductionist installation, curated by Andy Kenyon, Oct.
1991	Thunderbear Gallery, Santa Fe, *Group Show*
1991	Windsor-Betts Gallery, Santa Fe, *Permanent display*
1991	DataCorp, Isi As, Oslo, Norway, *Odalisques*
1991	Galleri Aktuell Kunst, Oslo, Norway, *Group Show*
1991	Hidden Images Studio, Boulder, *Macrodimensional Visions*
1991	Matthias Schossig Gallery, Berlin, Germany, *Neue Arbeiten*
1991	Amherst Art Associates, Amherst, *Recent Works*
1991	Blue Creek West Gallery, Denver, *Works on Paper,* Group Show
1991	Weir Gallery, Berkeley, *War & Peace,* Group Show
1991	Sergei Diaghilev Art Centre, Leningrad, *USA-USSR,* Group Show
1991	Estonia, *USA-USSR,* Group Show
1991	The Ukraine, *USA-USSR,* Group Show
1991	Bucharest, Romania, *USA-USSR,* Group Show
1991	Latvia, *USA-USSR,* Group Show
1991	Museum of Ancient & Modern Art, Penn Valley, *Rhythm & Movement,* a livre d'artiste
1991	Shayna Fine Art, Sacramento, *Permanent display*
1991	Keith Fields Fine Arts, Fremont, *Group Show*
1990	Peninsula Gallery, Palos Verdes, *Contemporary Creations,* Group Show
1990-91	Charles Jones, Cincinnati, *E.J. Gold, Macrodimensional Artist*
1990	Landsbanken As, Oslo, Norway, *E.J. Gold, Odalisques*
1990	Rod Goodwin, Sacramento, *The Goodwin Show*, with the Grass Valley Graphics Group
1990	Peter Heineman Fine Arts, Denver, *Dark Hours*
1990	Kreditkassen, Oslo, Norway, *Odalisques*
1990	Emrose Art Corporation, Albertson, *Corridors*
1990	Thunderbear Gallery, Santa Fe, *Group Show*
1990	Yesternow Gallery, Fremont, *E.J. Gold,* October 31

1990   Kimber Woods Tennis Club, Fremont, *E.J. Gold,* October 25
1990   Printemps, Denver, *Experimental Lithographs by E.J. Gold*
1989-90 Galleri Albin Up, Oslo, Norway, *Group Show*
1989   Galleri Heiberg, Oslo, Norway, *The White Folio*
1989   Misty Harbour Gallery, Cape Cod, *Gold Presents Gold*
1989   Cathy Inslee Gallery, Mannheim, *Group Show*
1989   Michael J. McDonnell, Santa Rosa, *Group Show*
1989   Fifth Ave. Gallery, Nevada City, *The Mayan Lady & Other Recent Works*
1989   Connell Foundation for the Fine Arts, East Haven, *Portraits*
1989   Hoho Gallery, Holyoke, *Artists in Resonance: Nona Hatay & E.J. Gold*
1989   Cafe Olsen, Oslo, Norway, The Livre d'Artiste
1989   Amherst Art Associates, Amherst, *Recent Works*
1989   Fifth Ave. Gallery, Nevada City, *Recent Works*
1989   Quintessence, Vancouver, B.C., *E.J. Gold: Works on Paper and Multiples*
1989   Thunderbear Gallery, Santa Fe, *Works on Paper*
1989   Gian Piero Cara Gallery, Rome, Italy, *Olio su tela*
1989   Emrose Art Corporation, Albertson, *E.J. Gold, Recent Oils*
1988   Connell Foundation for the Fine Arts, East Haven, CT, *Form and Color,* Group Show
1988   Amherst Art Associates, Amherst, *Odalisques*
1988   Peter Heineman Fine Arts, Denver, *Behind the Mirror*
1988   Spiral Gallery, Los Angeles, *Inside Outside*
1988-89 Peter Heineman Fine Arts, Denver, *Dimensional Tweak*
1988   Fifth Ave. Gallery, Nevada City, *Safe from the Rain*
1988   Isis Unlimited, Beverly Hills, *Gold at Isis:* Bronze Sculpture & Gold Jewelry
1988   Salon des Artistes, New York, *The Dark Hours*
1988   Galleri Heiberg, Oslo, Norway, *Odalisques*
1988   Thornes Marketplace, Northampton, *Group Show*
1988   Coleman-Greene Gallery, New York, *Recent Works on Paper*
1988   Grafin Gallery, Pasadena, *The Nude*
1988   Connell Foundation for the Fine Arts, East Haven, *The Dark Hours*
1988   EAC Gallery, Albertson, *Pure Gold*
1988   Fifth Ave. Gallery, Nevada City, *Odalisques*
1988   Amherst Art Associates, Amherst, *Pure Gesture,* Pastels by E.J. Gold
1988   Spiral Gallery, Los Angeles, *City Scapes*
1988   Schossig Gallery, Berlin, Germany, E.J. Gold, *Neue Arbeiten auf Papier*
1987   Hilton Hotel, Santa Fe, *Group Show*
1987   Galerie Matrix, New York, *E.J. Gold*
1987   Connell Foundation for the Fine Arts, East Haven, *Recent Acquisitions*
1987   Spiral Gallery, West Los Angeles, *Charcoals*
1987   Coleman-Greene Gallery, New York, *Works on Paper*
1987   Museum of Ancient & Modern Art, Nevada City, *Expressionist Landscapes*
1987   Grafin Gallery, Pasadena, *Dimensions in Art*
1987   Fifth Ave. Gallery, Nevada City, *Retrospective*
1987   Amherst Art Associates, Amherst, *Gold's Dancers*
1987   Panda East, Amherst, *Odalisques*
1986   Spiral Gallery, West Los Angeles, *Ink Washes*
1986   Fifth Ave. Gallery, Nevada City, *Recent Gouaches*
1983   Coleman-Greene Gallery, New York, *Workshop*
1976-74 Los Angeles, *Photographic Essays: Bardo Spaces*
1975   Forest Lawn, Los Angeles, *Gurdjieff Memorial Service*
1973   Carnegie Hall, New York, *The Shakti Experience*
1972   Happening, Los Angeles, *First Annual Hollywood Follies*
1970   Sy Amber, Hollywood, Performance Art, *Living Window Dressing*
1970   Elysian Park, Los Angeles, *Love-In*
1970   Santa Anna, *Love-In*
1970   Long Beach, *Love-In*
1969   Robert Comara Gallery, Los Angeles, *Group Show:* Shiro Ikegawa, Max Cole, Robert Hansen, Jeff Gold, Vic Smith, Roger Bruinekool, William Bradshaw, Jack Stuck, Suzuki
1969   The Gemini, Las Palmas, Los Angeles, *The Mystic Vision*
1969   California Federal Bldg. Wilshire Blvd, Los Angeles, Fellowship of the Ancient Mind
1969   Cosmo Street, Hollywood, *Vietnam Memorial*
1969   Happening, Hollywood, *The Cage Concert*
1969   Happening, Los Angeles, *The Great California Earthquake*
1969   Happening, Los Angeles, *Saints Rights Activists*
1969   Magical Mystery Museum, Hollywood, *Installations:* The Fake Mummy Mervin, The Vanishing Monks

Illusion, The Seance Room, The Davenport Spirit Cabinet, The Wyrd Sisters, The I-Ching Wheel, Hollywood Hooker

1969	Happening, Los Angeles, *Stele of Revealing*
1969	Happening, Los Angeles, *Meeting of Magical Minds*
1969	Happening, Los Angeles, *The New Kabbalah*
1968	Houston Fine Arts Museum, Houston, *California 9*
1968	Artisan Gallery, Houston, *California 9*
1968	Long Beach Museum, Long Beach, *California 9*
1968	Santa Barbara Museum, Santa Barbara, *California 9*
1968	The Gemini, Las Palmas, Hollywood, *Dimensions*
1968	Happening, *The Omnibus,* Hollywood, (with J.U.St. Michael)
1968	Robert Comara Gallery, Los Angeles, *Group Show:* Robert Hansen, Max Cole, Shiro Ikegawa, Jack Stuck, Suzuki, Vic Smith, Roger Bruinekool, William Bradshaw
1968	Robert Comara Gallery, Los Angeles, *Gold at Comara*
1968	Happening, Hollywood, *Green Power Be-In: Feed the Hippies*
1968	Palladium, *Psychic Fair*
1967	Los Angeles, *Back to the Egg,* A Satire on the Krishna Movement
1967	The Gemini, Las Palmas, Hollywood, *Super-Natural*
1967	Happening, Los Angeles, *Earth Day* (with Bea Stanley as the Earth Mother)
1967	Robert Comara Gallery, Los Angeles, *Life Forms; Kinetic Objects*
1967	Happening, MacArthur Park, Los Angeles, Lou Shaw's *MacBird* with Linus Pauling & Phil Bruns
1967-69	Hollywood Wax Museum, Hollywood, *Performance Art* with Bobby Shields
1967	Pierce Gallery, *E. J. Gold Retrospective: 1951-64*
1966-67	Aquarius Theatre, Los Angeles, *Rockathon*
1966-67	Spectrum 2000, Los Angeles
1966-67	The Store, Sunset Strip
1966	Robert Comara Gallery, Los Angeles, *Movable Feast*
1966	Robert Comara Gallery, Los Angeles, *Breathers*
1965	Robert Comara Gallery, Los Angeles, CA, *Group Show:* Max Cole, Shiro Ikegawa, Robert Hanson, Ed Keinholz, Jack Stuck, Jeff Gold, Suzuki
1965	Robert Comara Gallery, Los Angeles, *Softies*
1965	Otis Gallery, Los Angeles, CA, *Permanent Collection*
1959	Julliard, New York, NY, *Multi-Media Show*
1953-56	Woodstock Art Students' League, Woodstock, *Summer Fair*
1948-49	Museum of Modern Art, New York, *Children's Art Carnival*
1952	Museum of Modern Art, New York, *Children's Art Carnival*

BACKGROUND: Art History

2001-02 Western Plein-Air Workshop, Penn Valley, Founder/Instructor
1969-70 Instructor, Otis Art Institute
1964-65 Otis Art Institute, Los Angeles
1964-65 Arthur Ames, Otis, Los Angeles, Instructor
1964-65 John C. Braun, Otis, Los Angeles, Instructor
1964-65 Edmund Carpenter, Otis, Los Angeles, Design Instructor
1964-65 Samuel Clayberger, Otis, Los Angeles, Drawing, Painting & Design
1964-65 William Enking, Otis, Los Angeles, Oriental Art History
1964-65 Renzo Fenci, Otis, Los Angeles, Sculpture Instructor & Dept. Head
1964-65 Harry Finestone, Otis, Los Angeles, Instructor
1964-65 Joe Funk, Otis, Los Angeles, Instructor, Graphics & Design
1964-65 Bob Glover, Otis, Los Angeles, Instructor, 3-D Design
1964-65 David Green, Otis, Los Angeles, Instructor, Carpentry, Art, Plumbing & Mechanics
1964-65 Rico Lebrun, Otis, Los Angeles, Instructor
1964-65 Bentley Schaad, Otis, Los Angeles, Painting Instructor
1964-65 Millard Sheets, Los Angeles, Instructor
1964-65 Tom Van Sant, Otis, Los Angeles, Instructor
1964-65 Helen Watson, Otis, Los Angeles, Instructor
1964-65 Charles White III, Otis, Los Angeles, Instructor
1964-65 Alan Zaslove, Otis, Los Angeles, Drawing Instructor
1964-66 Fritz Schwaderer, Los Angeles
1964-65 Gutai School of Art, Japan
1961-64 Rico Lebrun, Los Angeles
1961-64 Russell Cangialosi, Los Angeles City College, Sculpture Instructor

1958-60 Franz Kline, New York
1958-59 George Rosenberg, New York, mentor
1953-56 Isamu Noguchi, Woodstock, family friend
1952-55 Ben Shahn, New York, family friend

BOOKS WRITTEN BY E.J. GOLD:

2001	*The Great Adventure* (illustrated by author), Gateways Books and Tapes
2001	*The Great Laws,* Gateways Books and Tapes
2000	*American Book of the Dead*, celebrating 25 years in print (illustrated by author), Gateways Books and Tapes
1997	*Angels Healing Journey* (illustrated by Tom X), Gateways Books and Tapes
1996	*Book of Sacraments* (illustrated by author), Gateways Books and Tapes
1995	*The American Book of the Dead,* Harper SanFrancisco
1994	*The Lost Works* (illustrated with photos by author), Gateways Books and Tapes
1993	*Virtual Reality Gamester's Manual #1:* Solstice
1993	*Virtual Reality Gamester's Manual #2:* Zelda
1991	*Hidden Work* (illustrated by author), Gateways Books and Tapes
1991	*Man On the Cross,* Gateways Books and Tapes
1989	*Practical Work On Self* (illustrated by author), Gateways Books and Tapes
1989	*Seven Bodies of Man* (illustrated by author), Gateways Books and Tapes
1989	*Visions in the Stone, Journey to the Source of Hidden Knowledge* (illustrated by author), Gateways Books and Tapes
1987	*Objective Art* (illustrated by author), Gateways Books and Tapes
1987	*Triad,* Gateways Books and Tapes
1986	*Life in the Labyrinth* (illustrated by author), Gateways Books and Tapes
1986	*Manifesto of Reductionism* (pamphlet, co-authored) Heidelberg Editions International
1986	*Creation Story Verbatim,* Gateways Books and Tapes, a story and a play
1986	*Songs My Dead Mother Sang Me,* Gateways Books and Tapes
1985	*Human Biological Machine as a Transformational Apparatus* (illustrated by author), Gateways Books and Tapes
1983	*Lazy Man's Guide to Death & Dying,* Gateways Books and Tapes
1983	*Redfin,* Gateways Books and Tapes
1982	*Brother Godfrey's Journal,* Gateways Books and Tapes
1981	*Labyrinth Reader's Course,* Gateways Books and Tapes
1979	*Baa Baa Black Sheep* or *The Black Sheep Massacree,* Gateways Books and Tapes
1979	*Child's Guide to the Real World,* Gateways Books and Tapes
1978	*Nimbus,* Gateways Books and Tapes
1978	*Joy of Sacrifice,* Gateways Books and Tapes
1977	*A Child's Guide to Altered States,* Gateways Books and Tapes
1977	*Autobiography of a Sufi,* Gateways Books and Tapes
1976	*Journeys to Inaccessible Monasteries,* Gateways Books and Tapes
1976	*Movements Workbook,* Gateways Books and Tapes
1975	*Science of Objective Hypnotism,* Gateways Books and Tapes
1975	*Gabriel Papers,* Gateways Books and Tapes
1975	*Tales of the Mexican Sufis,* Gateways Books and Tapes
1974	*Holy Hobo Handbook,* Gateways Books and Tapes
1973	*Shakti: The Gestalt of Zap,* Gateways Books and Tapes
1972	*Work of Groups,* Gateways Books and Tapes
1969	*Autobiography of God*
1968	*Villains from Vega IV*, H.L. Gold & E.J. Gold

SATIRE:

1988	*It's Murder in Here*
1978	*Brother Godfrey's Journal,* Gateways Books and Tapes
1967	*Creation Story Verbatim,* Gateways Books and Tapes
1967	*Hare Chickenah, Back to the Egg,* Satire on Krishna Movement
1966	*Vampire Rose*
1965	*Back to the Egg,* Satire on Krishna Movement
1964	*Jump, God, Jump*

COMEDY:

1985   *Lazy Man's Guide to Death & Dying*, Gateways Books and Tapes
1978   *Juan Tepozton*, Gateways Books and Tapes
1978   *Tales of the Jewish Sufis*, Gateways Books and Tapes
1975   *Gabriel Papers*, Gateways Books and Tapes
1975   *Tales of the Mexican Sufis*, Gateways Books and Tapes

SCIENCE FICTION AND FANTASY:

2003   *Dark Storm*, E.J. Gold, Gateways Books and Tapes
2002   *Dark Side Dream Walker*, E.J. Gold, Gateways Books and Tapes
1999   *How To Get Yourself Abducted*, E.J. Gold, Gateways Books and Tapes
1995   *I, Vampire, Interviews with the Undead*, Collected Stories, edited by Jean Stine and Forrest J Ackerman, Longmeadow Press
1979   *Heimie the Barbarian*, E.J. Gold
1975   *The Glass Wall*, E.J. Gold, Gateways Books and Tapes
1968   *Villains from Vega IV*, H.L. Gold & E.J. Gold
1967   *The Torso Affair*, co-authored with H.L. Gold
1966   *Schmuckslayer*, E.J. Gold
1964-65 *Joy of the Leopard*, E.J. Gold
1963   *Tork Travelling Trousers*, for Ralph Benner.

PAMPHLETS:

Over 75 pamphlets on as many subjects. Mostly written between 1965 and 1980; 1990 on. Many of these have been lost.

2000   *How to Become a Powerseller: The Online Auction Bible*, Insane Investor
1976   *Psyche and Essence, The Nature and Construction*
1976   *Ashram Dharma*
1976   *Family Information Packet for the Church of Thanathology*
1976   *The Song of the Guide*
1974   *A Child's Guide to Altered States of Consciousness*
1974   *A Child's Guide to the Real World*
1974   *A Child's Guide To Prayer*
1974   *Prayers from a Truely Great Tempel*
1974   *A Child's Guide to Transubstantiation*
1974   *The Great Sacred Hymns and Canticles of the Sufi Order*
1974   *The Holy Bugger's Gazette*
1974   *Cosmic Acupuncture*
1974   *The Butterfly of Retribution*
1974   *Dynamic Entity*
1974   *Brother Godfrey's Journal*
1974   *On Group Work*
1974   *The Mala Manual: A manual on the Observation, Cataloguing, and Conscious Direction of the DNA Code Package*
1974   *Table of DNA Code Corrections*
1974   *Brother Judas, The Compassionate Betrayal*
1974   *You Look Somehow Familiar Forever*
1974   *Sacrifices, The Letters of Pir Al-Washi*
1974   *Spontaneous Surrender*
1974   *White-Eyes Medicine Lodge*
1971   *The Creation Story Verbatim*
1971   *The Book of Archetypes*
1971   *The Avatar's Handbook*
1971   *The One Word*

BOOKS AND MAGAZINES ILLUSTRATED BY E.J. GOLD

2002   Art Matters, *Notation, A Few Moments in Time,* George Schroder, Volume 19, Issue 1
2001   Tandem, The "New Mainstream" Lifestyle Weekend Paper, Toronto, *Dark Gestures,* front page illustration, March 18
2001   Tandem, The "New Mainstream" Lifestyle Weekend Paper, Toronto, *Art Gallery Offers Up New Classical Experimental Work,* Donna Lypchuk, March 18
1993-94 *Shared Vision,* Vancouver's Creative Arts and Life Resource Magazine
1992   *Moonbeam,* featuring the poetry of Harry Nilsson
1991   *Lecture on Nothing* from *Silence* by John Cage
1990   *The Old Cedar Bar,* visual and written memoirs, a collaboration with Margaret Randall
1991   *Ennea-type Structures* by Claudio Naranjo, M.D.
1989   *The Golden Buddha Changing Masks* by Mark Olsen
1989   *Society's Problems* by D. Stanley Eitzen (cover), Allyn and Bacon, Simon and Schuster
1988   *Floating* Magazine (cover)
1988   *Radiance Technique Journal* (cover)
1978   *Wings*
1979   *Playwings*
1979   *Better Wings*
1964   *Citadel* (cover)

SCIENCE FICTION CLASSICS ILLUSTRATED BY E.J. GOLD:

2002   *None But Lucifer,* Horace L. Gold, Gateways Retro SF
1994   *E.J. Gold's Guide to the Galaxy and Beyond the Unknown* (Anthology Series), Vol II, Gateways Science Fiction
1994   *Double Whammy,* Fredric Brown, Gateways Science Fiction
1994   *Hell to Pay,* Randall Garrett, Gateways Science Fiction
1994   *I'd Give a Dollar,* Winston Marks, Gateways Science Fiction
1994   *Not According to Dante,* Malcolm Jameson, Gateways Science Fiction
1994   *Sine of the Magus,* James E. Gunn, Gateways Science Fiction
1994   *The Wall Around the World,* Theodore R. Cogswell, Gateways Science Fiction
1994   *Mists of Dawn,* Chad Oliver, Gateways Science Fiction
1992   *E.J. Gold's Guide to the Galaxy and Beyond the Unknown* (Anthology Series), Vol I, Gateways Science Fiction
1992   *Sense of Wonder,* edited by Forrest J Ackerman, Gateways Science Fiction
1992   *Skulking Permit,* Robert Sheckley, Gateways Science Fiction
1992   *Jesus Christs,* A.J. Langguth, Gateways Science Fiction
1992   *Four in One,* Damon Knight, Gateways Science Fiction
1992   *Keep Your Shape,* Robert Sheckley, Gateways Science Fiction
1992   *Satan's Shrine,* Daniel Galouye, Gateways Science Fiction
1992   *We Never Mention Aunt Nora,* Frederik Pohl, Gateways Science Fiction

LIVRES D'ARTISTES:

1993   *A Visitor's Guide to Cosmo Street,* Heidelberg Editions International
1993   *In-a-Gadd'n Aveed'n,* Heidelberg Editions International
1993   *An Abbreviated Practical Guide to the Darkside,* Gateways Books and Tapes
1992   *Faces of War,* Gateways Books and Tapes
1992   *Bardo Visions,* Gateways Books and Tapes
1991   *A Short Waltz Through the Bardos,* Gateways Books and Tapes
1991   *A Pleasant Conversation,* Gateways Books and Tapes
1991   *Abstract Impressions,* Gateways Books and Tapes
1991   *Asylum,* Gateways Books and Tapes
1991   *Dark Hours,* Gateways Books and Tapes
1991   *The Planar Contiguities,* Gateways Books and Tapes
1991   *In Old Greenwich Village,* Gateways Books and Tapes
1991   *La Corrida,* Gateways Books and Tapes
1991   *Mes Voyages,* Gateways Books and Tapes
1991   *The Nude,* Gateways Books and Tapes
1991   *Rhythm & Movement,* Gateways Books and Tapes

1991	*Spirit Photography*, Gateways Books and Tapes
1991	*Views from an Open Casket*, Gateways Books and Tapes
1991	*The Prisoner in the Velvet Mask*, Gateways Books and Tapes
1982	*Juan Tepozton* , Gateways Books and Tapes

BOOKS ABOUT THE ARTIST:

2002	*Master in Black, The Charcoals of E.J. Gold,* Linda Corriveau, Gateways Fine Art
2002	*More Color... Less Soul, The Photobiography of E.J. Gold,* Linda Corriveau, Gateways Fine Art
1998	*A Visual Tour of the Art of E.J. Gold*, Linda Corriveau, Gateways Fine Art
1993	*The White House Commemorative Folio*, a visual narrative of the White House art adventure, Barbara Haynes, Gateways Fine Art
1990	*Pure Gesture, an Introduction to the Gestural Work of E.J. Gold,* including a Catalogue of over one hundred gestural works on paper and paintings, including pastels, charcoals, ink washes, acrylics, and oils, with an Essay by Linda Corriveau, Gateways Fine Art
1988	*Miro's Dream,* Drawings by E.J. Gold, Poetry by Iven Lourie, Commentary by Linda Corriveau, Gateways Fine Art

FOREIGN LANGUAGE EDITIONS:

2002	*La Gran Aventura*, Prologue by Elizabeth Kubler-Ross, Ediciones LaLlave, Spain
2001	*El Libro Contemporaneo de Los Muertos*, (with illustrations by E.J. Gold), Editorial La Llave, Spain
1999	*La Machina Biologica Umana, La Trasformazione dell'Essere Umano*, Edizioni Crisalide, Italy (with illustrations by E.J. Gold)
1995	*La trilogie du labyrinthe, Volume I, La machine biologique humaine comme appareil transformateur,* Editions du Relié, Paris (with illustrations by E.J. Gold), France
1993	*A Maquina Biologica Humana Como Aparelho de Transformacao*, Dimensoes Humanas Ltda., Sao Paulo, Brazil
1991	*Los Siete Cuerpos del Hombre* (with illustrations by E.J. Gold), Edaf Sa Jorge Juan 30, Spain
1990	*La Maquina Biologica Humana Como Aparato Alquimico,* Nova - Siglo XXI, Lima, Peru
1988	*Die Menschliche Biologische Maschine als Apparat der Transformation*, Sphinx Verlag, Basel, Switzerland
1986	*Dem Tod is es Egal wie du Stirbst,* (German ed.), Sphinx Verlag, Switzerland

PUBLISHERS:

2002	Editorial La Llave, Spain
1999	Edizioni Crisalide, Italy
1995	Editions du Relié, France
1995	Harper SanFrancisco, San Francisco
1994	Galaxy
1974-2002	Gateways Books and Tapes
1985-2002	Heidelberg Editions International
1993	Dimensoes Humanas Ltda., Sao Paulo, Brazil
1991	Edaf Sa Jorge Juan 30, Spain
1990	Nova Siglo XXI, Lima Peru
1987	Simon & Schuster, Allyn & Bacon
1986	Sphinx Verlag, Basel, Switzerland
1985	Penthouse / OMNI
1982	Signet
1981	Abandonment Press
1974	New American Library

MAGAZINE CONTRIBUTIONS:

1994	GALAXY, Editor
1984	OMNI, *Last Word*, July
1979	Playwings, editor & illustrator
1979	Wings, The New Age Satire Magazine, editor & illustrator

> *Strange Passages,*
> *Tales of the Ukranian Sufis,*
> *A Matter of Babble,*
> *The Science of Idiots,*

1979   *Heimie the Barbarian*, May-June
1979   Tuesday's Child
1974   WSL Newsletter, *Instant Mythologies,* 1974 (an early example of fictiles)
1968   Mod Teen, editor
1968   Fifteen, editor
1968   Monkee Spectacular, contributing editor
1968   *Yes, Yes, Yes, The Monkees Play Their Own Instruments* by Their Instruments
1968   *How I Sneaked In To Meet the Monkees* by Guess Who
1968   *The Monkees Meet the Magic Jeannie and Get Three Wishes* by Jeannie-In-the-Bottle,
1968   Galaxy, *Villains from Vega IV,* co-authored with H.L. Gold, 1968, (Ed. Frederik Pohl)
1967   Tiger Beat, photography and articles
1967   Towne & Country, photographer
1966   Jet, photographer
1966   Adam, photographer
1966   Knight, photographer
1966   Cavalier, photographer

MEDIA REFERENCES:

2002   University of Niagara Film Department, *Floating World,* film interview with Greg Virc
2002   FCAT, Channel 10, Cable Television Nevada County, *Master Class with E.J. Gold,* series to be syndi-cated and distributed nationally
2002   What Is Enlightenment? *Interview* with Andrew Cohen, Fall-Winter
2001   FCAT, Channel 10, Cable Television Nevada County, *Jazz Art Will Warm You*
2001   The Union, *Jazz, Art in Grass Valley,* Cam Miller, November
2001   The Union, *County Jazzed After Festival,* Carol Feineman, November 26
2001   The Union, *Marsalis and Friends Leave Audience Captivated,* Cam Miller, November 26
2001   The Union, *Festival Features Art from 16 Local Artists,* Carol Feineman, November 26
2001   The Union, *Making Artists' Lives Easier,* David Mirhadi, October 22
2001   Tandem, The "New Mainstream" Lifestyle Weekend Paper, Toronto, *Art Gallery Offers Up New Classical Experimental Work, Donna Lypchuk,* March 16
2000   Renudo Magazine, Italy, *Interview* with Fabio Pelegrini in the issue about *Death & Dying*
2000   Magical Blend Magazine, *Potentials,* Editorial, Michael Peter Langevin
2000   New Dimensions Radio, *Wisdom Radio,* Interview with Michael Toms
1999   Team Fortress, *Interview* for Adair Equipment Corporation with Craig Dibble
1999   Crafts Report, *Selling Art on the Internet,* James Joyner
1998   Magical Blend Magazine, *The Game's Afoot, Taking Computer Gaming to a New Level,* Interview, Michael Peter Langevin, May
1998   Magical Blend Magazine, *Potentials,* Editorial, Michael Peter Langevin, May
1998   Buzz, The Talk of Los Angeles, *L.A. Style, Soulful Bowls,* Andrea Feldberg, January
1997   Toronto Life, *Paintings by E.J. Gold,* Donald Brackett, August
1997   *The Book of Enlightened Masters, Western Teachers in Eastern Traditions,* Andrew Rawlinson
1996   Fred Alan Wolf, *Spiritual Universe, How Quantum Physics...,* Simon & Schuster
1994   Los Angeles Reader, *A Touch of Schmilsson in Santa Monica,* Leslee Komaiko, May 13
1994   Preview of the Visual Arts, *Spiritual Life, Dance of the Warrior,* Llewellyn Vaughn-Lee, April
1994   Woodstock Times, Woodstock, *California Dreaming,* Kathi Norklun, March 3
1994   The Link, Marketplace, *The Art Lover,* Tinu Mathur & R. Paul Dhillon, July 16
1994   Vancouver Sun, *The Lord Must Be,* March
1994   News, Round & About, Vancouver, *Singer Nilsson's Work 'On Display',* March 26
1994   Hudson Valley Newspapers, Coming Events, *Art Exhibits,* March 2
1994   Gnosis Magazine, *Editorial,* Richard Smoley, Summer
1992   Village Voice, New York, *Gallery Directory,* November 3
1992   The Argonaut, Santa Monica, *Reductionist Art Show Opens In Venice,* David Hirning
1992   Dagens Naeringsliv, Oslo, Norway, Etter Bors, *Utstillingsguiden,* May 30
1992   Lewisboro Ledger, Cross River, NY, *E.J. Gold at Nardin*
1992   Oslo Business, Oslo, Norway, *Gallerier Salonger,* November 4
1992   Friday Magazine, *Best of the Week,* Jan. 24
1992   New York Post, *The Old Cedar Bar,* Jerry Talman

1991	Shared Vision, Vancouver's Creative Arts and Life Resource Magazine, *Women in Discovery* , October, Issue #38
1991	Esoterica (Italy) Gianpiero Cara, *Sciamani ad alta technologia: E.J. Gold*
1991	Magical Blend, Timothy Leary/Eric Gullichsen, *22 Common Sense Alternatives to Involuntary Death*
1991	Colorado Daily, *More News Muses, Hidden Images Gallery,* November 15
1991	Westword, *Galleries to Visit,* November,
1991	Icon, *The Arts Alternative*
1989-91	Meditation Magazine
1990	Magical Blend, *The Great Human Potential Debate; a dialogue between Claudio Naranjo, M.D. and E.J. Gold*
1990	Esoterica (Italy), Gianpiero Cara, *Intervista a E.J. Gold*
1990	Palos Verdes Peninsula News, Diane Kaminski, *Art Nouveau Deco's Gallery,* May 3
1989	Interview by Larry Roberts
1989	Universita Degli Studi Di Roma, Facolta di Lettere e Filosofia. Dipartimento di Musica e Spettacolo, (Italy) *La Sapienza*
1989	Westfield Evening News, Holyoke, MA, *Schlock Art* , April 24
1989	Amherst Bulletin, Suzanne Mitchell, *Building Art Without Walls,* May 3, 1989
1989	Daily Hampshire Gazette, Marietta Pritchard, *Artists in Resonance*
1989	Transcript Telegram, Holyoke, *Local Exhibit Features Work by Artist & Photographer*
1988	Hologramm (Verlag Bruno Martin, Germany, Brigitte Donvez, *E.J. Gold, Ein Portrat*, May
1988	Small Press Book Review
1988	New Haven Arts, Forum
1988	Fairfield County Advocate, Winter Times, *Color and Form: Matisse, Miro, and Gold, Dec. 14*
1987	East Haven Advertiser, *Color and Form: Matisse, Miro, and Gold,* Dec 12
1987	Branford Review, *This Week*
1987	Shore Line Times, *Bulletin Board, Color and Form: Matisse, Miro, and Gold,* Dec. 17
1987	New Haven Advocate, *Winter Times,* Dec. 14
1985	KVMR *Sacred Dance* Interview with Justyn Vallori
1985	Auburn Journal, *A Sacred Dance Performance featured at the American Victorian Museum*
1984	Critique, Bob Banner, ed. *Sheep in Sleep*
1984	Omni, *Last Word*
1984	Seattle Post-Intelligencer, *Eager Crowds Start Holiday Buying Spree, Nov. 24*
1983	KPFK interview
1983	WBAI, Mary Houston interview with E.J. Gold, *Inner Awakening & Transformation*
1983	KPPC interview
1983	KRLA interview
1983	KRON interview
1980	CBC Radio Television
1980	The Movement, *Interview: E.J. Gold, Developing the Harmonious Human Being*
1980	San Francisco Examiner, *More Than the Unconventional*, by Allan Ulrich
1980	Winnipeg Free Press, *Actors Perform in Ancient Ways*
1979	KPFK interview with Amanda Foulger
1978	New Horizons, *Cat & Mouse with E.J. Gold*, Interview with Dr. Bundolo
1978	*North American Bunraku Puppetry Theatre,* by Daniel Sckolnik
1978	The Union, Grass Valley/Nevada City, CA, *A Conversation with a Tall Puppet*, Dave Carter
1977	Today's World
1977	Tribune, Winnipeg, *Fun, High Ideals Mix in Ancient Puppetry*, Lee Rolfe, Sept. 1
1975	The New Yorker, *Three Days in L.A. Part I & Part II*
1973	KPFK interview with Amanda Foulger
1972	KPPC interview with Barbara BirdFeather
1971-72	KPFK *Enterview* interview with Amanda Foulger
1972	AUM, *Crystalballing for Fun & Profit*, Julie Russo
1969	TIME, *Doomsday in the Golden State*, April 11, 1969
1969	NEWSWEEK
1969	The New York Times Magazine, *Warning! California will Fall Into the Ocean in April!* by Steven V. Roberts
1969	LIFE, Sally O'Quinn
1969	Los Angeles Times, *Doomsday in April? Experts Ridicule Mystics' Warnings* by Linda Mathews,
1969	KHJ-TV, *Tempo interview* with Richard Dawson
1969	*Gorilla My Dreams, radio interview*
1969	Huntley/Brinkley interview
1969	Walter Cronkite interview
1969	Arizona Daily Sun, Flagstaff, AZ, *Los Angeles Repair Permit Too Costly*, March 14
1969	Manhattan Mercury, Kansas, *Earthquake Predicted in April, Doomsday Set for California*, March 31

1969   Leader, Lexington, KY, *Many in State of Fear as California's Earthquake "Doomsday" Date Draws Near*, March 31
1969   Escanaba Daily Press, MI, *Doomsday Rumor Has California Jittery*, March 31
1969   The Lima News, Lima, OH, *Ancient Minders Seeking Salvage*, March 13
1969   Garden City Telegram, Kansas, *Society Seeking Salvage Permit for Los Angeles*, March 14
1969   Arizona Daily Sun, Flagstaff, AZ, *Scientists Scoff at Rumor of Huge California Quake*, March 31
1969   Union-Bulletin, Walla Walla, WA, *Doomsday Prophets Predict Quake Will Destroy Half of California*, April 1
1969   Press Citizen, Iowa City, IA, *Devastating Quake in LA Next Month?*, March 15
1969   Independent, Gallup, NM, *Doomsday Nears for Californians*, March 31
1969   Fargo Forum, ND, *April Seen as Month for California Quake*, April 1
1969   Sun-Democrat, Paducah, KY, *Scientists Scoff but Californians Fear Earthquake Destruction*, March 31
1969   Wellington Daily News, Kansas, *April is the Month, Doomsday Prophets Continue California Quake Prediction*, March 31
1969   Denver Post, Denver, CO, *Quake Forecasts*, March 14
1969   Liberal Southwest Daily Times, Kansas, KS, *Last Days*, April 1
1969   Grand Rapids Press, MI, *Mystics Would 'Save' L.A.*, March 14
1969   Wellington Daily News, KS, *Ready for Quake but Not $66 Fee*, March 15
1969   Fairbanks News Miner, Fairbanks, AK, *Prophets of Doom Expect Big Quake*, April 1, 1969
1969   Evening Reporter News, Abilene, TX, *Group Seeks LA Salvage Permit*, March 13
1969   Capital Annapolis, MD, *Los Angeles Earthquake Predicted*, March 12
1969   News-Times, York, NE, *Prophets of Doom Forecast Quakes*, March 31
1969   Fresno Bee, Fresno, CA, *South Staters Tremble, Many Flee as 'Disaster' Time Nears*, March 23
1969   Marshalltown Times, Minneapolis, MN, *Quake Talks Rattle California's Nerves*, March 31
1969   Mt-Pleasant Times-News, MI, *Bad Vibrations Threaten the Golden State*, April 1
1969   Evening Tribune, San Diego, CA, *Quake Jitters Still Gaining*, March 31
1969   McPherson Daily Sentinel, KS, *Prophets of Doom Shake Californians*, April 1
1969   The Reporter, Independence, KS, *West Coast Getting Jumpy; April Doomsday Predicted*, March 31
1969   Adrian Daily Telegram, MI, *Many People Believe CA Earthquake Happening this Month*, April 1
1969   Herald-Courier, Bristol, VA, *Telepathic Society Seeks Salvage Permit*, March 13
1969   PARIS-MATCH (France)
1969   STERN (Germany)
1969   Los Angeles Free Press, *Activists March for Saints' Rights* by Julie Russo
1969   TIME, June 20, 1969
1969   Between 1969 and 1970 Gold generated over 6 million words of written news coverage in hundreds of newspapers from coast to coast too numerous to list here. More than 60 hours of radio and television coverage were generated at the same time.
1969   Tuesday's Child, *The Magical Mystery Museum*
1968   Houston Chronicle, Betty Ewing, *Alligators and Easter Eggs*, April 10, 1968
1968   Houston Chronicle, David D. Dolin, *Artisan's Nine*, April 7, 1968
1968   Houston Post, Eleanor Freed, *Surrealism & Op*, April 7, 1968
1967   Joe Pyne (several interviews)
1967   *Better Living,* Don Burgess, weekend LA Times supplement
1967-69 New York Times
1967   VARIETY, *Macbird*
1967   Los Angeles FM & Fine Arts, *MacBird Flies West, Pop Culture or Lousy satire*
1966   Los Angeles Times, Henry J. Seldis, *Jeff Gold Offers Sophomoric Whimsy*, Dec. 18, 1967
1966-67 Los Angeles Free Press

NOTABLE COLLECTORS:

Foundation for the Study of Objective Art, Toronto, Canada
King Hussein of Jordan, Jordan
President and Mrs. Clinton, Washington, D.C., USA
Catherine Oxenberg, Beverly Hills, California, USA
Oliver Stone, Beverly Hills, California, USA
Han and Sukie Huskey, Los Angeles, California, USA
Peggy Lee, Beverly Hills, California, USA
Harry Nilsson, Beverly Hills, California, USA
Greg Mosher, Denver, Colorado, USA
Bill Taubman, Los Angeles, California, USA
Tom Waits, Valley Ford, California, USA

Meryl and Lenny Beck, Cincinatti, Ohio, USA
James Anthony, Toronto, Canada
Denbridge Capital Corporation, Toronto, Canada
Steven and Suzanne Vorous, Sacramento, CA, USA
Sylvia Andrews, Beverly Hills, California, USA
Joyce Kenyon, Beverly Hills, California, USA
Joseph Bowman, San Francisco, California, USA
Doris Davenport, Los Angeles, California, USA
Lee Lozowick, Prescott, Arizona, USA
Oyvind Engen, Oslo, Norway
John and Ena Estes, Lake Wildwood, California, USA
Dick and Linda Fields, Fremont, California, USA
Don and Pam Harley, Sacramento, California, USA
Mike and Lisa Fields, Pleasanton, California, USA
Helen Mullen Fink, New York, New York, USA
Lin Larsen, Nevada City, California, USA
Richard Frey, Chico, California, USA
Rod and Debra Goodwin, Sacramento, California, USA
Bobbie Greenfield, Los Angeles, California, USA
Hannah King, Beverly Hills, California, USA
James King, New York, New York, USA
Landsbanken As, Oslo, Norway
Ginger Baker, USA
Per Heiberg, Oslo, Norway
Terje Tonne, Oslo, Norway
Tom Lavin, Vancouver, Canada
Annette Levey, Marina Del Rey, California, USA
Robin Mueller and Wayne Pantley, Pleasanton, California, USA
J. Nesgaard, Spain
Chris O'Banks, Silicon Valley, California, USA
H. Oseid, Oslo, Norway
Howard and Gloria Pontier, Suquanesh, Washington, USA
Bruce and Caryn Renfrew, Reno, Nevada, USA
Larry Roberts, Pasadena, California, USA
Dr. James and Gloreen Rowe, Santa Barbara, California, USA
Stan Sanders, Los Angeles, California, USA
Ed and Betty Ann Schneider, Armonk, New York, USA
Fera Sodeghiegh, Vancouver, Canada
Paul Soderburg, Nevada City, California, USA
June and Donald Suckling, Lancashire, UK
Dr. Paul Swanson, Topanga Canyon, California, USA
Sheldon and Sheila Swift, Sacramento, California, USA
Richard Hart, Grass Valley, California, USA
Peter Heineman, Denver, Colorado, USA
Evan Lurie, New York, New York, USA
Hans Vanderhill, Chicago, Illinois, USA
Carol Taubman, Sun Lakes, CA, USA
Karen Bryan, Beverly Hills, CA, USA
George Stein, Michigan City, Indiana, USA
Patricia Vaughan, Midlothian, Virginia, USA
Joanne Evans, Paradise Valley, Arizona, USA
Brad Haas, Brinklow, Maryland, USA
Henry Josephson, Shelburne, Massachusetts, USA
Liz Rosenberg, Binghamton, New York, USA
Mathews K. Varghefe, Belton, Texas, USA
Steve Carroll, Tenafly, New Jersey, USA
Kevin P. Brosnan, Belmont, Massachusetts, USA
James R. Lance, Richmond, Virginia, USA
Blake Martell, Palo Alto, California, USA
Renee Wilson, Tulsa, Oklahoma, USA
Luis Sequeira Dias, Acores, Portugal
David Harris, Toronto, Ontario
David Giezen, Toronto, Canada

DIRECTORIES/LISTINGS:

World Wide Art Resources
AskArt.com
ArtCyclopedia.com
Library of Objective Art
Print World Directory, Selma Smith, editor
California Art Review, Les Krantz, editor
ArtNet.com
Davenport's
Gordon's Print Price Annual
ArtistBiography.com
ArtPrice.com
ArtFact.com
Science Fiction Writers Association
Who's Who In American Art
AAM
American Artist, ed. Les Krantz
Annual Guide to Museums, Galleries and Artists, published by Art in America
Art & Antiques
Art & Auction
Art in America
Art News
Art Scene
Berliner Kunstblat
ICOM
International Directory for Collectors, published by Art & Auction
National Gallery Guide

FILM:

2002   FCAT, Channel 10, Cable Television Nevada County, *Master Class with E.J. Gold,* series to be syndi-
cated and distributed nationally
2002   Film Documentary Interview by the University of Niagara, Fim Department, Welland, Canada,
Floating World, a documentary about John Lilly and the Floatation Tank
2001   *The Insane Investors Quartet* live performance by satellite uplink to *Squawk Box,* CNBC, Audience
of 150 million viewers worldwide
2000   Script Collaboration with Peter Clausen Productions, Germany

INTERNET:

1994-2002 over 550 websites owned, created or in the process of development including award-winning
newbie.org and *nevadacitytours.com*
1997   *Paparazi, a virtual reality game,* over 1 millon downloads in less than 2 days after its creation

MULTI-MEDIA / VIDEO GAMES:

2001   *Harry Poddy,* Gamexx
2001   *Zeldar,* Gamexx
2001   *Dungeon Party,* Gamexx
2001   *Necronomicon,* Gamexx
2001   *Necromania,* Gamexx
2001   *Bardomania,* Gamexx
2000   *Wonderland,* Gamexx
2000   *Factory,* Gamexx
1999   *Exploding Lips,* Gamexx
1999   *Slimeworld,* Gamexx
1999   *Hot Night in Hell,* Gamexx
1999   *Temples,* Gamexx

1999	*Lucid Dreaming*, Gamexx
1999	*Gemini*, Gamexx
1999	*Cosmo*, Gamexx
1999	*Museum of Ancient and Modern Art*, Museum of Ancient and Modern Art
1998	*Beta 9*, G.O.D.D.
1998	*Bardo Town*, PGL I, Gateways Books and Tapes

TELEVISION INDUSTRY:

1998	*Randy*, Paramount Studios
1998	*Sister, Sister*, Paramount Studios
1971	*Snoop Sisters*
1969	*The Name of the Game*
1968	*The Wild, Wild West*
1968	*Rat Patrol*
1967	*Dundee & the Culhane*
1966	*Man from Uncle*
1966	*Lost in Space*
1966	*Get Smart*
1966	*Vampire Rose*
1964	Samart Enterprises, for Arthur Silber, Jr.

MUSIC VIDEOS / VIDEOTAPES BY OR ABOUT E.J. GOLD:

2002	*Art as T'ai C'hi with E.J. Gold*, Gateways Fine Art
2002	*The "I Can't Draw" Series with E.J. Gold, Pastel Class #1, A House and a Tree*, Gateways Fine Art
2002	*Masters Class Critique*, Gateways Fine Art
2002	*Motivation, How I Made One Million Dollars in Art $1.00 at a Time*, Gateways Fine Art
2001-02	*Western Plein-Air Workshop* series, Gateways Fine Art
2002	*Creation Story Verbatim*, Cloister Recordings
1999	*Beatless Forever*, Cloister Recordings
1997	*Ride That Carousel*, Cloister Recordings
1996	*Bardo Reaction Video Test*, Cloister Recordings
1996	*Darkside DreamWalker*, Cloister Recordings
1996	*Shop at House*, satire, Cloister Recordings
1996	*Angels Healing Journey*, Cloister Recordings
1996	*Past Lives Healing Journey*, Cloister Recordings
1994	*An Afternoon with E.J. Gold*, Gateways Books and Tapes
1992	*City in the Sky*, a Virtual Reality Video, Gateways Books and Tapes
1989	*Get Me Down From Here*, Cloister Recordings
1989	*The Movements at American River College*, Gateways Books and Tapes
1988	*Sculpting in Light, Sound and Color*, Gateways Fine Art
1988	*In the Garden / Uncommon Scents, The Lost Arts*, Gateways Fine Art
1987	*Color and Radiation I-VI*, Gateways Fine Art
1987	*Labyrinth Voyager with E.J. Gold*, Gateways Books and Tapes
1987	*Macrodimensional Models I-III* , Gateways Books and Tapes
1987	*Revenge of the Fly*, Gateways Books and Tapes
1986	*Hooray for Hollywood*, Cloister Recordings
1986	*Songs of the Spanish Sufis*, music video, Cloister Recordings
1989	*The Artist in the Studio*, Gateways Fine Art
1986	*Village Dancing, Village Drums* with E.J. Gold, Claudio Naranjo & Antonio Asin, Cloister Recordings
1986	*The Origins of Dance*, Cloister Recordings

AUDIO CDs:

2000	*How to Overcome Writer's Block*, Robert Sheckley and E.J. Gold
2000	*Chanting Induction*
2000	*Spiritual Gaming*
2000	*Sacred Prayers from The Original American Book of the Dead*
1997	*The Making of the American Book of the Dead*
1997	*A Walking Tour of BardoTown*

1994	*GAP, Galaxy Audio Project:*
	-Volume I, Catherine Oxenberg reading *Wells of Wisdom, by* Brad Linaweaver.
	-Volume II, Catherine Oxenberg reading *Dragon Lady* by Evelyn E. Smith; *The Words, The Names* by Don Webb.
	-Volume III, Catherine Oxenberg reading *Three Wish Habit* by Janni Lee Simmer; *The Biography Project* by H. L. Gold; *Nothing Changes* by Chuck Rothman; *The Vilbar Party* by Evelyn E. Smith; *The Fornicators* by Barbara Johnson.
	-Volume IV, Catherine Oxenberg reading *Not Fit for Children* by Evelyn E. Smith; *Extraction* by Jeffry Dwight; *Perchance to Scream* by Janet Berliner.
	-Volume V, Catherine Oxenberg reading *Mr. Monster Waits in Heaven for an Angel* by Forrest J Ackerman; *Ants in her Attic* by Kent Brewster
1993	*The Tank Talks*
1989	*The Rembrandt Tape*
1889	*A Treasury of British Humour*
1988	*Hi-Tech Shaman at the Spiritual Olympics*
1988	*Origami I / Guidelines for the Practitioner*
1987	*Waging Work*
1986	*The Great Comedy Challenge*
1986	*The Unseen Part of Art*
1986	*Objective Art*
1986	*Objective Theater*
1986	*Is There Life After Zelda?*
1985	*The Lazy Man's Guide to Death & Dying*
1985	*Journey through the Great Mother*
1985	*Adventures of the Hi-Tech Shaman*
1985	*Bardo Dreams*
1985	*Hart of the Labyrinth Tape*
1983	*Inner Awakening & Transformation, WBAI Radio Interview* by Mary Houston
1980	*Baa Baa Black Sheep*
1980	*Secrets of the Illuminati* with Robert Anton Wilson
1980	*The Secret Teachings of Star Wars* with Robert A. Wilson
1977	*Comedy Album* Illustrated by George Metzger
1977	*About Drumming*
1977	*Composite Waveform Technology*
1977	*Creation Story Verbatim,* Studio recording
1974	*The Spiritual Olympics* with Amanda Foulger at WPFK
1971	*How I Raised Myself from the Dead*

MUSICAL RECORDINGS:

2001	*Shapeshifter / Timetripper,* E.J. Gold & Friends
2001	*Send $ or the Fairie Dies,* Insane Investors Club
2001	*Wonderland,* Gorebag & the Grunts
2000	*Spirit of Woodstock,* E.J. Gold
2000	*California Dreams,* E.J. Gold
2000	*Spirit Drums,* E.J. Gold
2000	*Gorebag in the Morning,* Gorebag and the Grunts
2000	*Gorebag at Midnight,* Various Artists
2000	*Regularity,* Soundtrack from the Off Broadway play, music and lyrics by Accardi/Gold
2000	*Christmas Album,* Insane Investors Club
2000	*It Pays to be Ignorant,* The Morons
2000	*Mostly We'll Rock,* Zaphod & The New Harmonics
1999	*Hippie Heaven,* The Satin Experience
1999	*Wall Street,* Insane Investor Quartet
1999	*God Bless America!,* E.J. Gold and Friends
1999	*Quake II,* Sound effects produced with American McGee
1999	*Chanting Induction,* E.J. Gold
1998	*Hot Night in Hell,* Gorebag and the Grunts
1998	*Miles from the Dead,* The Cool Jazz Ensemble
1998	*Accardi/Gold Songbook,* Accardi/Gold
1998	*Bag Ladies From Hell,* Gorebag & the Grunts
1998	*Banned In 93 Countries,* The Terminators
1998	*Bardo Reggae / Bardo Bop,* E.J. Gold & Friends

1998   *Beatless: Together Again,* Various Artists
1998   *Best of Elwood Strutter Sutton,* Elwood Strutter Sutton & Friends
1998   *Blues From Hell,* Zaphod & The New Harmonics
1998   *Born to Be Mild,* The Satin Experience
1997   *Harlem Daze,* Accardi & Gold
1997   *Liberation* with Jimmi Accardi and E.J. Gold
1997   *In Your Face,* Gorebag and the Grunts
1997   *No Bread Lotsa Jam,* Accardi/Gold & Friends
1997   *One Single Outbreath,* E.J. Gold & Friends
1997   *Post Pop Festival,* Accardi/Gold
1997   *Return of Children of the Night,* Accardi/Gold
1997   *Ride That Carousel,* E.J. Gold & Friends
1997   *Songs We Wrote Tomorrow,* Accardi/Gold
1994   *Surrender,* Overlords of Jazz
1994   *Only Sleeping,* E.J. Gold and the Galaxians
1994   *Sax Offender,* E.J. Gold
1994   *Sax Pistol,* E.J. Gold and Friends
1994   *Children of the Night,* E.J. Gold and Friends
1994   *Wizzards,* Accardi / Gold
1993   *The Jazz Koto of Eugene Yamamoto,* with Eugene Yamamoto
1992   *Jazzmobile,* Jeff Spencer Trio
1992   *Lycanthrope,* E.J. Gold/Jimmi Accardi
1992   *Superjam,* E.J. Gold and Friends
1992   *Romulan Rap,* Zaphod and the New Harmonics
1992   *Galaxians,* Zaphod & The New Harmonics
1992   *Alto Sax Zarathustra,* Zaphod & The New Harmonics
1992   *The Drone ,* E.J. Gold
1992   *Ducks with Breasts,* Zaphod and the New Harmonics
1990   *Music from the Heart of the Galaxy,* Zaphod and the New Harmonics
1990   *Newport Live,* The Jeff Spencer Trio
1990   *Wizzards,* The Jeff Spencer Trio
1990   *Zaphod and the New Harmonics,* Zaphod and the New Harmonics
1990   *Star Barf,* Zaphod and the New Harmonics
1990   *Evolver,* Zaphod and the New Harmonics
1990   *Visions in the Stone,* E.J. Gold and Friends
1990   *The Tokyo Tour* with Evan Lurie and E.J. Gold
1989   *Way Beyond the Veil,* E.J. Gold and Friends
1989   *Childhood's End,* E.J. Gold and Friends
1989   *Fourth Dawn,* E.J. Gold and Friends
1989   *Good Vibes,* Jeff Spencer Trio with Bob Bachtold
1989   *Live at the Philharmonic, I-III,* E.J. Gold
1989   *Ritual of the Cave,* E.J. Gold and Friends
1989   *School Days,* E.J. Gold and Friends
1989   *Spacing Out,* E.J. Gold and Friends
1988   *Golden Age,* E.J. Gold and Friends
1988   *Mystical Journey of the Hi-Tech Shaman,* E.J. Gold
1971-88 *Cogitate Tape* with John C. Lilly, M.D.
1985   *E.J. Gold's Private Reserve,* E.J. Gold
1985   *Adventures of the Hi-Tech Shaman,* E.J. Gold and Friends
1985   *Saturday Night in the Higher Dimensions,* E.J. Gold and Friends
1985   *Night Blooming Jazzman,* E.J. Gold
1984   *Dance of the Hi-Tech Shaman,* E.J. Gold and Friends
1984   *Rates of Passage,* E.J. Gold and Friends
1984   *Blue Smoke,* E.J. Gold
1984   *Venus Rising,* E.J. Gold
1972-74 *Pythagorean Harp and Harmonium Improvisations with E.J. Gold,* E.J. Gold
1972   *I Can Free You with E.J. Gold at RCA,* E.J. Gold
1971   *Epitaph for An Ego,* E.J. Gold

ALBUM LINERS AND/OR DESIGN:

1967-69 RCA
        Harry Nilsson
        Family Tree
        Jefferson Airplane
1966-67 Columbia Recording Studios
        Turtles
        Paul Revere and the Raiders
        The Monkees
        Don & the Goodtimes

ANIMATION CREDITS:

1966 with Jim Carmichael
        Pointdexters in Paradise
        Rocky The Flying Squirrel
        Gullibles / Culligan Man
1965-66 with Lin Larsen
        George of the Jungle

STAGE PERFORMANCES:

2001   *Creation Story Verbatim*, Nevada County Center for the Arts
2000   *Creation Story Verbatim*, Grass Valley Masonic Lodge
1991   *Carnival of the Animals*, Museum of Ancient and Modern Art Children's Theatre
1991   *The Gold Rush Days*, Museum of Ancient and Modern Art Children's Theatre
1991   *Oh, The Places You'll Go*, Museum of Ancient and Modern Art Children's Theatre
1990-91 *Triad*, Museum of Ancient and Modern Art, Penn Valley
1989   *Tokyo Tour with Evan Lurie*
1989   *Hi-Tech Shaman, Red Lion Inn*
1987   *Ancient Dances*, American River College
1986   *Ancient Dances*, American Victorian Museum
1986   *Creation Story Verbatim*, Nevada Theatre,
1986   *Creation Story Verbatim*, NewFoundland Theatre Space
1986   *Labyrinth*, St Joseph's Hall, Grass Valley
1985-87 *North American Bunraku Puppet Theatre*, California State Fair, Sacramento
1985   *Creation Story Verbatim*, American Victorian Museum
1985   *Jazz Performance*, Westercon, Embassy Room, Sacramento
1985   *The Oracle & the Garden*, Academy of Ancient Dance, American Victorian Museum, Nevada City
1984   *Redfin*, American Victorian Museum, Nevada City
1983   *The Gabriel Project*, with Mark Olsen, Jane Hinders, Jeff Burnett, Gruber Theatre, New York
1983   *A Dinner to Remember*, Riverside Church, New York (with Lin Carter, Chip Delaney, and others)
1985   *Ancient Dances, Ancient Ways*, Cubiculo, New York
1985   *The Hi-Tech Shaman*, American Victorian Museum
1983   *Objective Theatre*, New Foundland Theatre Space
1983   *Objective Theatre*, Gruber Theatre
1983   *The Village of the Idiots*, Ohio Theatre, Soho
1982   *Magic Show* with Ormond McGill, at Ross Relles
1981   *Corridors*, The New American Dance Theatre, The Julia Morgan Theatre, Berkeley
1980   *The Shaping*, Theatre Absolute North American Tour
1980   *The Shearing*, CBC Radio Television
1980   *Seance*, A Rock Opera Ballet, Vancouver
1980   *Strawberry Man*, a mystery play
1980   *The Shearing*, Victoria Theatre, San Francisco, Theatre Absolute
1980   *The Shearing*, Robson Square Theatre, Vancouver, Theatre Absolute
1980   *The Shearing*, The Empress Theatre, Victoria, Theatre Absolute
1980   *The Shearing*, Granville Island Community Center, Theatre Absolute
1980   *The Shearing*, The Planetarium Theatre, Winnipeg, Theatre Absolute
1980   *Ancient Dances*, Lake Tahoe Summer Festival
1980   *Ancient Dances*, Granlibakken, Lake Tahoe
1980   *Rites of Spring*, Theatre Absolute, Victoria Theatre, San Francisco

1980	*Ancient Dances*, The Victoria Theatre, San Francisco
1980	*Ancient Dances*, St. Joseph's Hall, Grass Valley
1980	*Theatre Absolute Workshop*, False Creek, Granville Island
1979	*Inaccessible Monasteries*, Theatre Absolute, Boulder
1979	*Black Sheep*, Theatre Absolute, False Creek, Granville Island
1979	*Science of the Idiots*, Theatre Absolute
1979	*Yassun Dede & the Magic Christian*, Planetarium Auditorium, North Amer. Bunraku Puppet Theatre
1979	*Daisy and the Galactic Kid*, North American Bunraku Puppet Theatre, Nevada Theatre, Nevada City
1979	*The Truly Magical Child*, False Creek, Granville Island, North American Bunraku Puppet Theatre
1979	*Rites of Spring*, False Creek, Granville Island, Theatre Absolute
1978	*A Talk on Silence*, E.J. Gold & Samuel Avital, Grass Valley
1978	*North American Bunraku Puppet Theatre*, Resh House, Mill Valley
1978	*North American Bunraku Puppet Theatre*, A Halloween Matinee
1978	*North American Bunraku Puppet Theatre*, Planetarium Auditorium, Winnipeg, Manitoba
1978	*North American Bunraku Puppet Theatre*, American Victorian Museum
1978-83	*North American Bunraku Puppet Theatre*, Pier 39, San Francisco
1978-83	*North American Bunraku Puppet Theatre*, Renaissance Faire
1978	*Mime/Puppetry Workshop*, Grass Valley
1977	*North American Bunraku Puppet Theatre Workshops:* New York, Los Angeles, Tucson, Winnipeg, Vancouver
1977	*First American Puppetry Workshop*, Crestline
1977	*Supergame*, Winnipeg
1977	*Founded North American Bunraku Puppet Theatre*
1977	*Supergame*, Queen Elizabeth Theatre, Vancouver
1974	*Hallucination*
1969	*Agrippa, Nostradamus & Solomon*, Magical Mystery Museum
1969	*Hallucination*, Magical Mystery Museum
1968	*Supergame*, Los Angeles
1967	Comedy Store, Sunset Boulevard
1967	*Rockathon '67*, Spectrum 2000 and Aquarius Theatre
1967	Lou Shaw's *MacBird*, Player's Ring Gallery
1967	*Odyssey Theatre*, with Ron Sossi, director
1964	*Playhouse*, New York, comedy performance by E.J. Gold and a musical act by Peter and Antonia Stampfel.
1959	*The Boyfriend/Visit to a Small Planet*, Cherry Lane Theatre
1959	*Juno & the Paycock/Master Builder*, Minetta Lane Theatre
1958-59	Elon Players Shakespeare Repertoire Company
1958-59	Playhouse Theatre, with Peter & Antonia Stampfel
1958-59	Gaslight Cafe, with Hugh Romney, Peter, Paul & Mary, Dave van Ronk
1958-59	Gertie's, with Dave Guard, Judy Henske, Carol Hunter, Woody Allen
1958-59	Feenjon's, with Shep Sherbell, Carol Hunter, Gabrielle Martin
1956	*The Calico Indian Uprising* with Pete Seeger, Bob and Louise Decormier
1953	*The Lonesome Train*, a cantata by Millard Lampell

CREATIVE CONSULTANT:

2001	*Harry Fest*, RCA Los Angeles, an annual Tribute to Harry Nilsson organized by Curtis Armstrong
2000	*Harry Fest*, Los Angeles, an annual Tribute to Harry Nilsson
1997	Sound effects for *Quake II*, the 3D Action Adventure Game, under the direction of American McGee of id Software
1991	Nevada County School Board Supervisors consultation
1972-73	RCA Hollywood
1972	Toad Records
1971	Elektra Records, Hollywood
1971	Fidelity Studios
1970	Desilu
1970	RCA Special Products, Grelun Landon
1969-70	Universal Studios
1969-70	Paramount
1968	RCA
1968	Bruce Lansbury Productions
1967-70	CP
1967-69	Colgems

1967-68 Simon Oppenheim Collins (Design Director)
1967-68 Screen Gems
1967-68 20th Century Fox
1967   Columbia Recording Studios
1966-67 Samart Enterprises
1966-67 Chrislaw Productions
1966-67 RCA Hollywood
1966   The Bob Crane Show
1966   Arena Productions
1965-66 Metromedia
1959-60 Macy's
1958-59 Hammacher-Schlemmer (Design consultant to:)
         Dr. & Mrs. (Ingrid Bergman) Lars Schmid
         Eva Gabor
         Victor Borge and others

SET AND COSTUME DESIGN:

2001   Veteran's Hall, Grass Valley, Wynton Marsalis Concert, Stage Design, Nov. 23-25
1998   *Randy,* Jazz art and ceramics used as props for TV set design
1998   *Sister, Sister!* Jazz art and ceramics used as props for TV set design
1993   *Amityville: A New Generation*, movie set prop with *Monumentals*
1970   Odyssey Theatre
1969-70 Universal Studios
1969   *Name of the Game*, Universal Studios
1969   *Magical Mystery Museum*
1967-68 Players Ring Gallery
1967   Aquarius Theatre
1951-53 Hope & Morey Bunin (Pinhead & Foodini, Alice in Wonderland)

ARCHITECTURAL DESIGN:

1975   Sportmen's Lodge, Crestline
1973   Kung Fu, Bluejay
1972   Thieves' Market, Santa Monica
1971   Alpine Village, Lake Arrowhead
1971-91 Residential homes
1970   Markham Building, Hollywood

PHOTOGRAPHIC ESSAYS:

2000   *Nevada City Tours*
2000-02 *The Zen Garden*
1995   *Bardotown*
1992   *Catherine Oxenberg*
1978   *Frank Herbert*
1978   *Randall Garrett*
1974-76 Bardo Spaces, Photographic Essays
1974   *Princess Leda*
1974   *Theodore Sturgeon*
1974   *Damon Knight*
1969   *José Ferrer*
1968   *Bob Segarini and the Family Tree*
1968   *Peter Hirschfeld*
1968   *Jefferson Airplane*
1967   *Bill Lucking*
1967   *Bill Callaway*
1967   *Dale Morse*
1967   *Bob Doqui*
1967   *Davy Jones*

1967   *Don & the Goodtimes*
1967   *George Tipton*
1967   *Harry Nilsson*
1967   *Jerome Guardino*
1967   *Jill Andre*
1967   *Jimmy Piersall*
1967   *Leanna Gaskins*
1967   *Mark Lindsay*
1967   *Mickey Dolenz*
1967   *Phil Bruns*
1967   *Spike Jones Jr.*
1967   *Roger Hart*
1967   *Terry Melcher*
1967   *Turtles*
1967   *Vito*
1966   *Sammy Davis, Jr.*

ARCHAEOLOGICAL PROJECTS:

Attributions & Restoration, Theodora van Runkle Collection of Ancient Gold, Museum of Ancient and Modern Art
Cataloging, Conservation and Installation, Oxford Collection, 18th Dynasty Amarna, Museum of Ancient and Modern Art
Installation Design, Ancient Faces, Museum of Ancient and Modern Art
Curator, 18th Dynasty Collection, Museum of Ancient and Modern Art

SCIENTIFIC PAPERS PUBLISHED WITH CLAUDE NEEDHAM, PH.D.:

The Perhapsatron, A D-Ring Cyclic Accelerator
A plan for a quad-meg thermister-barriered overload capacitance induction control system for a 50MEV linear-fed cyclotron.

Ambient Temperature Plasma Dynamics
Preliminary work concerning high temperature ceramic superconductors has established a regimen for the investigation of ambient temperature plasma dynamics. Considerations of fuzzy boundary fluctuations have led to a possible doppling protocol.

Transformative Waveform Analysis
This paper explores the potential utility of waveform-waveform interaction as a direct tool for neo-analog computation in a formally transformed wavespace. Considerations of dynamic, self-imposed boundary conditions are discussed.

Fuzzy Boundaries and the Event Horizon
Dynamically variable fuzzy boundaries are incorporated into prime consideration of the Event Horizon, Zero-field fluctuations within a fuzzy-boundaried domain are investigated as a potential source of cross-field information transfer through an Event Horizon.

The Effect of Various Substances on Barrier Tension of Cell-cell Communication.
This paper tests the effects of several wetting agents and their effect on the barrier tension of cell-cell communication. The authors find a common modality for the effect of wetting agents on barrier tension. A model test system of cell-cell communication is discussed.

DNA in Metals and Plastics.
A previously unexplored model of metalomer and polymer self-catalysis is presented with possible application to molecular engines.

Velocity Dependence of Blob-blob Fusion in Iso-thermal Vertical Transfer Systems.
An experimental model is constructed using a stationary receiving blob in conjunction with a second blob of variable velocity. A velocity threshold of fusion is discovered and preliminary work is begun to isolate significant secondary variables. Temperature and will of fusion are primary candidates.

Dynamic Imbalance - A Mathematical Model
A non-set theory model of dynamic imbalance is presented. This paper makes use of the recent developments in cross-kernel dynamic variables with reference to a possible physical model.

Storage of Survival Based Processes in the Environmental Field.
A mechanism is discussed that would explain the as-if storage of survival based processes in the environmental field. New work with perceptual programming has uncovered response programming stored within the base field to perception mapping matrix.

Perception Threshold Clairvoyant Vision, Part I
A threshold plot of IOM and ESI-IOM clearly demonstrates the asymptotic nature of the clairvoyant vision threshold. As the IOM increases the differential of ESI and IOM necessary to allow perception of the clairvoyant vision increases with the nth root of IOM. In the higher values of IOM the value of n appears to be directly dependent on IOM.

Field Stripping Clairvoyant Vision, Part II
A technique has been found effective for the laboratory application of field stripping. Using this technique, we have been able to reproducibly strip the perceptual field of significance routines in participating subjects. This allows for the systematic study of field overlays and perception self generation.

Percepton-Percepton Interaction Clairvoyant Vision, Part III
A variable field-field mapping between perceptons of the clairvoyant vision and significance modules. The study of strain lines in this field-field mapping prove serviceable in the analysis of primary distortions and as a diagnostic tool in the generatton of field stripping routines.

Acoustic Stimulation of Electronic Transitions
Multi-level optical transitions in select models are found to be tunable through activation of selective channels by phonon excitation. A new model of enzyme regulation is proposed.

Non Black-Body Distribution of Emission Spectra in Living Systems
Using advances in low frequency single photon detection systems, a careful study of emission spectra from living subjects has revealed distribution of frequencies not attributable to black-body radiation. A differential spectra reveals structure that can be partially explained by reabsorption of deep tissue emissions in surface cells. The remaining spectral structure is related to macromolecular events.

LITES Part I, Application in Cancer Research
Living Tissue Emission Spectra (LITES) has been shown to have some application in specific carcinomas. Attempts have been made to push the sensitivity allowing for detection in earlier stages.

LITES Part II, Application to Metabolic Studies
Living Tissue Emission Spectra (LITES) has proven serviceable for real time analysis of sucrose metabolism and insulin stress. Comparing the time-dependence of fingerprint peaks in the LITES of test subject undergoing a simple insulin stress test have shown two frequencies to be of potential use in the real time tracking of this important metabolic test.

LITES Part III, Application to Sleep Studies
Modification of Living Tissue Emission Spectra (LITES) in select subjects has shown itself to be related to the REM and standard brain wave indicators of sleep activity. No explanation is offered to this dependence of LITES on the sleep phase of participating subjects.

Macrodimensions: A Mathematical Model
Drawing on experimental work in the fields of morphology of attention: a mathematical model for the macrodimensions is derived. The clarity and obscurity functions are described.

Macrodimensions: A Physical Perspective
The physics of macrodimensional transitions is explored with special attention to the effects of temporal functions. The effects of latent field memory on the free form expansion of the morphology of attention is discussed.

Microclimates in Bonsai
Experiments in self-regulated micro-environments with special application to Bonsai.

New Food Sources For Acellular Slime Molds or Is there life after E. Coli?"
Reporting on ongoing experiments in Dictyostelids nutrition, special mention is made of efforts at converting the acellular slime moulds from mammalian intestinal bacteria to flora based bacteria.

1978　　*Fictiles A New Art Form*
The challenge of found art or ready-mades is to use the artist's eye "to locate *objets d'art* that appear before the artist within the context of the environment as-it-is". Within the framework of this art form, it is permissible to juxtapose objects in new and stimulating fashions and to set objects within modified environments that may evoke the art from the ready-made. Altering the object itself is disallowed by the rules of the form. In fictile art no force is exerted on the environment, the environment is left unmodified. The creative force of the artist is exerted directly on the world view of the viewer. Through the modification of the world view, the environment as a whole becomes the art form. This use of the plasticity of the world view gives rise to the term fictile art. Through the molding of the world view into a new and unusual form, the environment itself is set into a strange juxtaposition with itself, thereby evoking the art form.

Non-Adrenalin Producing Taboos, A New Source of Fictiles
It is found that the breaking of a taboo will lead to the formation of a fictile when performed in the absence of adrenalin. The presence of adrenalin is found to have an overriding negative affect on the utility of a fictile. Because of the counterindication of adrenalin, taboos of violence and sexual taboos are found to be useless in the formation of fictiles under normal circumstances.

Paranoic Tendencies and the Production of Fictiles
Study of paranoic tendencies in non-clinical individuals is elucidative of the non-obsessive production of fictiles through these attributes. When stripped of compulsions, paranoic tendencies are potent tools for the production of fictiles. Suggestions are presented for future work.

Faux-Papers, A Review of Current Work
Current work in the use of faux-papers and mock scientific abstracts clearly demonstrates their utility in the production of fictiles for the intellectually centered. By awarding the foundation of precept, the plasticity of the viewer's world view is increased, allowing for an increased ease of art form production. In suitably prepared subjects, the papers are found to be non-adrenalin productive and friendly to the overall process of fictile generation. Specific recommendations for extensions of this art form are discussed.

An Immunological Analysis of Information Part I
When an information bit (logon) is presented to a host system, the host looks at the logon to determine whether or not it is host compatible. If the logon is deemed alien, attempts are made to either consume and reject the alien logon or it may be coated with bipolar translators that will yield the alien logon harmless.

An Immunological Analysis of Information Part II
A system of binary logons is studied analogous to binary gases in chemical warfare. Using this approach, potent fictiles have been produced that will not sensitize the host system or be rejected by anti-logons. The introduction into the host system of separate benign elements will bypass host's natural immunity to world view altering information. After incorporation and ownership by the host system, the binary logons can combine to form powerful fictiles. This system has proven useful in the softening of crystallized system-held belief.

An Immunological Analysis of Information Part III
The methods of genetic engineering are converted for use with ideological analysis. Infection vectors and evolution of logons is studied in its relationship to social fictiles.

Linda Corriveau

An insatiable curiosity seems to have always guided Linda Corriveau in her important life choices. Torn between a love for literature and philosophy, she postponed making the decision and decided instead to travel to Europe and North Africa, a trip which lasted a year and a half and would provide an endless source of inspiration.

Ultimately opting for a degree in philosophy, she now had the perfect excuse to dabble in areas of deep uncertainty—the frontiers of knowledge. What better venue upon graduation than the directorship of a pavilion at MAN AND HIS WORLD, Montreal, the site of the legendary 1967 EXPO, called *Strange Strange World* which was a celebration and exploration of just such a thing.

In a highly dramatic setting, subjects at the frontiers of knowledge and science were explored usually leading to open questions. Research for her groundbreaking exhibits put her in contact with sought-after Nobel-prize winners, erudite scholars, respected scientists, famous writers and researchers around the world.

The esthetic level was uncompromisingly high. The atmosphere of the exhibit was magical, and like all things magical, it had a scary aspect because it dared to address certain questions and to face the universe open-minded, with a will to understand one's place as it exists in its broadest reality. Skirting the edges of science, perusing the frontiers of knowledge became a *modus operandi* of every subject approached. Where lay the limit of knowledge in any explored domain, there lay the focus of attention. From there it was a matter of penetration towards the unknown and beyond the limits of current knowledge. This became the fuel of the exhibits.

The themes she delved into were virtually unlimited, reflecting her own thirst for knowledge. They included archaeology, astronomy, space exploration, biofeedback, unexplained phenomena, parapsychology, UFOs, abductions, ancient astronauts, advanced technologies, holography, the intelligent universe, mind/matter relationships, and countless others.

The overall experience was exhilarating and the results speak for themselves: the exhibit typically attracted more than 250,000 visitors for the two-month period it was open each summer during the five years she was its director. Nearly two million visitors streamed through its doors during the whole of its thirteen years of existence, and every single one of them was awed by the scope and beauty of its 10,000 square feet of exhibit space.

One legacy of this unique exhibit is veiled in controversy and speculation. In 1978, Corriveau created an alien sculpture she called *The Man of My Dreams* which has since taken on a life of its own and become famous worldwide. It slipped into the netherland of international hoaxes and now officially occupies a definitive post in the mythology of the late twentieth century. It can be found all over the Internet. It has been published in books in Germany, Australia, China, Italy and probably several other countries and languages. It has appeared in documentaries, newspapers and magazines. It has been the subject of panel discussions,and of much correspondence between UFO experts. It has baffled scientists. Most accounts of it are highly inaccurate. A French language magazine titled *ENIGMA* printed her alien on the cover of its premier issue in 1995. Documentaries such as *Strange Universe, The UFO Evidence* and others have also shown it. The mystery that keeps it alive is simply that it is so convincing that it is believed to be a real alien corpse. Corriveau is delighted that the exhibit with her sculpture was effective beyond her wildest dreams...

After this early exposure to working with some of the best designers in Canada, and long before this amusing turn of events cropped up, Corriveau, a bilingual French Canadian, went on to work as a design consultant for a variety of top-notch museums and design companies, including Design + Communication Inc. on the *Cartier Historical Museum* in Montreal, and the *Tyrrell Museum of Palaeontology*—the largest paleontology museum in the world—in Alberta's haunting badlands.

Her views on museum exhibits became more widely recognized when she delivered a paper at a seminar on science museums and new trends in museology at an annual meeting of the French chapter of the Association for the Advancement of Science in the early eighties.

Corriveau subsequently branched out into television reporting, scientific journalism for popular science magazines such as *Québec-Science*, book translations, computer manual editing, and editorial consultation for everything from a dance journal specializing in traditional Indian Kathakali dance to *MEDIUM*, a magazine exploring contemporary religious phenomena throughout North America.

Another significant step was taken in her career when she turned down an offer to work on the biggest science museum in the world, the *Cité de la Villette*, in Paris. In typical adventuresome fashion, she opted for innovation, rather than prestige by moving to California, where she became the designer for the *Museum of Ancient and Modern Art*, a small but dynamic and creative museum run by artists rather than administrators. It was from these artists that a few years later the Grass Valley Graphics Group emerged.

In this stimulating setting, Corriveau designed over forty exhibits covering such themes as *Mummies, Meteorites and Dinosaurs, Miniature Worlds, Beautiful Butterflies and Beastly Bugs, Ancient Faces, Jewels of the Ancients, The Goddess in the Ancient World*, and a host of other exotic themes that have thoroughly spoiled her. She has even broadened her palette by acting as an auctioneer for the *Museum of Ancient and Modern Art's Annual Fine Art Benefit Auctions*, a challenging educational and entertaining function which has been both demanding and enjoyable for her.

The beauty of the ancient world captivated her in more ways than one and was instrumental in her co-founding with E.J. Gold, Jewels of Ancient Lands, a jewelry company whose designs are inspired by ancient Western Asiatic jewelry. JAL has made a name for itself based on its exquisite designs and fine craftsmanship. Its one-of-a-kind jewelry is sold in museum gift shops and fine galleries throughout North America. Corriveau and Gold see no end to the inspiration that guides their hands in these creations.

Corriveau has maintained a high profile in writing which she feels provides a balance in her hectic life and an inner centering. Other projects to which she has devoted herself include writing the commentaries for *Miro's Dream*, an art book focussed on pen and ink drawings of E.J. Gold, followed by *Pure Gesture*, an attempt to introduce the gestural aspect of E.J. Gold's art. She has worked on *More Color ...Less Soul* for well over a decade in the midst of designing exhibits for the Museum of Ancient and Modern Art, and gallery shows for the Grass Valley Graphics Group and E.J. Gold. All this while curating Gold's artistic production which is steadily climbing to the 100,000 or so range.

In addition to these artistic themes, Corriveau has been an editor in the area of transformational psychology with titles such as *The Human Biological Machine as a Transformational Apparatus, Life in the Labyrinth, Visions in the Stone, The Book of Sacraments, Angels Healing Journey* and most recently *The Great Adventure*.

Corriveau has interviewed some prominent individuals in the field of transformational psychology including Claudio Naranjo and Heather Valencia. The interviews are available as audio recordings and published articles.

Bringing *More Color...Less Soul* to completion has been enormously rewarding for Corriveau. She is already looking forward to writing and editing more books about the art of E.J. Gold whom she strongly feels deserves to be known and appreciated by a wider audience. She already has plans for a new title and can't wait to get started. Meanwhile, she has begun a career in landscape painting and looks forward to painting some glorious light-filled scenes inspired by Bierdstaat and Turner.

INDEX

Fine Art Books About E.J. Gold
from Gateways Fine Art

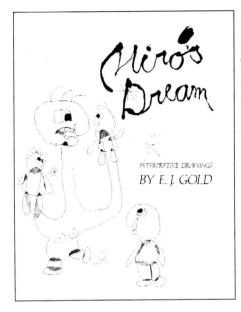

INTERPRETIVE DRAWINGS
BY E. J. GOLD

Miro's Dream.
Drawings by E.J. Gold, poetry by Iven Lourie, commentaries by Linda Corriveau. In the French art-book tradition, poetry and drawings on facing pages. A delightful and instructive book.
$16.95

Pure Gesture
An extended monograph by Linda Corriveau on the transcendental possibilities of contemporary art, as demonstrated by the entire body of work coming from E.J. Gold's studio. Includes photo art by rock star photographer Nona Hatay.
$49.95

MACRODIMENSIONAL GLIMPSES OF OTHER REALITIES

E.J. Gold
Text by Linda Corriveau
PhotoArt by Nona Hatay

Master Art Classes with E. J. Gold

The "I Can't Draw" Series
with E.J. Gold
Pastel Class #1
A House and a Tree

I Can't Draw
Pastel Class #1: A House and Tree
(2 VHS Tapes: 120 mins.)
VID 140. $69.95

E.J. Gold demonstrates the essentials of drawing to a private gathering of students. Valuable as an exceptional lesson in art.

Art As T'ai Chi
with E.J. Gold

Art As T'ai Chi
(2 VHS Tapes: 72 mins.)
VID 152 $69.95

Many of E.J. Gold's students are calling this video one of his very best presentations on art and its creation ever given! Watch as Gold demonstrates the magic of painting, revealing along the way numerous methods of using art as a tool for developing higher attention.

Masters Class Critique
(2 VHS Tapes: 120 mins.)
VID 151. $69.95

Sit in with E.J. Gold as he provides critique and commentary on dozens of paintings produced by his top students especially for this master class! An extraordinary chance to get an in-depth understanding of what makes a great (and not so great) work of art!

Masters Class Critique
with E.J. Gold

"How I Made One Million Dollars in Art $1 at a Time"
(2 VHS Tapes: 120 mins.)
VID 150. $69.95

E.J. Gold shares some of his adventures and stories from his years in the art world, including practical suggestions on how to become a selling artist! A must for anyone who has ever seriously considered earning a living through his art.

Motivation
How I Made One Million
Dollars in Art $1.00 at a Time
with E.J. Gold